Rebel City

'And so at an early age, I took my mind to this question of the ages – why are the many poor? It was true to me. I don't know whether the light of God or the light of humanity or the light of my own intelligence brought it to me, but it came to me like a flash. The thing was wrong because the basis of society was wrong'.

Jim Larkin

FOR LORNA

REBEL CITY

Larkin, Connolly
and the Dublin Labour Movement

John Newsinger

The Merlin Press

First published 2004 by The Merlin Press Ltd.
PO Box 30705
London WC2E 8QD
www.merlinpress.co.uk

British Library Cataloguing in Publication Data
is available from the British Library

ISBN. 085036518X

Printed in Great Britain by Antony Rowe Ltd., Chippenham

Contents

Acknowledgements

My greatest debt is to my partner, Lorna Chessum, whose support, encouragement, inspiration and advice was beyond value. I also owe a continuing debt of gratitude to my colleagues in the History Department at Bath Spa University College, in particular Alan Marshall, Brian Griffin, Graham Davis and Fiona Montgomery. Special thanks are due to my typist, Carol Slade. Also to Tony Zurbugg at Merlin. Once again, the Inter-Library Loans Service at Bath Spa provided a first-rate and indispensable service.

Glossary

Irish Citizen Army (ICA)	ITGWU militia established during the Dublin Lockout.
Independent Labour Party (ILP)	reformist socialist party affiliated to the British Labour Party.
Irish Republican Brotherhood (IRB)	underground republican organisation established in the 1850s.
Irish Transport and General Workers' Union (ITGWU)	the Dublin based union established by Jim Larkin after his break with the NUDL.
Industrial Workers of the World (IWW)	American revolutionary syndicalist trade union.
National Union of Dock Labourers (NUDL)	Liverpool based dockers' union.
Sinn Féin	nationalist organisation founded by Arthur Griffith that included both dual monarchists and republicans in its ranks.
United Irish League (UIL)	the Home Rule Party that was politically dominant in Ireland until post-1916.

Introduction

The first wave of Irish syndicalism that saw the rise of Jim Larkin's Irish Transport and General Workers Union and its eventual defeat in the Great Lockout of 1913-14 remains of considerable interest. The union succeeded in organising the poverty-stricken unskilled and casual working class of Dublin and by means of aggressive tactics of blacking and the sympathy strike was on its way to dominating the city. This militancy was accompanied by an ideological offensive mounted principally through the *Irish Worker* newspaper, but also in pamphlets and on the platform. The union stood for the socialist reorganisation of society and the raising up of the downtrodden working class. It championed women's rights and was an enthusiastic supporter of the campaign for women's suffrage. And it adopted a staunchly republican standpoint, indeed the ITGWU was the largest republican organisation of the day.

In the summer of 1913 the Dublin employers, led by William Martin Murphy, counter-attacked and imposed a six-month lockout that effectively broke the union, although working-class support for Larkin and 'Larkinism' remained strong. The Lockout saw the union under attack from employers, police and troops, the Hibernians, the clergy and the press, but nevertheless sustain a heroic resistance. It was assisted in this by an unprecedented level of financial support from the British labour movement, from trade unions, socialist organisations and individuals. The *Daily Herald* newspaper played a vital role in the organisation of solidarity. In the end, however, the ITGWU went down to defeat when, on 9 December 1913, the British Trades Union Congress (TUC) refused to take industrial action in support of Dublin workers, leaving them isolated in the face of large-scale importation of blackleg labour. The struggle remains the most important in Irish labour history and one of the most important in British labour history.

To a considerable extent the history of the first wave of Irish syndicalism has been distorted by arguments over the relative merits of Jim Larkin and Jim

Connolly. While the two men undoubtedly had their disagreements and on occasions their very different personalities clashed, nevertheless they worked together in the struggle with Connolly emerging as Larkin's chief lieutenant during the Great Lockout. The argument over their relative merits does not actually derive from the time, but from a later period when Jim Larkin and William O'Brien were battling for control of the ITGWU.[1] O'Brien, who moved the union decisively to the right, used Connolly, who was safely dead, as a club with which to beat his arch-rival in a conflict that lasted from 1923 until Larkin's death in 1947 and beyond. This use of Connolly's reputation to damage Larkin was given academic credibility by C. Desmond Greaves in a number of influential books: his biography of Connolly, his official history of the ITGWU and his study of the Larkinite playwright, Sean O'Casey. He celebrated Connolly as the great Messiah of Irish labour and as part of building Connolly up, sought to diminish Larkin. This denigration of Larkin was to be carried to occasionally grotesque lengths in his official history of the ITGWU.[2] The most recent biographer of Larkin, Emmet O'Connor, arguably Ireland's foremost labour historian, continues in this vein. Larkins's personality is not only systematically maligned, but somewhat incredibly he is also described as 'a reluctant and inferior trade unionist'.[3] O'Connor is confusing trade unionism with trade union officialdom here.

Larkin, of course, has had his defenders, not least the tens of thousands of working-class Dubliners for whom he was a hero and an inspiration. The standard biography of the man, Emmet Larkin's *James Larkin*, presents a sympathetic and balanced, if somewhat dated account.[4] More recently, Donal Nevin's collection, *James Larkin: Lion of the Fold*, is a tremendous celebration of the man that indisputably establishes his importance, warts and all.[5] This is reinforced by Padraig Yeates's massive study of the Great Lockout, a work that does not hesitate to criticise Larkin, although not always correctly.[6] More recently, there have also been attempts to arrive at a more balanced assessment of Jim Connolly, breaking away from the Greaves' mould. The best of these accounts is Kieran Allen's, *The Politics of James Connolly*.[7]

What of this present study? It is informed by the insight of British working-class intellectual, Jack Murphy, who described Larkin as the tornado and Connolly as the lighthouse. Larkin could whip up a storm, while Connolly could explain the situation. This captures the distinctive contribution of both men to working-class struggle in Dublin, to the phenomenon of 'Larkinism'.[8]

As well as providing accounts of Ireland's two great socialists, the study seeks to delineate the contours of the labour revolt in Dublin, to provide an account of 'Larkinism'. It examines the movement's aspirations, its methods, its rhetoric, its republicanism, its relations with the Catholic Church and its struggles. It provides an account of the Great Lockout that identifies the solidarity campaign in Britain as decisive, focusing in particular on the efforts of the *Daily Herald* and of the Daily Herald League. It discusses the ITGWU's relations with the republican underground and the Irish Volunteers and its attitude towards the outbreak of War in 1914. The differences between Larkin and Connolly over relations with the republican underground were resolved by Larkin's departure for the United States, leaving Connolly free to tread the road to Easter Week. The study examines the Easter Rising from a working-class perspective before proceeding to an account of the Irish working class during the War of Independence. Inevitably, the discussion of the War of Independence involves a shift from the perspective of Dublin to a wider national perspective. While the study has aspired to accuracy, it will be evident to readers that it is wholeheartedly and unashamedly on the side of the Larkinites.

Readers in search of the history of the Irish working-class and socialist movement before the advent of Larkinism are recommended to consult John Boyle's *The Irish Labour Movement in the Nineteenth Century* and Fintan Lane's *The Origins of Modern Irish Socialism 1881-1896*.[9]

Notes

1   See for example *The Attempt To Smash The Irish Transport and General Workers Union*, Dublin 1924.
2   C. Desmond Greaves, *The Life and Times of James Connolly*, London 1961; *The Irish Transport and General Workers Union: The Formative Years*, Dublin 1982; and *Sean O'Casey: Politics and Art*, London 1979. Greaves, a lifelong Communist, was primarily concerned with arguing for an alliance between the Irish left and Irish republicanism rather than with developing independent working-class organisation and Connolly became the symbol of this alliance. Larkin offered a different politics.
3   Emmet O'Connor, *James Larkin*, Cork 2002.
4   Emmet Larkin, *James Larkin*, London 1968.
5   Donal Nevin, ed, *James Larkin: The Lion in the Fold*, Dublin 1998.
6   Padraig Yeates, *Lockout: Dublin 1913*, Dublin 2000.
7   Kieran Allen, *The Politics of James Connolly*, London 1990.
8   J.T. Murphy, *New Horizons*, London 1941, p. 38.
9   John W. Boyle, *The Irish Labour Movement in the Nineteenth Century*, Washington 1988 and Fintan Lane, *The Origins of Modern Irish Socialism 1881-1896*, Cork 1997.

PART ONE

Chapter I
Jim Larkin, Syndicalism and the Rise of the ITGWU

Writing in the *Freeman's Journal* in the early days of the Great Lockout, Professor T.M Kettle of the National University, certainly no great friend of Jim Larkin, nevertheless confronted the social conditions that he believed had produced Larkinism:

> Labouring Dublin is the blackest scandal of the Empire with which we are associated. And its housing? As a citizen of Dublin I rend my garments and cry for forgiveness at the word. The mansion-slums of Dublin go as close as any material fact can to a denial of the ways of God. You can walk through broken street after street of this proud capital, and as you absorb into your eyes – and your nose – the realities there presented, you will understand the degradation to which this city has condemned the caryatides of labour .... The houses in which too many of them now live are not so much houses as camps pitched in the cemetery of the eighteenth century. If you seek for a parallel to the houses in which so many of our fellow-citizens are endeavouring to enact the Ten Commandments on fifteen shillings a week you must go to some city in the Balkans.

It was not, he insisted, that Dublin was poor. Indeed, there 'is no luxury so recondite that Dublin is not able to afford it'. A walk 'along that glorious coast-line, jewelled everywhere with rich and beautiful villas, which runs from Lansdown Road to Greystones' provided ample evidence 'of substantial incomes gained in the professions, the public service, or business, or accruing to annuitants'. The problem was that there was 'a terrible and wide gulf between the very rich and the very poor' so that on the one hand Dublin had 'some of the finest shops in the world' and on the other, there was 'that mass – that ragged and hungry mass' that had rallied to Larkin.

Kettle explained 'the terrible and wide gulf' between rich and poor in Dublin as deriving from the city's economic structure. Manufacturing, with a few exceptions, ('that will readily come to mind'), was weak, and the majority 'of the manual workers live by carrying things from one spot to another'. Dublin was 'a transport city' that offered a large proportion of its working population low paid casual employment with all the poverty and its consequences that went with it.[1] Modern studies bear out this contemporary analysis.

The Dublin Slums

In her discussion of Dublin's economy, historian Mary Daly observes that the city's spread of occupations reveal a city much closer to London than to industrial cities such as Birmingham or Manchester. Indeed, manufacturing had been in decline in Dublin in the course of the nineteenth century. Whereas in 1841, manufacturing had provided employment for 33.8 per cent of the city's working population, by 1911 that figure had fallen to 24 per cent. The percentage employed in transport, however, had risen from 2.97 to 15.46 per cent although she makes the point that many of the city's general labourers (16.3 per cent of men in 1841, 19.5 per cent in 1911) would also have worked in the transport sector but on a casual basis. While manufacturing had declined, Dublin's importance as a port had increased, exporting cattle, sheep, pigs, beer and biscuits and importing coal, flour and wheat. Even while port work became increasingly important to Dublin's economy, however, the relative importance of Dublin as a port declined. In 1875 Dublin had been the largest port in Ireland and the fifth largest in Britain as a whole, but by 1907 it had been overtaken by Belfast as Ireland's largest port and was twelfth in Britain. The consequence of this was, in Daly's words, that 'Dublin failed to provide adequate employment, either for the indigenous Dublin population or for even a small proportion of the surplus population of rural Ireland'. Over a third of the women in employment were in domestic service, while a large proportion of men were only in casual employment. Many were only able to earn at best a subsistence living and at worst a below subsistence living. As Daly puts it once again, it was the labourers who 'constituted the hardcore of the Dublin tenement problems, were disproportionately represented among tuberculosis victims, while their children were those most likely to die in early childhood'.[2]

There was a contemporary survey of poverty in Dublin carried out by T.J. Stafford, the Medical Commissioner of Health of the Local Government Board, although as he pointed out, his survey did not include the circumstances 'of the very poor'. He examined 1,254 families and concluded that over half of the working population of the city was living in poverty. A more detailed study of 21 families that he considered typical revealed that only nine families had an income that could 'satisfy the simplest of wants' while twelve families could not 'procure a competency of the barest necessities of life'. Seventeen of the families were malnourished, including the families of skilled workers. They had no savings and spent most of their income on food (63 per cent) and rent (15 per cent) with ten families not able to match income with expenditure. The condition of the very poor, he acknowledged, defied belief.[3]

The housing conditions of a large proportion of the Dublin population reflect-ed their low earnings and casual employment. Visitors soon noticed the 'star-tling contrasts' between wealth and poverty. Arnold Wright, a supporter of the employers in the Great Lockout nevertheless noticed the contrast between the 'Gothic pinnacles of St. Patrick's Cathedral' and 'O'Connell Bridge with the re-ally magnificent vista of soaring monuments and noble buildings' and the slum districts 'where the degradation of human kind is carried to a point of abjectness beyond that reached in any city of the Western world, save perhaps Naples'. He described the Dublin slums as 'a thing apart in the inferno of social degrada-tion'.[4] Dora Montefiore, a staunch supporter of the workers in the Great Lock-out, echoed this: 'in no city of the world have I seen such degrading poverty'. She had seen something of slums, 'but Dublin slums just beggar description. They have to be seen and smelt to be realised'. Outside her hotel 'in the main street of Dublin' every morning 'ragged kiddies aged from four or five' rummaged through the bins, threw the ashes into their bags and wolfed the pieces of broken bread and meat they found.[5]

One middle class Dubliner, Todd Andrews, a future republican and Fianna Fáil supporter, recalled in his memoirs, *Dublin Made Me*, how

> Even in winter the children of the poor were mainly without boots. They were rag-ged and frozen looking and sometimes had newspapers tied round their legs with string, in the manner of puttees. Sacking was commonly used instead of overcoats; all the coalmen wore it over their shoulders. Smells are very evocative of places and times past, and of all the unpleasant smells I recall the worst was that of a slum tenement. One of the girls who looked after me often brought me home with her. She lived with her parents in one room in Gardiner Street. The stench of the house when you entered the hall was disgusting. Urine and excrement (visible as well as smelling) mingled with all the stinks that the human body can exude. There was no indoor lavatory and only one outdoor lavatory and one outdoor tap for the whole building. The room where the girl lived with her father, mother and two sisters, had two beds with old rags for bed clothes, and no other furnishings except a table, a few chairs, a china dog, and statues of the Blessed Virgin and the Sacred Heart.[6]

The experience never left him.

In 1914, in response to the Church Street tenement disaster in which three adults and four children were killed when a slum property collapsed, the Dublin Housing Inquiry investigated conditions. This found that 25,822 families were living in 5,322 slum tenements. Of these families 20,108 lived in one room, 4,402 in two rooms, 821 in three rooms and 491 in four rooms. According to the 1911 Census in Dublin 22.9 per cent of the population were living in one room com-pared with 13.2 per cent in Glasgow, but only 0.59 per cent in London, 0.56 per cent in Edinburgh, 0.23 per cent in Liverpool and 0.04 per cent in Birmingham.

Without any doubt Dublin had the worst living conditions of any city in Britain and among the worst in Europe.[7] The *Freeman's Journal* in an article, 'The Slums of Dublin', published in January 1913, commented that 'the existence of such conditions of life as many of the poor live under is the greatest blot on our Western civilisation'. It went on:

> the number of people who live in the slums, four in a room, is 39,000. That is a fact to make people think. But it is an infinitely more shameful fact that of these 39,000 people living under these terrible conditions six thousand live seven in a room and three thousand eight in a room. Even at eight to a room the terrible record does not stop. People live ten to a room – there are nearly five hundred of them in Dublin – eleven to a room, even twelve to a room. The figures are harrowing enough, but what must the reality be.[8]

There were also the homeless, those sleeping rough or in the night shelters provided by the Catholic Church.

With the terrible conditions and overcrowding of the slums came disease, disability and premature death. Jacinta Prunty has used the rate of mortality as a yardstick with which to compare the condition of Dublin's poor with other cities. In 1905, a very favourable year for Dublin, the mortality rate in the city was 22.3 per 1000 of inhabitants. This compared with 15.6 per 1000 for London, 17 per 1000 for Glasgow and 16.1 per 1000 for Edinburgh. 'Dublin death rates', she observes, 'were closer to that recorded for cities such as Prague, Budapest and Moscow'. Moreover within the city itself there were wide differences with some working-class districts reaching mortality rates 'that might bear comparison with cities such as Cairo, Moscow or Madras'. In his 1906 report, Surgeon-Colonel Edgar Flinn identified a slum district with a mortality rate of 38 per 1000 in 1899. The crucial factor in sustaining these mortality rates was pulmonary tuberculosis.[9] Of the 1,254 families examined by T.J. Stafford, in his study of poverty, tuberculosis was present in 150 families and he quite explicitly identified ' poverty as ... the most potent predisposing cause of the malady'.[10]

There is, of course, another dimension to the terrible conditions in the Dublin slums. No cloud is without a silver lining and these bastions of poverty and squalor were the source of considerable profit. Rented property 'was the greatest source of unearned income for Dublin's middle class'. In 1913 no less than seventeen members of Dublin city council owned slum property, the city's greatest capitalist, William Martin Murphy, owned slum property, and even such a staunchly Catholic and Nationalist family as the Plunketts (Joseph, a 1916 martyr and his father George, a founder of Sinn Féin in 1917) owned slum property.[11] Poverty in Dublin was not a thing in itself, but a relationship and it is difficult to disagree with Larkin's assessment that while some of the middle class 'close their eyes and pass on', there were others 'who in their selfishness are satisfied to know that poverty exists because they recognise the fact that as long as one class are content to endure the cruelties of poverty, just so long can they themselves enjoy to the full the luxuries of abundant wealth'.[12]

The Coming of Jim Larkin

The extent of poverty and casual employment in Dublin made the city very difficult territory for trade union organisation. Historically, only the organisations representing skilled workers had survived, not least because of the difficulty of replacing their labour during strikes. There was no such difficulty with unskilled workers. In the event of a strike, there were large numbers of casual workers, underemployed and unemployed, readily available to be recruited by the employers to replace those who had walked out. This was, of course, not just a Dublin phenomenon, but the situation in Dublin was particularly difficult because of the extreme nature of social conditions. Nevertheless, at a time when unskilled workers, both men and women, in Ireland and in Britain, were beginning to stir, were set to make another attempt at organisation, Jim Larkin appeared in Dublin, In Sean O'Casey's words:

> Through the streets he strode, shouting into every dark and evil-smelling hallway. The great day of change has come; Circe's swine had a better time than you have; come from your vomit; out into the sun. Larkin is calling you all …. From a window in the building, leaning well forth, he talked to the workers, spoke as only Jim Larkin could speak, not for an assignation with peace, dark obedience, or placid resignation; but trumpet-tongued of resistance to wrong, discontent with leering poverty, and defiance of any power strutting out to stand in the way of their march upward … 'who will stand, who will fight, for the right of men to live and die like men?' he called out, the large strong hand stretched out the window gesturing over the head of the crowd.

Larkin was O'Casey's 'Prometheus Hibernicus' bringing fire to the Irish working class. Typically mixing his mythologies, O'Casey likened Larkin's arrival in Dublin to the arrival of a Biblical prophet, striding through the streets and calling on the poor to come forth 'and fight with the son of Amos … come out that we may smite the winter house with the summer house; till the houses of ivory shall perish and the great houses shall have an end'.[13] Amen to that!

Who was Jim Larkin? There is continuing dispute even about his place of birth with most historians arguing that Liverpool has that honour, but his descendents still insist on Newry in Ulster. Even the year is disputed: 21 January 1874 or 1876, but whatever, he was the son of poor Irish parents, and certainly raised in Liverpool.[14] He left school when he was eleven years old and had a number of jobs before becoming a docker in the late 1890s. By this time he was already a socialist, having joined the Independent Labour Party (ILP) in 1892-93. Outside of work, his life was dominated by his propagandist efforts on behalf of the ILP and he became well-known as a public speaker, advocating the overthrow of capitalism and the introduction of a socialist commonwealth. Like many of his contemporaries in the socialist movement, Larkin had little time for trade unionism, which he regarded as at best a palliative and at worst as an accomplice of the capitalism system. He considered strikes to be counter-productive, hurting the working class more than the employers. The only way forward for the working class was not to engage in diversionary trade union agitation, but to elect socialists into office both locally and nationally, through the ballot box. Only in 1901 did he join the Liverpool-based National Union of Dock Labourers (NUDL), influenced, according to Eric Taplin by the Labour leader, Keir Hardie, who was urging that the unions should be won over to socialism. He was not a union activist, however. Indeed, by 1903 he had been promoted to foreman with the firm of T. and J. Harrison, with the reputation of being a 'rusher'.[15]

Larkin was transformed from a cardholding union member into a militant activist in 1905 when the NUDL attempted to impose the closed shop on seven of Harrison's thirty-five foremen who had either refused to join the union or had allowed their membership to lapse. In June 800 men walked out on strike and Larkin went with them. Already a powerful public speaker, he was elected onto the strike committee and soon became the driving force behind the conduct of the dispute. The employers' strike-breaking organisation, the Shipping Federation, provided the firm with some 500 scabs and after thirteen weeks the union went down to a crushing defeat. The company withdrew union recognition altogether, let alone imposing the closed shop on its foremen. It took back only those workers it wanted, and Larkin was not among them. During the dispute, though, Larkin had emerged as the most effective of the strike leaders and had made a name for himself as an organiser and an agitator. The dispute had taught him the need for working-class organisation and solidarity and the consequences when it was found wanting. Being blacklisted brought home the need for strong trade unions now rather than putting faith in an eventual electoral victory ushering in socialism. Larkin was transformed by the hard school of experience into an aggressive, determined trade union organiser who was to preach the virtues of industrial militancy and class solidarity with tremendous effect for the rest of his life.

Belfast 1907

In the aftermath of the defeat at Harrison's, Larkin was taken on by the NUDL as a full-time organiser, working the ports of Scotland and Ireland. His militant methods made him very popular with the rank and file but were soon to bring him into conflict with the union leadership. It was in Belfast in 1907 that he was to achieve his most famous success, uniting Protestant and Catholic workers against the employers. Working with Michael McKeown, a veteran trade unionist and one of the founders of the NUDL, Larkin began organising the dockers, holding meetings and signing up members: 'years afterwards men remembered the impact of Larkin's words. William Long, who first heard him in Corporation

Square recalled "as fine a speech as ever I had or as ever I heard". While Joseph
Cooper summed up his feeling thus: "half a dozen words from Jim Larkin and
you were all together"'.[16] In early May 1907 dockers working for the Belfast
Steamship Company went on strike, beginning what was to quickly become a
general offensive to secure union recognition, shorter hours and improvements
in pay. On 20 June the NUDL presented its demands to the dock employers, and
while some smaller companies conceded, the larger companies were not even
prepared to negotiate, and strike action became general. The employers' expectation was that they would be able to break this challenge in the traditional way
by importing blackleg labour, but Larkin spread the dispute to the carters who
were on strike by the end of the first week of July. Even if the employers could
work the docks, they could not move goods to and from, at least not without
considerable difficultly. While the police, the Royal Irish Constabulary (RIC),
could provide the scabs on the docks with some protection, it was a different
matter altogether protecting hundreds of carts, vans and wagons. The striking
dockers and carters were joined on the picket lines by hundreds of shipyard
workers, skilled Protestants, who joined in stoning the police and attacking
blackleg vehicles. On 9 July at least ten vehicles were wrecked by the crowds
throughout the city, overturned, set on fire or thrown in the harbour. Larkin
himself was arrested for assaulting a scab who had stabbed three pickets before
being felled with a shovel.

   Mass meetings in support of the strikers were held in both Protestant and
Catholic areas of the city, as solidarity, at least temporarily crossed the sectarian
divide. As John Gray has pointed out in his standard history of the conflict, *City
in Revolt*: 'The success of these meetings made it clear that the strike had mass
working class support in all areas of the city'.[17] The Independent Orange Order,
a working-class breakaway, gave its enthusiastic support to the strike. Skilled
and unskilled, Protestant and Catholic, men and women, all had rallied behind
the strikers. Larkin, McKeown and their comrades had successfully orchestrated
a working-class insurgency in that bastion of sectarian division, Belfast. Moreover, on 19 July a police constable, William Barrett, refused to ride on a scab
vehicle, prompting a mutiny in the RIC, a mutiny which NUDL leader, James
Sexton gave Larkin credit for. Troop reinforcements were rushed to the city. On
10 August a mass meeting attended by over 10,000 people was held with Lindsay
Crawford, Grand Master of the Independent Orange Order speaking alongside
Joseph Devlin, the Home Rule MP and leader of the Ancient Order of Hibernians. This great demonstration of unity, only reluctantly attended by Devlin,
it has to be said, was a testimony to popular support for the strikers and their
cause. The following day saw serious fighting between troops and working-class
crowds break out in both Protestant and Catholic districts of the city, fighting
that culminated in troops opening fire on the Falls Road, killing two Catholic
bystanders, on 12 August. These shootings prompted large demonstrations in

support of the Belfast workers in the East End of London and in Liverpool. Back in Belfast it brought the Catholic priests out against the socialist agitators who were misleading their flock, while the Unionist press portrayed events as a Fenian uprising.

What became of this impressive display of militancy and solidarity? It was not defeated by repression or by sectarianism. What accomplished its defeat was the intervention of NUDL leader, James Sexton and officials from the General Federation of Trade Unions (GFTU). At a time when the strike still had enthusiastic mass support, Sexton, together with Allen Gee and Isaac Mitchell of the GFTU, set out to divide the strikers and to get them back to work as quickly as possible on terms acceptable to the employers. As John Gray observes, even moderate trade unionists unsympathetic to Larkin's methods were 'horrified at the peremptory fashion in which they had been sold down the river'.[18] The carters were persuaded to return to work with a pay rise but without union recognition, leaving the dockers isolated and doomed to defeat. Larkin, it has to be said, did not mount any opposition to this betrayal, but there can be no doubt that the lesson of having a strike sold out from under him by the intervention of British trade union officials was to be something that he remembered and was determined should never happen again.

Why did Sexton and co behave in this way? This is an important question, indeed it is crucial for understanding the syndicalist dimension of the Great Labour Unrest that was going to overwhelm both Britain and Ireland. As trade union leaders of longstanding, Sexton, Gee and Mitchell saw themselves not as leading their members in struggle, but rather as arbitrating between their members and the employers. Their position as trade union officials gave them interests and perspectives that were distinct from those of the rank and file. For them trade unionism had become a middle-class career, opening up considerable opportunities for personal advancement. This career was forwarded by strong trade unions, but not by militant trade unionism. As far as they were concerned good relations with the employers were essential and working-class insurgency was as big a threat to this objective as were anti-union employers. For Sexton and co the objective was the establishment of sweetheart deals with the employers whereby the employers were convinced that trade union recognition was in their interests. They had no interest in class warfare or industrial confrontation. This is not to say, of course, that all trade union officials are the same or that there are no differences between right-wing and left-wing officials but rather that their peculiar position between workers and employers inevitably encourages a certain trajectory, subjects them to the same pressures and concerns. How else to explain how so many left-wing officials, former militants, end up in the House of Lords. Isaac Mitchell of the GFTU is a useful example of the career trade union official. An engineer by trade and member of the Amalgamated Society of Engineers (ASE), he had in his youth been a Deleonite socialist, but had matured, in the words of the official historian of the GFTU, into 'a pragmatist, a negotiator and inevitably also therefore a master of compromise'. Nevertheless, we are assured that he remained 'a trade unionist first and foremost' which presumably explains why after his Belfast performance he secured a government post at the Board of Trade as a full-time conciliator, a post where 'he won golden opinions for his negotiating skills'.[19]

Sexton himself is an even more interesting example of the successful trade union official and his or her trajectory. A former Fenian, he had bitter personal experience of the callous disregard that the dock employers had for their workers. In 1882 Sexton had a serious accident at work that left him disfigured for life. He was left waiting at the dockside while unloading was completed and was then sent to hospital in a cab. After two months in hospital, he was taken back by the firm (he got no compensation) and started on light work. The company stopped the cab fare out of his first week's wages.[20] Sexton, at this time, was certainly no moderate. He was sacked for assaulting a foreman and in his memoirs fondly remembered the use of 'applied vigour' to deter scabs – much more effective than mere 'politeness'.[21] But once he became general secretary of the NUDL in 1893, the strength of the employers convinced him that the union could only survive if the employers could be persuaded to tolerate it. From this point of view the members' demands were no longer what the union was all about, but a potential danger to the union, militancy was a threat rather than an opportunity. Indeed, by 1907 the same James Sexton, who had organised attacks on imported blacklegs in the early 1890s, carried a pistol in Belfast to protect himself from his own members.[22] This was the road to a knighthood, a seat in the Commons and friendship with the likes of Andrew Bonar Law, Stanley Baldwin and Sir Austen Chamberlain, friendships that, as he acknowledges, 'made me the object of fierce attack by some of my comrades of the proletariat'. Conflict between Sexton and Larkin was inevitable because, even though Larkin was a full-time organiser for the NUDL, he remained a rank-and-file leader rather than a trade union official. As Sexton observed, Larkin's 'cloven hoof', his rank-and-file orientation, showed itself very early on.[23]

The particular analysis of the trade union official put forward here has, of course, a very respectable pedigree. As long ago as 1894, the Fabian socialists, Sidney and Beatrice Webb, in their pathbreaking, *The History of Trade Unionism*, had written of the 'Civil Service of the Trade Union world', which had been non-existent in 1850, but 'numbers at the present time between six and seven hundred'. Identifying the emergence of this trade union bureaucracy is one of the most important achievements of the Webbs' work. They argued that the salaried official 'of a great Trade Union occupies a unique position. He belongs neither to the middle nor to the working class', but instead finds himself (and at this time they were writing about men), in a contradictory position. If he avoids succumbing to drink, his structural position inevitably brings about a change in his outlook. They quote the observations of an anonymous 'thoughtful artisan' who described for them the fate of the career trade unionist:

> To the ordinary Trade Unionist the claim of the workman is that of Justice. He believes, almost as a matter of principle, that in any dispute the capitalist is in the wrong and the workman in the right. But when, as a District Delegate, it becomes his business to be perpetually investigating the exact circumstances of the men's quarrels, negotiating with employers, and arranging compromises, he begins more and more to recognise that there is something to be urged on the other side. There is also an unconscious bias at work. Whilst the points at issue no longer affect his own earnings or conditions of employment, any disputes between his members and their employers increase his work and add to his worry. The former vivid sense of the privations and subjection of the artisan's life gradually fades from his mind; and he begins more and more to regard all complaints as perverse and unreasonable.

Their astute commentator went on to describe how the union official 'is courted and flattered' by the middle class, comes to admire and envy them, 'insensibly adopts more and more of their ideas' and, in the end, finds himself looking down on common workmen. And then a 'great strike threatens to involve the Society in desperate war' and he finds himself transformed into the enemy of his members' interests, 'and eventually arranges a compromise on terms distasteful to a large section of his members'. Or more colloquially, 'sells them down the river'.

This trajectory is, of course, only illustrative, but it is the contention here that it provides the necessary basis for an understanding of trade union bureaucracy. There are still matters left unresolved: the extent of democracy within the trade union, the militancy of the membership, the attitude of the employers (some employers can force even the most reluctant union officials to fight), and relations with the State. And, of course, there are important differences between left- and right-wing trade union officials, although whether these are fundamental differences is another matter. A comparison of J.H. Thomas and Ben Tillett during the Dublin Lockout would suggest they are not. And lastly, there is that category the Webbs describe as 'the apostles of the unconverted', the 'professional agitators'. These are the men for whom trade unionism is and remains a crusade to bring justice to a world of oppression and exploitation, a weapon with which to break the employing class, rather than the means to an accommodation with them. Jim Larkin was arguably, the greatest of these 'apostles'.[24]

This leaves consideration of the importance of Larkin's achievements in Belfast. Emmet Larkin (no relation) in his classic biography of Larkin provides the best assessment:

> The myth that has grown up around James Larkin claims Belfast as one of his

greatest achievements. What happened in Belfast can, of course, be conceived in the most grandiose terms. It could include the destruction of religious bigotry, organising workers for the revolutionary act, and contributing to the dignity and integrity of the working classes. The rub is that Larkin did achieve all these things, but only to a limited extent .... In the long run Larkin achieved little of a tangible nature in Belfast, not because he was something less than he should have been, but because his enemies were too powerful and circumstances too adverse. In the short run he shook Belfast to its roots.[25]

Founding The Irish Transport and General Workers' Union

Even while the Belfast strikes were still underway, Larkin was at work establishing the NUDL in Dublin. At a meeting launching the Dublin branch Larkin regretted the injury inflicted on an army officer with a broken bottle in Belfast with the observation that 'it was a bad thing to disgrace a common bottle by using it on an officer.' He went on:

> no man in that room could guarantee that tomorrow night he would be in a job. Four out of every eleven men in that room were going to die in the workhouse, asylum or jail unless they altered the laws, and they could only alter them if they combined. He would alter this state of things or go under ....[26]

1908 was to be the critical year in Dublin with Larkin conducting major disputes involving both the dockers and the carters, and promising the employers either 'peace with honour or war to the knife.' This brought him into increasing conflict with Sexton and the NUDL executive, who ordered him out of Ireland. Larkin carried on regardless.

Aggressive picketing played an important role in the Dublin carters' strike of November-December with serious clashes between police and strikers taking place. Strike-breaking carts and vehicles were attacked, overturned or tipped into the Liffey as the ranks of the strikers were swollen by thousands of sympathisers. On one occasion a lorry was stopped and its load scattered over the road only for the driver to protest that he was not a scab and that his firm was not in dispute with the union. The pickets reloaded the lorry and sent it on its way. Against all the odds, the dispute was won and the union's position was secured. This particular dispute was, as the historians of the Dublin Trades Council have observed, 'the most important strike that had occurred in Dublin since the 1890s'. Larkin, they go on 'came to personify the fundamental changes taking place in the Dublin working class .... Trade unionism took on a new meaning'.[27] Even Dermot Keogh, a historian generally sceptical with regard to Larkinism, acknowledges that in the 1908 carters' strike, 'Larkin's achievement was really quite remarkable'. He had conducted a major dispute without any official support and brought it to a successful conclusion.[28] Moreover, by the end of 1908 Larkin and his supporters had established NUDL branches in every major port in Ireland. By now his relations with Sexton had gone beyond breaking point.

Larkin was urging a campaign to organise the unskilled workers throughout Ireland while Sexton was still refusing to support strikes and concerned with maintaining good relations with those employers prepared to recognise the union. On 8 December Sexton suspended the mutinous Larkin from his post.

Larkin's response was, together with an important group of activists and sympathisers (P.T. Daly, Thomas McPartlin, W. P. Partridge, William O'Brien and others), to launch the Irish Transport and General Workers' Union (ITGWU). The membership of the NUDL was to be enlisted in a crusade to establish a great general union throughout Ireland. On 28 December a meeting of delegates from the Irish branches of the NUDL voted to establish the new union and it came into being on 4 January 1909. One important point worth making here is that the Irish breakaway from the NUDL was not unique. Sexton's authoritarian and conservative leadership, his refusal to support strikes, had alienated a large proportion of the union's membership. Militancy and democracy were becoming the order of the day not just in Dublin but throughout the British working-class movement as well. In Glasgow, for example, in a little-known episode, dockers, sympathetic to Larkin, voted with their feet, abandoning the NUDL, which had virtually collapsed on the Clyde by the end of 1910. In July 1911 they launched the Scottish Union of Dock Labourers (SUDL) which ,after hard fought strikes in 1911 and 1912, succeeded in organising the Glasgow dockside.[29] In both Dublin and Glasgow, rank-and-file dockers rebelled against Sexton's leadership and established successful breakaway unions. The critical difference between the two ventures was that in Dublin, Larkin and his comrades were determined to use their hard-won support among the dockers and carters as a base from which to strike out and organise all the workers.

The ITGWU and the Great Labour Unrest

While the new union had no difficulty in winning over the NUDL membership throughout most of Ireland, it did encounter serious difficulties in Belfast. Here Michael McKeown's efforts were successfully beaten off by Sexton, a one-time Fenian, who now played the 'Orange card', setting Protestant and Catholic against each other. The NUDL allied itself with the employers to exclude IT-GWU members from employment. This was very much in line with Sexton's strategy of ingratiating himself with the employers, but, of course, once the Larkinites had been defeated, the employers dispensed with the NUDL as well and the Belfast docks became effectively non-union.[30] Elsewhere, determined efforts were made to strangle the new union at birth. In Cork, it was plunged into a bitter dispute that was to end with the union organiser, James Fearon, receiving six months in prison and the union suffering a crushing defeat.[31] Soon after in August 1909, Larkin was arrested and charged with conspiracy to defraud, a charge got up by the Cork Employers Federation, aided and abetted by Sexton. During the 1908 carters' strike, Larkin had transferred funds from the Cork branch of the NUDL to help the struggle in Dublin. He was now charged with having defrauded the union membership in Cork, first because the Cork branch had never been officially recognised by the NUDL and second because he used the money for illegitimate purposes. Sexton appeared as a key prosecution witness (once again he went armed with a pistol) and played a crucial part in securing Larkin's conviction. On 17 June 1910 Larkin was sentenced to one year's imprisonment, an astonishingly harsh sentence for what was, in effect, a technical offence. The sentence was clearly designed to destroy, if at all possible, both Larkin and the new union, but it seriously backfired. Protest was such that the authorities backed down and Larkin was released after only three months. On 1 October 1910 a huge torchlight procession marched through the streets of Dublin in his honour. The ITGWU had survived the attempt to strangle it at birth and now set about the great task of organising the unskilled workers of Ireland.

The ITGWU's drive to organise Ireland's unskilled workers has to be seen as part of the great labour unrest that swept over Britain from 1910 to 1914. In many ways, Larkin's efforts in Belfast in 1907 and in Dublin in 1908 presaged the great explosion of militancy that was to come throughout Britain. In the words of one historian:

> The mass strike wave of 1910 to 1914 remains unique in British history. A wild, elemental, pent-up force seemed suddenly let loose, disregarding precedents and agreements, impatient of compromise, shaking the old complacent trade unionism by the ears, sometimes, as in the rail strike of 1911, forcing conservative leaders ahead of it like fallen leaves driven before an autumn wind. The trade union leaders, almost to a man, deplored it, the government viewed it with alarm … yet disregarding everything, encouraged only by a small minority of syndicalist leaders, the great strike wave rolled on, threatening to sweep everything away before it.[32]

Beginning with unofficial strikes in the mines in Durham and South Wales in 1910, followed by a seamen's strike in 1911 that brought out the dockers and turned into a general strike in Liverpool, where the railwaymen came out in sympathy, producing an unofficial strike wave on the railways that the union leaders had to race to catch up with, the movement spread. In 1912 a national miners' strike involving over a million workers gripped the country. The following year, 1913, saw 1,500 recorded strikes with the Dublin Lockout occupying a central place in the concerns of the British labour movement. And in 1914 there was the great building workers' lockout with major strikes threatening in the mines and on the railways as the Great War approached. Alongside the great setpiece confrontations, hundreds of thousands of workers, many of them women, took courage to confront their employers with demands for union recognition, better working conditions and higher pay. With or without official support militant, often violent, disputes were conducted in factories and workshops throughout the country, signifying not just a dramatic rise in union membership, but also a historic shift in the balance of class forces.[33] According to the Webbs, in the revised 1921 edition of their classic *The History of Trade Unionism*, the period saw 'an outburst of exasperated strikes designed, we may almost say, to supersede Collective Bargaining'. The country was gripped by a 'spasm of industrial "insurrectionism"' that seemed 'to repudiate any making of long-term agreements, to spring demand after demand upon employers, to compel every workman to join the Union, avowedly with the view of building up the Trade Union as the dominant force'. By the summer of 1914, they thought the unions were 'working up for an almost revolutionary outburst of gigantic industrial disputes'. This, they sagely acknowledge, would have been 'seriously embarrassing' to the British Labour Party. Within the context of this general revolt, they identified the Dublin Lockout of 1913-14 as 'an epic in itself'.[34] This is, however, to run ahead of ourselves.

1911 was the year that the ITGWU securely established itself, growing from 5000 members at the beginning of the year to some 18,000 at the end. The union played a major part in organising the wave of unrest that swept over Ireland, but it certainly cannot claim to have conjured it up. As Emmet Larkin observed: 'labour unrest was general throughout Ireland and Larkin was again only a convenient focus for what was a national picture'.[35] So many groups of workers made demands of their employers that in August the *Freeman's Journal* introduced a regular column for 'Irish Labour Troubles'. The position was consolidated through 1912 but in 1913 the great wave of unrest burst out again. Before the year was out agricultural labourers, blacksmiths, bill posters, biscuit workers, bottle makers, box makers, brass finishers, bricklayers, building labourers, cabinet makers, canal loaders, carpenters, carters, coach makers, confectioners, dockers, electricians, engineers, gas workers, glaziers, hairdressers, iron founders, linen workers, market gardeners, match workers, millers, newsboys, painters, pavoirs, plasterers, plumbers, poplin workers, seamen and firemen, sewage workers, soap makers, stevedores, stone cutters, tobacco workers, tramway workers, van drivers, wood machinists – even schoolchildren – were to be involved in industrial action.[36] According to the *Freeman's Journal*, 'strike fever' had gripped the Dublin working class.[37]

Between January and August 1913 there were over thirty strikes in Dublin, including a three month long stoppage on the docks that ended in a decisive victory for the ITGWU. Larkin, in the words of his biographer, was 'master of the port'.[38] At the same time, the union was busy organising the agricultural workers of County Dublin. A large enough membership had been built up by August for the union to threaten strike action and thereby secure an unprecedented 20 per cent pay rise for this most downtrodden section of the working class. By the summer of 1913, the ITGWU had achieved a membership of 30,000 and Larkin was claiming that Dublin was the best organised city in the world. This, comments the ITGWU's official history, 'was possibly true'.[39] The union seemed in control of events and the working class was confident and full of hope. Discussions were actually underway to establish a Dublin Board of Conciliation. The employers' counterattack was imminent.

Larkin and Larkinism

What was the nature of the labour unrest in Ireland? According to Dermot Keogh, in his history of the Irish labour movement in this period, all that was at stake in the years before 1914 was the principle of trade union organisation. There was, he insisted, 'a growing trade union consciousness' but not 'a social revolutionary one'. 'I do not accept', he went on, 'that any significant section of the fledgling ITGWU … were either politicised revolutionary socialists or syndicalists'.[40] In some ways, of course, his argument is a useful corrective to those who have seen Dublin in 1913 as an Irish Petrograd with Connolly as an Irish Lenin and the Citizen Army as the Red Guards, but in his eagerness to dispel the red mist surrounding the period, he has emptied it of colour altogether. The 'growing trade union consciousness' he writes of cannot be just left at that. It was more than routine, everyday, official trade unionism founded on compromise and collaboration, accepting employers' prerogatives and the capitalist system. It was a revolt against the authority of the employers, a rejection of the place the working class had been given in society and it contained within it elements capable of developing into a coherent challenge to the employing class and the capitalist system. Certainly, this was what well-informed contemporaries believed. According to Arnold Wright, putting the Dublin employers' view, Larkin's 'movement stands quite outside the ordinary category of labour disturbances'. It was a 'revolutionary rising', the promoters of which intended 'the destruction of Society quite as much as the betterment of the wage conditions of the workers'.[41] While Lord Askwith, the government's chief conciliator, observed that while 'the disputes in the ports and inland cities of Great Britain had been chiefly based upon economic causes, the serious riots in Dublin, although founded upon poverty, low wages and bad conditions, included determination to establish the transport workers' union as the "one big union" in Ireland and put into practice the doctrines of syndicalism …. The influences of "ca'canny" propaganda, the overthrow of Capitalism and revolution against existing authority were all present'.[42] What we are confronted with has been best described by Bob Holton, the historian of British syndicalism as 'proto-syndicalism', something less than social revolutionary but more than trade union consciousness.[43] In its Irish incarnation, this 'proto-syndicalism' was known as Larkinism.

As a movement, Larkinism involved a combination of very diverse elements: syndicalism, industrial unionism, labourism, socialism, republicanism and Catholicism. Holding them all together was the principle of working-class solidarity. This was the central ethic of the ITGWU, the core around which everything else revolved. Any section of workers in dispute could rely upon the active support of the rest of the union. Picket lines were scrupulously respected and 'tainted' goods were never touched. The sympathy strike was a crucial instrument for breaking employer resistance so that no group of workers ever went down to defeat in isolation. Every section of the working class had to be enrolled in the one big union, so that there were no gaps for the employers to exploit, so that everywhere they turned they confronted a united working class stood shoulder to shoulder. Larkin's approach to trade union organisation was evangelical. He came not just to secure union recognition and better wages, but to raise the working class up and to create a new world. As one Dublin employer observed: 'You can't argue with the prophet Isaiah'.[44] There was no place for the non-unionist or the scab in his scheme of things. This was the core of Larkinism and by the summer of 1913 it had given the union an ascendancy in Dublin.

Writing in the British *Daily Herald* newspaper at the height of the 1913 Lock-out, Jim Connolly produced a powerful defence of the Larkinism and of sympathetic action. He argued that the doctrine of the sympathy strike had been developed in 1911 when the ITGWU had come to the rescue of the National Seamen's and Firemen's Union (NSFU). Every ship putting into the port of Dublin was 'held up by the dockers under the orders of Larkin until its crew joined the Union and signed on under Union conditions and rates of pay'. To achieve this result, 'the delegates of the Transport Union up and down the docks preached most energetically the doctrine of the sympathetic strike, and the doctrine was readily assimilated by the dockers and carters'. Since then, the ITGWU had applied the doctrine 'ruthlessly in every Labour dispute' and for the benefit not only of its own members, but of other unions as well. The Dublin mill sawyers had been denied union recognition for twenty years, but 'the sympathetic strike by our Union won them recognition and an increase in pay'. ITGWU control of the carting industry was decisive in winning pay increases for stationary engine drivers, cabinet makers, sheet metal workers, carpenters, building workers and others. Sympathy action or the threat of sympathy action brought employers to heel. Moreover, the ITGWU won increases and improvements for its own members, many of them among the most downtrodden. 'All of these increases', Connolly insisted, 'were the result of the sympathetic strike policy'. And this policy derived not from any 'theories or theorists' but 'was hammered out of the hard necessities of our situation' by the working class itself. For Connolly, it was 'the struggle (that) was forming our theories and shaping the policy ....
We fight as conditions dictate'.[45] This account lacks the inspirational dimension that Larkin brought to the class struggle, but it nevertheless brings home how central sympathetic action was to the success of the ITGWU and the organisation of Dublin.

Larkin, of course, has to be seen as central to this, preaching solidarity and sympathetic action as the moral economy of the working class, but he too has to be related to the circumstances that produced him, to the exigencies of the struggle. Larkin was the product of working-class experience and practice. He had been formed within the working class. There were many militants and activists who shared his attitudes and outlook, but his exceptional abilities and forceful personality had pushed him to the fore and made him the spokesman of the movement. His strengths and virtues, his weaknesses and inconsistencies were those of the most advanced section of the Irish working class that constituted Larkinism. He made this plain himself when he told a meeting:

> Don't bother about cheering Larkin – he is but one of yourselves. It is you that want the cheers, and it is you that deserve them. It is you and the class from which I come – the downtrodden class – that should get the cheers … I don't recognise myself – a mean soul like myself in a mean body – as being the movement. You are the movement and for the time being I have been elected as your spokesman.[46]

This is an important point. One of Larkin's great strengths was his ability to articulate, indeed to shout out, his members' bitterness and anger, their hopes and longings. It seemed to Constance Markiewiez when she heard him speak in public that 'his personality caught up, assimilated and threw back to the vast crowd that surrounded him every emotion that swayed them, every pain and joy that they had ever felt made articulate and sanctified'.[47] Even so hostile an observer as James Sexton, in a backhanded compliment, argued that 'If men were contented, Larkin could convince them that they were really miserable and ready for revolution'. He considered himself as having been something of a hot agitator in his younger militant days but 'I was more frigid than a frozen millpond in comparison with Larkin.' Larkin, he recalled, in Belfast in 1907 'actually succeeded in calling out the members of the Royal Irish Constabulary … I happened to be present at that meeting'.[48] To R. M. Fox, he 'was a crater through which volcanic rumblings emerged from the great upheaving force which was responsible for social tremors throughout the world'.[49] He was a great agitator, 'weak as a theorist … [but] a master of smashing technique when it came to Labour struggle'.[50] For Jack Carney,

> What impressed me most about Larkin was his ability to translate the feelings of his audience into sympathetic speech. One felt that through some mysterious means, he had investigated your personal position and was taking the opportunity of saying for you what you could not say for yourself. His language was not the language of tears but the language of hope …. More than any other man, Jim Larkin taught me that Socialism does not spread by itself because of its own inner beauty or logic or consistency. It spreads when there is something in it that makes it a response to the needs of the hour….[51]

Jim Connolly and Irish Marxism

In July 1910, the veteran socialist propagandist and organiser Jim Connolly had returned to Ireland from America, taking up the post of organiser for the small Socialist Party of Ireland. He initially showed little interest in the ITGWU, and, according to one account, was quite dismissive of the organisation.[52] Nevertheless, in the summer of 1911, Larkin appointed him the union's Belfast organiser and by the end of 1913 he had become his chief lieutenant. Theirs was always an uneasy relationship with inevitable disagreements over strategy and tactics and clashes between two very different personalities, the tornado and the lighthouse as Jack Murphy characterised them. But work together they did until Larkin's departure for the United States in October 1914. With Larkin gone, Connolly was to enter into his fateful alliance with the Irish Republican Brotherhood on the road to Easter Week 1916. We shall come to that further on, but for the moment, who was Jim Connolly?

Connolly was born in Edinburgh in June 1868. He enlisted in the British Army when he was fourteen and served seven years before deserting in 1889. He returned to his native Edinburgh, where he threw himself into the socialist movement as a member of its militant left wing. Despite his lack of formal education, Connolly became a socialist propagandist and working-class intellectual of the first order. His private studies, conducted in the most difficult circumstances, equipped him with a wide knowledge of history, Marxist economics and socialist theory. He developed a written style marked by a remarkable clarity and strength of purpose that can still grip the reader. Everything he said and wrote was informed by what even the Webbs acknowledged was a 'noble character and fine intelligence'.[51]

Victimised and blacklisted in Scotland, Connolly accepted the post of organiser for the Dublin Socialist Club in 1896. He quickly transformed it into the Irish Socialist Republican Party and issued a manifesto that proclaimed that 'the national and economic freedom of the Irish people must be sought in ... the establishment of an Irish Socialist Republic'.[54] His great claim to originality as a Marxist derives from his early assertion that the struggle for national liberation and the struggle for socialism were inseparable in Ireland, and that national freedom would only be accomplished with the overthrow of capitalism. He famously warned in January 1897 that 'If you remove the English army tomorrow and hoist the green flag over Dublin Castle, unless you set about the organisation of the Socialist Republic, your efforts will be in vain'. England, he insisted, would still rule the country 'through her capitalists, through her landlords, through her financiers'.[55] At the same time, he developed a sharp critique of the methods of Irish Republicanism. Revolution 'can only succeed in any country when it has the moral sanction of the people' and this was a lesson the republicans had never learned. What was needed was not an underground conspiracy but a Socialist Republican Party that would campaign openly for revolution. For the republicans to continue 'to counsel rebellion without first obtaining the moral sanction of the people would be an act of criminal folly which would only end in disaster'.[56] This powerful critique of Fenianism was, of course, to be completely forgotten twenty years later.

At this stage of his political development, Connolly's socialism derived from the Scottish left wing of the British Social Democratic Federation (SDF). He had very little time for trade unionism and saw socialist propaganda and nationalist agitation as the way forward but as part of an electoral strategy. The revolution would be accomplished by means of the ballot box. This certainly limited the impact of his ideas on the republican movement. Increasingly, though, he came under the influence of the American Socialist Labor Party (SLP) and its leader, Daniel De Leon. It is worth remembering that at this time Bolshevism was not available as a Marxist alternative to electoralism. With the collapse of the ISRP in circumstances of increasing acrimony, Connolly emigrated to the United States in September 1903. He had no intention of every returning to Ireland, indeed to do so would be 'to return like a dog to his vomit'.[57]

Connolly's time in America was an important phase in his political development with his ideas undergoing considerable change. He passed through De Leon's SLP, was active in the Industrial Workers of the World (IWW), and for a time was a paid organiser for the Socialist Party of America (SPA). At the end of this progress through the American left, he emerged as a political syndicalist, believing that industrial unionism was the decisive element in the future socialist revolution, with the socialist party playing only subordinate propagandist and electoral roles. His ideas were, in many ways, his own reworking of De Leonism. Throughout his American exile, he had devoted considerable effort to working among Irish immigrant workers and had continued to argue that the socialist movement had to take over the leadership of the national struggle in Ireland. This aspect of his political thinking remained unchanged.[58]

Larkin and Connolly

According to Emmet O'Connor, Jim Larkin's most recent biographer, when Connolly returned to Ireland Larkin had at first refused to offer him a post out of jealousy.[59] There is not really any evidence to support this assertion and indeed it is difficult to see what reason Larkin would have had to be jealous of Connolly in 1911. This is an important point because up to 1911 Connolly's political career had been one of failure. This was why he had left Scotland in 1896, why he left Ireland in 1903 and why he left America in 1910. With his return to Ireland, however, he found a situation where his skills and abilities could be put to good use. The defining characteristics of this situation were provided by the Larkinite revolt. The point was made by Jack Carney:

> The sound industrial organization that Jim Larkin had created gave Connolly a platform he had never enjoyed at any time either in England, Scotland or America, so far as his own written propaganda was concerned. Connolly (I have his own word for it) sold more of his pamphlets during the first two years he was in Ireland, after his return from the USA, than in the whole of his career. During my tour of England and Scotland in 1913 I sold 1,500 copies of Labour, Nationality and

Religion and at least two hundred copies of *Labour in Irish History*.

Of course, Carney goes on to allege that it was Connolly who was jealous of Larkin.[60]

Rather than focusing on the conflicts and tensions between the two men, something that derives from the later conflict between Larkin and William O'Brien and that was written into the historiography by C. Desmond Greaves, it is much more important to situate them in their context. This was a context of labour revolt where Larkin was the leader and spokesman of the movement and Connolly was its theoretician and Larkin's chief lieutenant. The *Daily Herald* captured the contrast between the two men when it referred to 'red-hot Larkin' and 'lucid Connolly'.[61] Whatever their conflicts and disagreements, what is important is the work they did together in the great labour revolt.

Notes

1   *Freeman's Journal*, 24 September 1913.
2   Mary Daly, *Dublin: The Deposed Capital*, Cork 1984, pp. 5-18.
3   Frederick Powell, *The Politics of Irish Social Policy*, Lampeter 1992, pp. 118-120.
4   Arnold Wright, *Disturbed Dublin*, London 1914, pp.2-3, 29.
5   Dora Montefiore, *From A Victorian To A Modern*, London 1927, p. 166.
6   C.S. Andrews, *Dublin Made Me*, Cork 1979, pp. 31-32.
7   Powell, op cit, p. 125. For the Church Street collapse see Padraig Yeates, *Lockout: Dublin 1913*, Dublin 2000, pp.106-107.
8   *Freeman's Journal*, 4 January 1913.
9   Jacinta Prunty, *Dublin Slums 1800-1925*, Dublin 1998, pp. 153, 157.
10 Powell, op cit, p. 121-122.
11 Yeates, op cit, p. 109; *Daily Herald*, 27 October 1913.
12 *Irish Worker*, 30 November 1912.
13 Sean O'Casey, *Drums Under The Window*, London 1945 pp. 273, 275.
14 See Jim Larkin, *In The Footsteps of Big Jim*, Dublin 1995, pp. 6-7 for Newry in 1876 and Donal Nevin, ed, *James Larkin, Lion of the Fold*, Dublin 1998, pp. 133-136 for Liverpool in 1874.
15 The best account of Larkin's early career as a political and trade union activist is Eric Taplin, 'James Larkin, Liverpool and the National Union of Dock Labourers: The Apprenticeship of a Revolutionary', *Saothar* 4, 1977.
16 John Gray, *City In Revolt: James Larkin and the Belfast Dock Strike of 1907*, Belfast 1985, p. 56.
17 Ibid, p. 92.
18 Ibid, p. 108.
19 Alice Prochaska, *History of the General Federation of Trade Unions 1899-1980*, London 1982, pp. 46, 48. This official history does not even mention the Belfast disputes.
20 Eric Taplin, *The Dockers' Union: A Study of the National Union of Dock Labourers 1889-1922*, Leicester 1985, p. 51.

21   James Sexton, *Sir James Sexton, Agitator*, London 1936, p. 98.

22   Lord Askwith, *Industrial problems and Disputes*, London 1920, p. 112.

23   Sexton, op cit, pp. 203, 290.

24   Sidney and Beatrice Webb, *The History of Trade Unionism*, London 1894, pp. 456-457, 462. The 'thoughtful artisan' they quote was probably Frank Galton, a former trade union secretary who worked as their assistant on the book. He went on to become secretary of the Fabian Society. In the later 1920 edition of the book, the Webbs write of 'the apostles of the unconverted' as a feature of the 'revivalist' phase of trade union development (p. 581).

25   Emmet Larkin, *James Larkin*, London 1968, p. 35.

26   Seamus Cody, John O'Dowd and Peter Rigney, *The Parliament of Labour: 100 Years of the Dublin Council of Trade Unions*, Dublin 1986, pp. 53-54.

27   Ibid, p 62.

28   Dermot Keogh, *The Rise of the Irish Working Class*, Belfast 1982, p. 133.

29   See William Kenewick, *"Rebellious and Contrary": The Glasgow Dockers 1853-1932*, East Lothian 2000, pp. 200-212.

30   Gray, op cit, pp. 201-203.

31   See Bill McCamley, *The Third James – James Fearon 1874-1924 – An Unsung Hero*, Dublin 2000.

32   Walter Kendall, *The Revolutionary Movement in Britain 1900-1921*, London 1969, p. 26.

33   There is really no adequate account of the Great Labour Unrest but Bob Holton's, *British Syndicalism 1900-1914*, London 1976, is a fine introduction to the politics of the revolt. Also of interest is Standish Meacham, *A Life Apart: The English Working Class 1890-1914*, London 1977.

34   Sidney and Beatrice Webb, *The History of Trade Unionism*, London 1920 revised edition, pp. 473, 690.

35   Larkin, op cit, p. 83.

36   Joseph V. O'Brien, *"Dear, Dirty Dublin": A City in Distress 1899-1916*, Berkeley, California 1982, pp. 222-223.

37   *Freeman's Journal*, 9 July 1913: 'The strike fever in Dublin has now reached a very high temperature'.

38   Larkin, op cit, p. 103.

39   C. Desmond Greaves, *The Irish Transport and General Workers Union: The Formative Years*, Dublin 1982, p. 91. This volume is unfortunately characterised by a degree of hostility towards Larkin that amounts on occasions to character assassination, a tribute to the passion that the man can still excite.

40   Keogh, op cit, pp. 3-4.

41   Wright, op cit, p. 255.

42   Askwith, op cit, p. 259.

43   Holton, op cit, pp. 207-208.

44   Askwith, op cit, p. 113.

45   James Connolly, 'The Solid Truth About The Dublin Dispute', *Daily Herald*, 6 December 1913.

46   *Irish Worker*, 29 July 1911.

47   Larkin, op cit, p. 145.

48   Sexton, op cit, pp. 201, 204.
49   R. M. Fox, *Smokey Crusade*, London 1938, p. 167.
50   R. M. Fox, *Jim Larkin: The Rise of the Underman*, London 1957, p. 73.
51   Patrick Lynch, 'Larkin in History' in Nevin, op cit, p. 118.
52   Austen Morgan, *James Connolly: A Political Biography*, Manchester 1988, p. 88.
53   Sidney and Beatrice Webb, *Trade Unionism* revised 1920 edition, op cit, p. 656.
54   Desmond Ryan, ed, *Connolly: Socialism and Nationalism*, Dublin 1948, p. 186.
55   Ibid, p. 25.
56   Owen Dudley Edwards and Bernard Ransom, eds, *James Connolly: Selected Political Writings*, London 1973, p. 169.
57   C. Desmond Greaves, *The Life and Times of James Connolly*, London 1972, p. 148.
58   For Connolly in America see Carl Reeve and Anne Barton Reeve, *James Connolly and the United States*, Atlantic Highlands, New Jersey 1978. See also James A. Stevenson, 'Clashing Personalities: James Connolly and Daniel De Leon 1896-1909', *Eire-Ireland* XXV 1990.
59   Emmet O'Connor, *James Larkin* Cork 2002, p. 34. This biography by Ireland's foremost labour historian is marred by its almost unremitting hostility to its subject.
60   Nevin, op cit, p. 399.
61   *Daily Herald*, 17 November 1913.

Chapter II
'Wrath, Hope and Wonder': The *Irish Worker* and the Dublin labour movement

On 27 May 1911 the ITGWU launched a weekly newspaper, the *Irish Worker*, edited by Larkin. The first issue sold 5,000 copies, the second 8,000, the third 15,000, with sales finally settling at around 20,000 a week. Circulation was largely confined to Dublin and, as C. Desmond Greaves points out in his official history of the ITGWU, it seems a fair assumption that it 'was read or discussed by the entire working class of the city'. This was, he acknowledges, 'something unprecedented in any city in the world'.[1] The pages of the *Irish Worker* offer a remarkable insight into the ideological contours of Dublin's labour revolt and help delineate the nature of Larkinism. As Larkin advised his working-class readers

> At present you spend your lives in sordid labour and your abode in filthy slums; your children hunger, and your masters say your slavery must endure for ever. If you would come out of bondage yourself must forge the weapons and fight the grim battle.
> The written word is the most potent force in our modern world. The Irish Worker will be a lamp to guide your feet in the dark hours of the impending struggle; a well of truth reflecting the purity of your motives, and a weekly banquet from which you will rise strengthened in purpose to emulate the deeds of your forefathers, who died in dungeon and on scaffold in the hopes of a glorious resurrection for our beloved country.[2]

The *Irish Worker* preached discontent and rebellion, urging its readers to join together and take up the fight for a new social order and for a free Ireland. When historian Dermot Keogh dismisses it as being merely 'vitriolic, scurrilous ... many of the issues were "a libel a line"', he seriously misjudges both the paper and its purpose.[3] Other historians have, of course, been more generous to Larkin and his newspaper. R.M. Fox, one of his early biographers, compared his 'eruption into Labour journalism' with that of Feargus O'Connor and the *Northern Star*. The *Irish Worker* was, according to Fox, ferociously partisan, warmly praising friends but directing a constant stream of abuse against "'scabs', employers who paid low wages and denied the right of trade union organisation, enemies of every description'. The newspaper kept up the fighting spirit at a time 'when struggle was very necessary'.[4] Emmet Larkin, in what is still the standard biography of the ITGWU leader, describes the *Irish Worker* as 'unique in the history of working class journalism'. 'Nothing like it has ever been seen since …. It was less a newspaper than the spirit of four glorious years'. Reading the newspaper was like feeling 'the quickening pulse of Dublin', as Larkin laid about him, attacking 'with a monumental perseverance the sweating, exploiting employers and the corrupt cynical politicians who in his eyes were responsible for the reprehensible social conditions of Dublin'.[5] Similarly, Robert Lowry, in an account of Sean O'Casey's involvement with the newspaper, describes it as 'an extraordinary newspaper, a milestone in the history of working class journalism'. He points out that over a period of forty-one months, as well as editing the newspaper, Larkin authored nearly 400 articles. Every week he wrote one or more editorials, which were always 'fresh and lively and, as often as not, explosive'. This journalistic achievement is staggering when one realises 'that he was also in charge of the Irish Transport and General Workers' Union, president of the Irish Women Workers' Union, a frequent candidate for political office, and often the main speaker at workers' rallies in all parts of Ireland.[6] Certainly, a close reading of the paper is essential for any understanding of Larkinism.

In its very first issue, the paper carried Larkin's 'Our Platform and Principles' where he introduced himself:

> To the working class of Ireland the Editor of the Irish Worker makes his bow – not in any humble manner, however, but as one who desires to speak to you and of you with honour and pride. Too long, aye! for too long, have we, the Irish working people been humble and inarticulate …. The Irish Working Class (capital letters, good Mr Printer) are beginning to awaken. They are coming to realise the truth of the old saying: 'He who would be free himself must strike the blow.'

He went on to attack the various nationalist organizations that competed for the allegiance of the working class: Arthur Griffith's Sinn Féin, William O'Brien's All-for-Ireland League (or the 'All-for-William League', as Larkin called it) and John Redmond's powerful Home Rule Party. The Home Rule party, in particular, 'have proved that they are not concerned in the material welfare of the Irish Worker by the fact that every Act passed by the British Parliament that in any way minimised the hard conditions of the English worker, or in any way improved his condition, the Nationalist Party have agreed, nay insisted on Ireland being deleted from such legislation, always excepting the Old Age Pensions Act, which they dared not interfere with'. What these parties understood by freedom was, according to Larkin, freedom for employers and landlords to continue their oppression and exploitation of the working class. The *Irish Worker* championed another definition:

> By freedom we mean that we, Irishmen in Ireland, shall be free to govern this land called Ireland by the Irish people in the interest of all the Irish people .... We owe no allegiance to any other nation nor the king, governors, or representatives of any other nation. That all such persons are interlopers and trespassers on this our land, and that we are determined to accomplish not only National Freedom, but a greater thing – Individual Freedom – Freedom from military and political slavery, economic or wage slavery! How then are we to achieve Freedom and Liberty?
> To accomplish political and economic freedom we must have our own party! There is no difficulty whatever about that.[7]

Interestingly enough, Dermot Keogh also quotes quite extensively from this article in order to illustrate the 'abusive', 'tendentious', indeed hateful way that Larkin abused his opponents. Certainly, there is more than a little of that in the article, but there is also much more. First of all, Larkin was clearly concerned to foster and encourage the self-respect of the working class, to argue that working people should hold their heads high with pride both in themselves and in their class. Their humility and inarticulacy were the badges of their downtrodden subordination and Larkin intended to banish these forever. This was a necessary precondition if the working class was to organize itself to fight for improvements in its material conditions. The working class could not look to others, he argued, but must themselves 'strike the blow'. The article also made clear that the *Irish Worker* was a wholeheartedly republican newspaper and that it stood not just for the achievement of national independence, but also for a socialist reordering of society. This required an Irish Labour party. Clearly the newspaper cannot be dismissed as a mere scandal sheet or a 'libel a line' rag. Over the next three and a half years it was to play a vital part in the struggle of the Dublin working class to raise itself up.

Over this period, the *Irish Worker* carried a number of detailed exposures of the appalling social conditions that existed in Dublin. On 11 November 1911 the whole front page was devoted to R. J. P. Mortished's 'Facts About Dublin', a statistical account of working-class poverty in the city. Through May and June 1912, the paper serialized James Connolly's 'Labour and the Reconquest of Ireland'.[8] Similarly, over a period of five weeks in August and September 1912, 'Euchan' (A. Patrick Wilson), one of the propagandist mainstays of the news-paper, contributed a series of articles on 'Labour and Frugality', arguing that no matter how careful a family was over its expenditure, the wages of the unskilled were simply not enough to live on.[9] These were all substantial pieces, written with controlled outrage and arguing a cogent, well-documented case against the iniquities of the capitalist system. However, the paper is best remembered, somewhat unfairly, for its exposure of more specific injustices and its pillorying of more particular villains. This was very much Larkin's own speciality.

Week after week, the newspaper exposed and condemned the sweat-shop conditions that existed in many Dublin workplaces and often attacked employers, overseers and foremen by name. The biscuit firm, Jacobs, was often complained of:

> If a girl who makes a collection for another work girl, either in the way of a wedding present or for some other purpose, deserves instant dismissal according to firm's rules, what do the snivellers who terrorise the employees into giving a donation (voluntary, moryah!) for a wedding present to Miss G. M. Jacob deserve? – the snivellers think promotion. I think a summons under the Truck Act ....[10]

And as Christmas drew near in 1911, the Jacob's management earned an editorial all of their own from Larkin's pen: 'Peace on Earth: Good Will to All Men':

> Let us take the philanthropic firm of Jacobs. Here on the eve of Christmas, so to speak, a large number of men, boys and girls have been dismissed, and a still larger number under notice of dismissal this week. The excuse is slackness of trade and shutting down of plant, the night shift having been dispensed with. One would naturally expect that the last persons employed would be dispensed with first. Not so in Jacobs. Men and youths, with from 6 to 12 years service have been discharged at a few minutes notice ... we ask George Jacob has his daughter's clock ticked; for if so she must be reminded that a number of the employees of Jacob and Co. who kept her and her family in affluence and luxury and who provided her wedding dowry – aye, even the clock that ticked – are now sacked on the eve of Christmas .... We wonder did Mr George Jacob ever read Charles Dickens' *Christmas Carol* – we wonder.[11]

In late January 1912 the *Irish Worker* carried another story that Larkin used to dramatize the nature of class relationships in Dublin. The newspaper's readership were reminded of how on Christmas morning, Larkin and the rest of the staff had entertained some 200 sandwich board men to breakfast and of how 'poor old John Carroll', 102 years of age, had proposed a vote of thanks. A few days later John Carroll went to Jameson's Distillery, where he had worked for forty-five years, for his regular Christmas box, 'but was heartlessly told to begone: that if he wanted to live he go could and make speeches for a living, telling him what had been seen in the Irish Worker'.[12] The newspaper opened a subscription list for the unfortunate Carroll and reported the contributions in succeeding weeks.

On another occasion, Larkin told his readers of how

While we write, two children accompanied by their poor, hungry, ill-dressed mother are telling their tale of woe. Two children – girls of 14 and 16 years of age – were slaving for Somersets, of Golden Lane, embroiderers and linen manufacturers. They supply finished goods to Roberts, of Grafton Street. These two hungry children worked 12 days for 10d – twelve days for ten pence! This is no exaggeration or mis-statement. They produced their dockets issued by these soulless blood-suckers.

He warned such employers that

The time is rapidly arriving when you will be called to a halt! The Worker is doing its share in educating the working class to their own want of knowledge, want of class loyalty, want of solidarity, want of earnestness, want of spirit, and their rights which they have forgotten to demand. A new nation is in birth, a newer type of man and woman is being formed amongst the working class; a new era opens out to us, and the Worker is one of the instruments to that end – the end being a mutual Commonwealth built on service, a broadening out of the perspective of life, a fuller and more complete life, the obliterating of class rule and distinction of caste – a day when work, useful and beautiful, will be the test; when the idler, the wastrel, the fop, the creature of an hour shall cease to be, and the builder, the beautifier shall take their rightful place in the land, and among other nations, there will be no child slaves in those good days to be working twelve days for tenpence.[13]

This is Larkin's journalism at its most powerful, moving from the particular to the general, from a specific, heart-breaking injustice to a vision of a new world.

Alongside exposé articles of this kind, highlighting particular acts of injustice and petty tyranny, the *Irish Worker* also regularly featured personal attacks on a variety of foes. In January 1913, for example, the newspaper began a series of 'Biographies in Brief', savaging the leaders of the Dublin Home Rule Party in the most abusive and uncomplimentary language. This treatment was meted out to anyone and everyone who stood in the way of Larkin's efforts at building the ITGWU and the Dublin Labour Party. The press, predictably enough, came in for its share of Larkin's wrath. In February 1913 he wrote of how 'the latest manifestation of vindictive cowardly lying' by the Dublin newspapers 'puts the hallmark on their ability in trying to destroy the confidence of the working class in an intelligent working class movement'. He singled out the newspapers owned by William Martin Murphy, 'the most foul and vicious blackguard that ever polluted any country', and castigated the 'journalistic renegades' who worked for him:

Take this foul lie that a child, famished for want of food, when spoken to by a good, generous gentleman who pens the filthy lying statement, the fainting hungry child explains that its daddy is on strike. What ho! Fancy William Martin Murphy sympathizing with a hungry child, the Ghoul, the creature who sweated and starved a whole countryside during the strike of the railway slaves in Clare, the ghoul who has sacked hundreds of men for trivial complaints, knowing that such dismissal meant actual starvation for the dismissed men's children .... When did he ever cherish or assist one human being who was in trouble?[14]

Larkin offered £100 to charity if the story of the child was shown to be true. When his challenge was ignored, he decided that the time for restraint was gone and returned to attack:

Let them produce the child whose daddy's on strike and fainted for food, and who received 6d from a philanthropic reporter, because this alleged reporter's heart bled for the child's sufferings. Oh, ye hypocrites! Oh, ye whited sepulchres! Oh, ye blasphemous hounds .... You sell your talent for a miserable thirty pieces of silver ... ye paid blacklegs of the press will be remembered ... and the men ye lied about will not forget .... Your attacks but spur us onward.[15]

What was the reason for the ferocity of Larkin's journalism? His great concern was to raise up the working class from subordination to a recognition of its own power and strength. His abuse of the multitude of oppressors that day after day lorded it over the working class was but the other side of this coin. Raising up the working class required pulling down its enemies, and this was the intention behind his rhetoric of vilification and abuse. This is an important point. Larkin's scabrous attacks on slum landlords, sweat-shop employers, lying journalists, various scabs, corrupt politicians and bullying policemen served a definite and calculated purpose. He was out to diminish them by ridicule, to cut them down to size and show them up as moral pygmies. The cloak of morality with which they covered their activities was to be stripped away as Larkin moved among them, come to cleanse the Temple. His recourse to biblical imagery and reference was intended to identify the working-class cause as the cause of righteousness and to damn its opponents. His attacks turned the world upside-down and made the rich and the powerful the object of working-class contempt. They were stripped of the respect to which their position in society normally entitled them, replacing the doffed cap with the challenging stare. His sarcastic, abusive and contemptuous journalism was a necessary means of rallying the working class and building up its self-confidence in the face of ruthless, determined employers who were accustomed to having things their way. The *Irish Worker*, as R. M. Fox notes, 'kept up the fighting spirit'.[16]

What remedy did the *Irish Worker* offer to its readership for the righting of their wrongs? The solution lay in trade union organization, in the building of one union embracing all categories of labour. As 'Euchan' argued:

How can the living wage be obtained? It can be obtained by the workers themselves without thanks to anyone. Let the workers stand firmly together, shoulder to shoulder, just as the masters do. Let the demand come from all – one union for all workers, and the capitalist class could not resist ... the workers are not making the class war for the class war has been forced upon them. Let the workers learn from the masters how to engage in the fight.

Federation! Consolidation! Organisation! These are the watchwords for the workers – the three-leafed Shamrock of Labour growing from the one stalk – the one great union for all workers.[17]

This was the *Irish Worker*'s rallying cry. Time and time again it urged the need for 'the one great union' and called on the workers to rouse themselves from their apathy and enlist in the struggle.

The Time of Dreams

In a powerful front-page article, 'The Time of Dreams and the Virtues of Discontent', that appeared at Easter 1913, 'Euchan' proclaimed that the workers' struggle was a holy struggle and that it had been sanctified by Christ's Easter passion:

Just as the stone was rolled away on that first Easter morning, so, too, are the stones which veil our eyes rolled away with the coming of spring, and we who are not yet grey of heart see visions and dream dreams – dreams, too, which we believe can be realised. And when we of the proletariat or working class dream these dreams and when we know they can be realised, we are filled with a holy discontent ... the working classes themselves are beginning to understand. They are beginning to understand that when they dream of freedom, and when they grow discontented with their chains, they are becoming real men and real women, real images of God, and not the beasts of burden they have hitherto been content to remain ... it was the falling away of the stone on that first Easter dawn that gave the workers the right to be discontented, for then, indeed, had the old order passed away and the new order of Christian Brotherhood had become the world's ideal ... it is the dream of the workers that this era of wage slavery shall cease, and this dream shall be realised, too, for its realisation depends upon the workers themselves, their combination and their solidarity; and they are already working for these things and working hard. The workers have awakened. They have seen the vision; they are working to realise their dream of freedom, and they will realise it undoubtedly.[18]

In this way, the *Irish Worker* waged a continual campaign to make the union central to the lives of its readership, endowing its trade union concerns with spiritual significance and advocating a spiritual transformation.

While as a union the ITGWU was primarily concerned with economic questions of wages and conditions, under Larkin's leadership it was also intended to prefigure the socialist commonwealth of the future, to begin the building of that future in the here and now. The union offered its members membership of a working-class community that embraced a whole view of society starkly at odds with the prevailing ideas. Brotherhood, fraternity and solidarity, the collective virtues, were championed over and against the possessive individualism that dominated capitalist society. As Emmet O'Connor has argued, Larkin offered 'an ethical vision to the working class' and tried 'to forge an alternative morality by the patient construction of a workers' counter culture'. This was often an uphill struggle and sometimes even Larkin was near to despair. On one occasion, he wrote of how working-class apathy had at one time seemed to 'stultify all our efforts' and of how the 'gospel of the materialistic school seemed to have captured the great mass of the working class'. Men replied to his appeals for fellowship and brotherly love in the words of Cain: 'Am I my brother's keeper?' But even when things seemed blackest 'and dark night enshrouds abroad, lo! the Sun, and lo! thereunder rises wrath and hope and wonder, and the worker comes marching on'.[19] This vision sustained him through all the many disappointments and set-backs of these years.

Larkin completely rejected any narrow economic view of trade unionism as a capitulation to the capitalist class. For him, the ITGWU was the means to build a new world, humane and just, and it was this philosophy that filled the pages of the *Irish Worker*. Early in January 1912, 'O'F' had asked

> Is it because a man joins a trade union he is never to think of anything but committee meetings; never to wish for anything but strikes; never to hope for anything better than a rise of a few shillings in his pay? Should he not love good books and plays, and the sun and the stars and fields and flowers? Ought he not to love his wife and children, and to teach them all he can? If he is expected to rear children, why is he not to seek all the information he needs on the subject? If home and family are not bad for the working man, then all things that in any way bear on either come within the scope of a Labour paper. There is no topic from stars to strikes in which the workers should not be encouraged to take an interest.[20]

The union tried to realize its breadth of vision in practice, and considerable effort was put into organizing a social life for its members. According to Emmet Larkin, 'the crowning achievement' was the acquisition of Croydon Park, a house and three acres of land in Clontarf, as a recreational centre for union members and their families.[21]

'Euchan' made clear how important this area of the union's activity was in an article, 'The Jovial Revolution', describing the celebrations which accompanied the opening of Croydon Park in August 1913. 'The Social Revolution, so far as Ireland is concerned, was', he wrote, 'ushered in last Monday.' There was no bloodshed and no violence, but nevertheless there had been a revolution:

> To watch a dock labourer walk into a mansion, saunter into the dining-room and proceed to put a tuppence doorstep sandwich and a penny bottle of minerals out of sight without the slightest air of surprise at his surroundings struck me as the most revolutionary sight I ever saw in my life .... Not so long ago a mansion was

a place which working men were supposed to pass with cap in hand and with a mumbled blessing or curse for the lord of the manor. Nowadays things have changed. Through organisation the workers of Dublin have secured a spirit of independence and self-reliance which enables them to snap their fingers at the lords of the manor, of the factory and of the workshop.

With this spirit of independence also the workers are realising that they require a fuller and more enjoyable life. If employers and their families need lawns and gardens to sport in, then the workers and their families need them also. If the sons and daughters of the employing class require tennis-courts and croquet greens, then the sons and daughters of the working class require them also. The idea may be revolutionary, but it is merely bare justice nevertheless ....

According to 'Euchan', Croydon Park provided a place for the children to play, and 'we wanted a place for their fathers and mothers to learn to play too'.[22] Already, however, the storm clouds had gathered that were to sweep away this vision and awake the dreamer to a harsh and unkind reality.

Catholicism and the Dublin Working Class

In his official history of the Irish Transport and General Workers' Union, C. Desmond Greaves almost completely ignores the degree of clerical hostility that greeted it, reaching a crescendo at the time of the Lockout. This neglects an important aspect of the struggle, because, as we shall see, on numerous occasions the *Irish Worker* was driven to respond to clerical attacks and they were clearly regarded as a serious threat.

According to Emmet Larkin, the rise of the ITGWU was from the very beginning greeted with 'nonsensical abuse' and 'hysterical anti-Socialism' by the Church.[23] This obviously created serious problems because both Larkin himself and the overwhelming majority of the union's members were practicing Catholics. The exact contours of working-class Catholicism in Dublin still remains to be delineated, but there can be no serious doubt that the great majority, both men and women, still identified with the Church and the Catholic faith. This was a stark contrast with the working class in most other Catholic countries.[24] Larkin himself was once to famously insist to a sceptical revolutionary audience in the United States that

There is no antagonism between the cross and socialism. A man can pray to Jesus the Carpenter, and be a better socialist for it. Rightly understood, there is no conflict between the vision of Marx and the vision of Christ. I stand by the cross and I stand by Karl Marx. Both *Capital* and the *Bible* are to me Holy Books.'[25]

While these sentiments were almost incomprehensible to an audience of European or American revolutionaries, in Ireland they were inevitable. How are we to explain this phenomenon? This is obviously a necessary preliminary to any examination of the *Irish Worker's* attitude towards the Catholic Church, and, more particularly, towards clerical hostility, but it is also essential to an understanding of the Irish working class.

The peculiar strength of Irish Catholicism has its beginnings in the Elizabethan conquest and the first manifestation of England rule in Ireland as a Protestant Ascendancy. The Protestant character of the conquest became more pronounced over time, reaching its highpoint in the penal regime that followed the Treaty of Limerick of 1691. Resistance to English rule during this period took the form of a Catholic Jacobite reaction. There was an opportunity in the 1790s for the emergence of an Irish nationalism uniting both Protestants and Catholics, both North and South, in the form of the United Irishmen, but this was decisively crushed by the British.[26] Modern Irish nationalism, as it emerged in the nineteenth century bore the marks of its long pre-history, including the United Irish defeat, so that Catholicism and nationalism became inseparably linked in the consciousness of the people. This identification was firmly fixed in place by the gradual disappearance of Gaelic Ireland. The Irish turned, in what Emmet Larkin, has characterised as a 'devotional revolution' to a particular brand of puritanical Catholicism for a new cultural identity and religion became the hallmark of their national identity.[27]

The Catholicism and the Church that the Irish people turned to in the nineteenth century were very much the creation of a particular class, part and parcel of the emergence of the Catholic rural and urban middle class as the dominant social group within Irish society. In some ways, what Emmet Larkin characterised as a 'devotional revolution' can be better characterised as a 'devotional conquest' whereby the large tenant farmers in the countryside and the middle class (businessmen, professionals), in the towns set about imposing their social values on the rest of society. The Church was to play a vital role in the disciplining of the working class on behalf of the Irish middle class. It was in a very real sense their Church. Whereas on the Continent, the Catholic Church was allied with the great Catholic landowners and with Catholic governments, in Ireland the great landowners and the government were Protestant. Instead, the Church became a middle-class Church. It was the rural and urban middle class who staffed the Church with their sons and daughters, who financed it with their contributions, and who constituted the respectable core of its congregation. Unsurprisingly, the Church reflected their worldview and represented their interests.

As far as the political history of the nineteenth century was concerned, the Catholic Church had rallied to O'Connell's Repeal movement, following very much in the wake of the Catholic middle class. Indeed, the Church provided the organisational framework within which O'Connell built a mass movement. Similarly with the Land League, the Church soon rallied to the cause of the farmers and the parish priest was to provide many of the organisational skills that sustained the movement. Archbishop Croke was one of the great propagandists of the farmer's cause, with the British government seriously considering imprisoning him. Indeed, the hierarchy was to go so far to defy Rome in its support for both the Land League and the later Plan of Campaign. The Church was able to play the decisive part in the overthrow of Parnell precisely because it had proven its nationalist credentials during the Land War. When the Church condemned revolutionary movements such as the Fenians in the 1860s, it did so not on behalf of the British, but because such movements were perceived as a threat by the large tenant farmers and the urban middle class, as a challenge to their ascendancy within the nation and as a threat to their material well-being. It was for this same reason that the Church was to condemn Larkinism.[28]

One consequence of the middle-class character of the Irish Catholic Church was the failure of a serious anti-clerical movement to develop in Ireland. The country was unique in this regard. Whereas on the Continent, in France, Spain and Italy, the rising middle class had to fight for power and influence against a feudal-royalist reaction that was allied with the Church and accordingly rallied popular support around a programme of anti-clericalism, in Ireland the Church supported the middle class against the Protestant Ascendancy and the British. Instead of having to combat the hold of Catholicism over the people, the Catholic middle class were able to make use of it and consequently did all they could to strengthen it. The absence of any serious anti-clerical tradition in Ireland had profound consequences for the Irish working class and neither Larkin nor Connolly were exempt from this.[29]

The religious devotion of the Catholic working class was incontestable. Todd Andrews, in his evocative memoir, remembered the Dublin working class as terribly poor and deeply religious:

> Their main concern was to provide food and lodgings for their children; they frequently failed to do either. Among them trachoma and rickets were endemic. They were religious on Sundays, and no matter how small their possessions there was always a statue of the Blessed Virgin, the Sacred Heart and perhaps the Infant of Prague on the mantelpiece. They accepted their misery as the will of God and in the certainty that their fortitude would be rewarded in the next life. They had abandoned hope in the here and now until Larkin, the great Labour leader and agitator, emerged to proclaim the dignity of the working man.[30]

Larkin, Connolly and the Church

Confronted with the Catholicism of the Irish working class, Jim Connolly argued that there was no incompatibility between socialism and religion, indeed that 'the most consistent socialist or syndicalist may be as Catholic as the Pope if he is so minded'.[31] Indeed, he looked forward to an accommodation between the Church and the socialist movement. While he countered clerical attacks on the left with considerable ferocity, he nevertheless rejected anti-clericalism because

To use a homely adage, the Church "does not put all her eggs in one basket", and the man who imagines that in the supreme hour of the proletarian struggle for victory the Church will definitely line up with the forces of capitalism ... simply does not understand the first thing about the policy of the Church ... in the future, the Church, which has its hand close upon the pulse of human society, when it realises that the cause of capitalism is a lost cause, will find excuse enough to allow freedom of speech and expression to those lowly priests whose socialist declarations it will then use to cover and hide the absolute anti-socialism of the Roman propaganda .... Thus it has been in the past. Thus it will be, at least attempted in the future. This forecast has infinitely more probability in it than the dreams of those who tell us so glibly of a coming Armageddon between the forces of socialism and Catholicism.[32]

This belief that the Church would inevitably come to terms with the growing socialist movement rather than go down with capitalism underpinned his view that religion as such was not inimical to the socialist project and that all that was necessary as far as the Church was concerned was for socialists to combat clerical efforts at interfering in matters that did not concern them. To this end he grasped at any hint of clerical sympathy. On 6 July 1912, the *Irish Worker* carried an enthusiastic report by Connolly of a paper on 'Strikes' delivered by a priest at the annual meeting of the Maynooth Union. Connolly acclaimed the paper as 'a welcome revelation that a new spirit is also at work among the clergy' and looked forward to the day the Church would rally to the socialist cause. He wrote of how

our minds travel back to the early days of the Irish Land League, the attitude of the clergy of Ireland towards that uprising of the poor, and the great change in their attitude when that movement became a dominant force in the struggle between the landlord and tenant. In the early days of the movement the higher clergy had practically nothing but condemnation for the agitation and vehement denunciation of the agitators .... The Bishop of Sligo, the same prelate who recently came out of his political silence to denounce Jim Larkin made himself an unpleasant reputation by his reckless denunciation of Michael Davitt .... But with the growth of the Land League and the increasing proof of the beneficent effects upon the fortunes of the tenants the attitude of the clergy underwent a change. In greater and greater numbers they entered the Land League and very soon this indiscriminate abuse of the Land League and its methods by the clergy was replaced by an equally indiscriminate praise .... If the Irish Labour Movement is destined to go through the same phases, no one will more heartily accept it than we shall.[34]

This, as the Dublin Lockout was soon to demonstrate, was somewhat optimistic.

Even after the experience of the Lockout, Connolly remained absolutely committed to this perspective. Only months before the Easter Rising in 1916 he welcomed a speech by Father Lawrence to the Dublin Trades Council as 'by far the most significant speech yet delivered in the Trades Hall'! He went on once again to conjure up the illusion of an alliance between the Church and the socialist movement:

> Here we had a great meeting of working men and women, overwhelmingly Catholic in their religious faith, gathering together to discuss problems of social life and national aspiration with a priest whom they held in affectionate esteem, but insisting upon discussing these problems in the spirit of comradeship and equality. Perhaps nowhere else in Europe could such a meeting on such terms be held, and in such harmony between the parties concerned .... It is safe to say that such meetings as that of Tuesday are safer guarantees for Ireland against the growth here of anti-clericalism of the French type than would be all the pamphlets of the Catholic Truth Society, without such friendly discussions between the clergy and the laity. They are a sign that the lesson of France has not been lost, that the church recognises that if it does not move with the people, the people will move without her.[34]

What was missing, of course, was any understanding of the class nature of the Irish Church.

While Larkin never had Connolly's understanding of Marxism and was himself a devout Catholic, he seems to have escaped Connolly's illusions about the Church. For him the priority was how to deal with clerical hostility that often amounted to little more than slander, lies and intimidation dressed up as religion. Two strategies were adopted to deal with the situation: first, every effort was made to avoid giving offence over questions of faith or morals, and second, any clerical trespassing on what was felt to be the territory of the trade union was censured. Problems still arose, however, and no matter how hard the union tried the clergy still found the opportunity to beat them with the club of morality.

Early in January 1912, for example, the *Irish Worker* was forced over a number of weeks to deny that it advocated birth control or so-called 'Malthusian doctrines'. This followed publication in its columns of an innocuous article by 'O'F in which he urged the poor not to have large families because this only worsened their poverty. The paper strongly denied that any writer 'would be allowed to use the columns of this paper to advance views which are contrary to common sense' and stated that at no time had it advocated 'limitation of families by artificial means'.[35] 'O'F himself subsequently replied somewhat limply to one clerical critic that 'I simply said that people should exercise self-control after marriage as they did before. If "purity" was possible then it is possible now'.[36] The question became the subject of considerable clerical sermonizing and was made much of by the press, particularly Murphy's *Independent*, in the Dublin municipal elections. On occasion, Larkin tried to play the same game himself and used the *Irish Worker* to defend Catholic morality. He powerfully editorialized against the showing in the city of a 'blasphemous' film, *The Miracle*, and demanded to know what the police and the Vigilance Committee were doing. 'Why some creatures', he wrote, 'would barter the Cross of Calvary for money'. But not, he added, 'Socialists or Labour men, mark'.[37] Both Connolly and Larkin on other occasions made clear their opposition to divorce. In his *Labour, Nationality and Religion*, Connolly condemned divorce in uncompromising terms as a product of capitalism, while during the Great Lockout, on one celebrated occasion, Larkin refused to share a platform in Grimsby with a divorcee. His place was taken by the young Harry Pollitt.[38]

There was a continual undercurrent of clerical hostility to the union that occasionally manifested itself in the pages of the *Irish Worker*. The paper carried stories of nuns telling children to refuse to buy copies of the *Irish Worker* if their parents tried to send them for it, and of priests making deliberate use of Fergussons the hairdresser where union members had been on strike for twelve weeks.[39] It was with the onset of the Great Lockout, however, that clerical attacks became a serious enough problem to merit a determined response. We shall return to this in subsequent chapters.

National Freedom

One aspect of the ITGWU and of the *Irish Worker* that is often neglected is the fact that from the very beginning the union was staunchly republican and this was reflected in its newspaper. Numerous articles made this commitment clear. In the very first issue, Larkin had written that 'we owe no allegiance to any other nation, nor the king, governors, or representatives of any other nation'. The *Irish Worker* stood quite unambiguously for 'National Freedom'. On 17 June 1911 the paper made absolutely clear its identification with left republicanism by starting a series of reprints from James Fintan Lalor's 1848 newspaper, the *Irish Felon*. The series ran for nine weeks until 12 August. The republican commitment was made even clearer in a front page article, 'Loyal – to whom?' by 'O'F' that appeared on the occasion of George V's visit to Dublin in July 1911:

Over one thousand persons deliberately chose to visit Wolfe Tone's grave on Saturday last in preference to staying in the city to watch the procession. Over one thousand young men and women, in Dublin alone, who cared more for the principles of a man, whom the British Government sentenced to death, than they did for all the tawdry pomp and bloody vengeance of the Pirate Empire.
Some may say that this is out of place in a labour paper; that we should not take sides in politics. We know what we are about. We know that until the workers of Ireland obtain possession of the land of Ireland and make their own laws they can only hope for and obtain partial improvement of their conditions .... Our ambition is to nationalise the wealth and production of the country; to do this we must first nationalise the people, then the Government .... The welfare of the people of Ireland is more important to us than the smiles of a king or queen. While there is a hungry man, woman or child in Ireland, while there is even one of

our people ill-clad, or ill-treated, we will join in no display of hypocritical loyalty. While there is one barefooted child in this country we cannot afford to buy flags or fireworks, nor present loyal addresses.[40]

The paper's attitude towards Home Rule is instructive. Larkin welcomed it in an editorial, 'Shall the Bill be a final settlement', but only because it would teach 'the class for whom we speak … that not in Bills nor Acts lies freedom – the only freedom worth enjoying – "economic freedom"'. As far as he was concerned 'this emasculated measure is not and cannot be a final settlement, and this statement will be supported by the vast majority of the working class in this country.' The good thing about it was that it would clear the way for the rise of 'a conscious working class party [that] will face the exploiting class in this as in every other country, and no longer will we be the helots of the world-wide working class movement'. He looked forward to 'a day of reckoning, and then for the final settlement'. The editorial ended with an appeal to the 'shades of Mitchel, Davitt, Lalor, Emmet and Tone …. Ever watching, ever waiting, still accepting, still pursuing, until the final settlement'.[41]

Larkin poured scorn on the idea of Home Rule as a final settlement, and in one extremely effective editorial hilariously satirized the position of the Irish Nationalist leader, John Redmond:

We regret to inform our readers from wireless messages received, signed Tone, Emmet, Russell, Lalor, Mitchel and Davitt, that the old barque 'Erin' struck an iceberg whilst bound for the port of Independence. From latest advice to hand, it seems that during the voyage of 800 years bound for the above port numerous skippers had commanded the craft, some of whom had given up the job in despair; other had given up their lives in bad weather in trying to keep her head to the wind; but not one of those who had gone before ever dared to suggest they should alter course. The port of Independence they were bound for – the port of Independence they had orders to reach; and if they had dared, we repeat, to go about and alter course by a point the crew who served under them would have keel-hauled them. But times have changed. The present skipper has thought it wise to discharge the crew and depend on the passengers to bring the old craft in … the boatswain will pipe God Save The King and persuade the crown in the forecastle it is a Nation Once Again.[42]

The paper often gloried in full-blown republican rhetoric. In November 1912 Larkin commemorated the Manchester Martyrs in a powerful editorial, 'Allen, Larkin, and O'Brien', that once again makes clear the paper's republican commitment:

And yet those three humble working men, who gave their all for the Irish nation, live on in the hearts of all true men, though dead they truly liveth …. Were Allen, O'Brien, and Larkin justified in protesting against the brutal power of the English

Government; were they right in trying to break the chains that shackled and still shackle their beloved country ...? We say emphatically, Yes .... Remember, if Esau sold his birthright for a mess of pottage it is not necessary for us to repeat that foolishness. Better the roadside starvation and Freedom .... No, to you our dead, lying in the cold clay of England, your bodies burned by the cursed quicklime, if it be our own fate to go through the furnace, we repeat our vow, as true as you were to Kathleen Na Hoolihan, so too we, bone of your bone as we are, will never disgrace you nor forget you.[43]

On other occasions he was to urge the social side of republican politics. The men and women who assembled at Bodenstown on 22 June 1913 were urged to 'try and understand Tone's life and work'. They were not to forget 'his historic words that having found it was useless to appeal to the landed and capitalistic section of the community he was forced to realise there was but one section, and one section only, who answered his call ... the working class'.[44] As for Arthur Griffiths, the Sinn Féin leader, Larkin offered a copy of his *The Resurrection of Hungary* as a prize to any reader who could 'quote a line written by Lil' Arthur in favour of organised labour'.[45]

There was never any problem in this forthright advocacy of 'National Freedom' as far as the *Irish Worker* was concerned. Without any doubt 'the cause of Labour is the same the world over', but this was 'a clear national issue, and one that deserves a clear and distinct answer':

We have not any fear of repudiation when we say that the majority of the Irish people are patriots, that they love their country with a love as passionate and as true as Mitchel or Tone, and as pure and as holy as maiden ever was honoured with by man; they love the grass of her fields, the pavements of her streets, and the wind that blows across her hill.

And why not? Great heavens, there is not a hill nor a valley that is not sanctified by the blood of her martyrs, and blessed by the footprints of her saints! Her cities and towns have been sacked and beleaguered; her altars have been desecrated; her temples razed, and you are the descendants of the men who fought to save her, and died to shield her from the foreign marauders.

And ever in the forefront of her fight for freedom was the working man, the national forces of Ireland were ever composed mainly of working men, and if there is future in Ireland it is the working men will achieve it.

The article emphasized 'again and again that the Irishizing of everything within the four seas of Ireland is our object'.[46]

Clearly, the *Irish Worker* has to be seen as an advocate of socialist republicanism, of the belief that the working class was the one true repository of republican virtue, and that only through the achievement of a republic would the working class be able to bring about a socialist reordering of society. At this time, moreover, it was easily *the most powerful public voice of republicanism*, dwarfing in circulation any of its rivals, and speaking for an increasingly powerful trade union. This has not yet been fully appreciated in the histories of the period that still, by and large, see Jim Connolly as almost the lone spokesman for working-class republicanism. As the pages of the *Irish Worker* make absolutely clear, this was not the case. There was much more widespread support for such a standpoint than is generally acknowledged, and it has to be seen as an integral part of the phenomenon of 'Larkinism'. Indeed, Connolly's particular contribution is best viewed as an attempt, in works like *Labour in Irish History*, to develop a basis for this working-class republicanism in Marxist theory, building on his theoretical breakthrough in the late 1890s.

The *Irish Worker's* nationalism was not without its darker side. On a number of occasions the paper carried anti-Semitic asides: for example, a particularly obnoxious cartoon, 'Gentlemen of the Jewry', that appeared on the front page in August 1911, with a pathetic disclaimer from Larkin, and even, in August 1914, an accusation that the war breaking out in Europe was the work of 'the Jewish financial ring that circumnavigates the globe'.[47] Although the paper never advocated anti-Semitism as such, not only did it not challenge it, but on a number of occasions it clearly capitulated to it. This was certainly Larkin's responsibility. Connolly was much more forthright and uncompromising in his opposition to anti-Semitism.[48]

The Savoy Strike

Let us end this chapter with an examination of one particular industrial dispute through the pages of the *Irish Worker*: the lockout at the Savoy Confectionary Company that began in the summer of 1913. This dispute began when the manager, M'Murty, sacked a number of women for joining the Irish Women Workers' Union (IWWU), at this time the women's section of the ITGWU, led by Larkin's sister, Delia.[49] From the beginning the union put every effort into having the firm blacked. The paper provides an interesting record of its successes and failures in this endeavour, taking the story up after nine pickets had been arrested by the police. On 5 July it was reported that 'Waytes, the scab motor firm', were supplying M'Murty with taxis, but the paper made clear that the union was 'going to deal with Waytes and make them understand that it won't pay to interfere in a dispute'. The paper also reported that there 'are unemployed at the Labour Exchange who have refused to go and drive M'Murty's van, although he offered 25/- a week', that 'the hackney car drivers … have refused to deliver his order or hire their cars to drive the blacklegs to their houses', that the clerks in the goods office 'refused to receive parcels from the Savoy', that parcels 'put on the trams were kicked off into the street' and that the carters 'pass the Savoy as though it were a place in which the plague was raging'. A week later the paper took great delight in telling its readers how M'Murty 'has been compelled to turn coalporter'. 'It was quite an inspiring sight', the reporter crowed, 'to discover M'Murty … pushing a truck with bag of coal on it, along Harcourt Street

Station at 6 o'clock in the morning'. The report continued:

> It is something to be proud of these days to find that no inducements are strong
> enough to get a man to go and scab on a few locked out girls …. Three more of
> the lady scabs have stayed away and the remainder will find it somewhat difficult
> to find another job when M'Murty puts them out. They will understand what
> organisation means among the women workers when they look for another job.

The following week, the paper continued the saga:

> During the past week he has met with many mishaps, due to the incompetency of
> the scabs he has employed. The van which was driven by the two seasoned scabs,
> Gleeson, the ex-policeman's son, and Gore, who scabbed it during the City of
> Dublin strike, came to grief and was smashed to bits in Parliament Street. Andrews,
> of Dame Street, gave shelter to the wreckage, not knowing the facts about the case.
> Upon being informed that the van belong to M'Murty, the scab, it was put out
> again on the road. He then went to Sheridan's, West Arran Street, and hired a van
> from him at the rate of 25/- per week for four weeks. However, Sheridans were
> informed to whom they had hired the van, and they like wise people, have taken
> back their van. Two chocolate mixers required repairing and were sent to Booth's,
> Stephen Street. We would like to know what the Society to which the Trades
> Union men in this firm belong, and who repaired the scab machinery, have to say
> for themselves. No matter, all things being considered, M'Murty is in just as nice a
> fix as it is possible for any employer to be in.

Further success followed when the nine arrested pickets were all acquitted,
and the paper celebrated by printing photographs of the 'Savoy Scab Octette'
who gave evidence against them. At the same time, readers were warned of
the standard of hygiene at the firm. It carried on its business 'in a condemned
premises where we are given to understand the previous inhabitants died from
CONSUMPTION'. The building was rat-infested, 'and time and again rats are
found in the large pans of liquid chocolate'. When this happened, the chocolate
was wiped from the rats, the rats were burned, 'and the chocolate … made up
for public consumption'.

Early in August, the paper proclaimed that 'M'Murty is well on the road to
oblivion'. The company was trying to divert its goods to escape the blacking, and
the paper warned that 'it would be well for the Insurance Company in Foster
Place and the Public-house in Temple Bar to take warning or they will require to
have their own goods diverted.' The following week the paper printed the names
and addresses of twenty-eight of M'Murty's scabs.[50] At this point the Savoy Confectionary dispute disappears from the pages of the *Irish Worker*, swallowed up
by the general lockout ordered by the Dublin Employers' Federation. One further episode reported in the *Freeman's Journal* is, however, still worth recording.
The Savoy van was sent to pick up 'goods shipped to Dublin.

The city company's men, all of whom belong to the Irish Transport Worker's Union, declined to have anything to do with the consignment. Under these circumstances, the driver set about loading the vehicle himself, and then adjourned to the shipping company's office to sign the necessary receipt form. Whilst he was so engaged the car was unloaded and the goods replaced in the stores. The Savoy driver did his best to collect his parcels, but was outnumbered and had to drive off, with but a scanty supply of goods in his van. Near the first bridge, a Union carter hauled his yoke across the road, but the Savoy driver charged full tilt over the bridge and made good his escape.[51]

Notes

1   C. Desmond Greaves, *The Irish Transport and General Workers Union: The Formative Years*, Dublin 1982, p. 58.
2   R.M. Fox, *Jim Larkin: The Rise of the Underman*, London 1957, p. 73.
3   Dermot Keogh, *The Rise of the Irish Working Class*, Belfast 1982, pp. 162-163.
4   Fox, op cit, p. 73-74.
5   Emmet Larkin, *James Larkin*, London 1977, p. 69.
6   Robert G. Lowery, 'Sean O'Casey and the Irish Worker', in Robert G. Lowery, ed, *O'Casey Annual* 3, London 1984, p. 42-43.
7   *Irish Worker* 27 May 1911.
8   *Irish Worker* 4, 11, 18 May and 1, 8, 15 June 1912.
9   *Irish Worker* 17, 24, 31 August and 7, 14 September 1912. The paper also published two plays by Wilson: *Profit* (12, 19, 26 October 1912) and a one-act play, *Victims* on 21 December 1912.
10   *Irish Worker*, 24 June 1911.
11   *Irish Worker*, 16 December 1911.
12   *Irish Worker*, 27 January 1912.
13   *Irish Worker*, 24 May 1913.
14   *Irish Worker*, 15 February 1913.
15   *Irish Worker*, 22 February 1913.
16   Fox, op cit, p. 74.
17   *Irish Worker*, 17 August 1912.
18   *Irish Worker*, 22 March 1913.
19   Emmet O'Connor, 'An Age of Agitation', *Saothar* 9, 1983, p. 68.
20   *Irish Worker*, 13 January 1912.
21   Larkin, op cit, p. 147.
22   *Irish Worker*, 9 August 1913.
23   Emmet Larkin, 'Socialism and Catholicism in Ireland', *Church History*, 33, 1964, p. 466.
24   While the historiography of the Catholic Church in Ireland is extremely rich (see my 'The Catholic Church in Nineteenth Century Ireland', *European History Quarterly* 25, 1995), the relationship of the Dublin working class to the Church has been sorely neglected. A study, preferably a comparative study, of the quality of Hugh McCleod's *Piety and Poverty: Working Class Religion in Berlin, London and New York 1870-1914*, New York 1996, is urgently needed. Even his edited volume, *Eu-*

ropean *Religion in the Age of Great Cities 1830-1930*, London 1995, does not look at Dublin, although there is an interesting chapter on Belfast.

25 Bertram Wolfe, *Strange Communists I Have Known*, London 1996, p. 55.

26 For the United Irishman see in particular Kevin Whelan, *The Tree of Liberty*, Cork 1996, and my own *United Irishman: The Memoirs of James Hope*, London 2001.

27 Emmet Larkin, 'The Devotional Revolution in Ireland 1850-1875', *American Historical Review*, 77, 1972.

28 See Newsinger, 'The Catholic Church' op cit.

29 See my unpublished paper 'Why Was There No Irish Anti-Clericalism?'

30 C.S. Andrews, *Dublin Made Me*, Cork 1979, pp. 12-13.

31 *Irish Worker*, 28 February 1914.

32 *The Harp*, September 1908.

33 *Irish Worker*, 6 July 1912.

34 *Workers Republic*, 29 January 1916.

35 *Irish Worker*, 6 January 1912.

36 *Irish Worker*, 20 January 1912.

37 *Irish Worker*, 29 March 1913.

38 On divorce see Connolly's *Labour, Nationality and Religion* which is reprinted in Owen Dudley Edwards and Bernard Ransom, *James Connolly: Selected Political Writings*, London 1973, pp. 100-103. He accompanies his condemnation of divorce with a strong attack on the Church's attitude towards women. For Larkin in Grimsby, John Mahon, *Harry Pollitt*, London 1976, pp. 41-42.

39 *Irish Worker*, 27 April 1912 and 27 August 1913.

40 *Irish Worker*, 15 July 1911.

41 *Irish Worker*, 13 April 1912.

42 *Irish Worker*, 27 April 1912.

43 *Irish Worker*, 23 November 1913.

44 *Irish Worker*, 21 June 1913.

45 *Irish Worker*, 9 September 1911.

46 *Irish Worker*, 4 January 1913.

47 *Irish Worker*, 26 August 1911 and 8 August 1914.

48 See Manus O'Riordan, 'Connolly, Socialism and the Jewish Worker', *Saothar* 13, 1988. In the *Workers Republic* of 24 September 1898, Connolly made clear his sympathy with Zionism, with 'the political ideal of that section of the Jewish race who are at present advocating the establishment of an Israelitish nation in Palestine'.

49 For Delia Larkin see Theresa Moriary, 'Delia Larkin: Relative Obscurity' in Nevin, op. cit. For the IWWU see Mary Jones, *These Obstreperous Lassies: A History of the ITGWU*, Dublin 1988.

50 *Irish Worker*. 5, 12, 19, 26 July and 9, 16 August 1913.

51 *Freeman's Journal*, 28 August 1913.

Chapter III
The Lockout: The Struggle Begins

Larkin's concern as 1913 unfolded was to consolidate the position of the ITGWU with a view to making Dublin a union city. The strike wave, with its routine displays of solidarity and sympathetic action, was successfully intimidating many employers and he proposed to take advantage of this. To this end, in an editorial of 26 April 1913, 'Open Letter To The People – how to stop strikes', Larkin proposed that the Board of Trade should be invited to establish conciliation machinery to be operated jointly by the employers and the unions with a view to resolving disputes without recourse to strike action, but more significantly involving full recognition of the unions and acceptance of the closed shop. Larkin proposed that if 80 per cent of the workers in any establishment joined a trade union then they should be able to insist on a closed shop. These proposals were put forward as a 'mutual arrangement' that was in the interest of both parties. According to Larkin

> the ultimate solution is the ownership and control of the means of life by the whole of the people; but we are not at that stage of development, as yet. Therefore it is essential that some means should be sought whereby the work of the nation may be carried out without constant yet at present necessary dislocation. The Strike is a damnable but necessary evil at present, and if it is possible to limit them in number, place and magnitude, all thinking people should assist to that desirable end.

This was a long way from any doctrine of unbridled militancy, and indeed smacks of opportunism. It has to be seen, however, as an attempt to exploit the union's strength by imposing what amounted to a general surrender on the employers while using the language of conciliation and moderation. In the circumstances of 1913 Larkin's readiness to formalise relations found a ready response among many Dublin employers even though the terms offered amounted to a crushing defeat. They were used to smashing trade union organisation, but Larkin had brought them to heel. A remarkable achievement.

By the end of July an agreement had been concluded between the Dublin Chamber of Commerce and the Dublin Trades Council to establish a Board of Conciliation. The sincerity of either side must be seriously doubted. At the beginning of June, 'Shellback', writing in the *Irish Worker* had warned against 'Conciliation and Arbitration Boards', which were only intended 'for the one great purpose of laying the Labour Unrest ghost'. When 'Capital had the whip hand', he quite correctly observed, there was no talk of 'settlements or agreements'. Only when 'Labour was sure of victory' did the employers become conciliatory. Neither side, he assured his readers, 'had any intention to remain bound by the terms of such an agreement any longer than it paid them to do so'.[1] The Great Lockout, coming only weeks after the agreement establishing the Dublin Conciliation Board, provides a powerful endorsement of 'Shellback's' understanding of class relations.

Murphy's Trams

While many employers were adopting a conciliatory pose in the face of union power, there was one important exception: Catholic Ireland's most powerful capitalist, William Martin Murphy. A former Home Rule MP, who had refused a knighthood, Murphy had opposed Parnell in the great leadership crisis, losing his Dublin seat to a Parnellite in 1892. When the Home rulers eventually reunited under John Redmond's leadership, he adopted an unremittingly hostile stance, supporting Home Rule, but bitterly critical of the Home Rule party. Murphy had extensive railway interests in Ireland and tramway interests that extended from Cork and Belfast to London and Glasgow, Bournemouth and Hastings, Ramsgate and Poole. He had been involved in the development of the tram system in Buenos Aires and effectively controlled the Dublin United Tramway Company. He owned one of Dublin's largest hotels, the Imperial, together with Clery's department store and the *Independent* newspaper chain. Although Murphy was prepared to tolerate the moderate, deferential, trade unionism of the skilled worker, he was completely opposed to any signs of militancy and resisted any attempts to organise the unskilled by means of victimisation and the blacklist. In 1911, when workers on the Great Southern and Western Railway had taken strike action in sympathy with the ITGWU, Murphy had threatened their union, the Amalgamated Society of Railway Servants (ASRS) with a lockout. The strikers were, in Murphy's words, 'beaten to the ropes' and returned to work on the company's terms.[2]

Now, in 1913, Murphy was determined not just to exclude the ITGWU from his own concerns, but to accomplish its destruction throughout the whole city. Interestingly, he had some difficulty convincing his fellow employers that the time was ripe. Few had his resources and Larkin had made blacking, picketing and the sympathy strike such powerful weapons that even the use of scab labour was no longer effective: it spread disputes rather than ended them. The working-class solidarity fostered by Larkin had defeated the methods that had been successfully used to destroy the unskilled unions in the past. Murphy would have to convince the Dublin employers that confrontation would be more effective than conciliation by the force of example. By the same token, Larkin was determined to organise the Dublin trams, and, moreover, had no reason to believe that this would put the union's very existence at risk. If it came to a strike, picketing, blacking and boycotting would inevitably bring the tram system to a halt and, sooner or later, Murphy, whether he liked it or not, would have to recognise the union.

At the end of July 1913 Larkin warned readers of the *Irish Worker* of the coming conflict with Murphy. He derided Murphy's claim that he was not anti-trade union in his establishments. He poured scorn on Murphy's claim that he was a good employer who had never had a strike and proceeded to lambast him with characteristic ferocity:

> For fifty years as an employer, he has had no strike. What a lie. What a damned lie. There is not a company or industry that you are connected with, directly or indirectly, that has not had disputes prolonged and otherwise. What about the Clare Railway Strike, you Christian? You were a member of Parliament; yes, but they found you out. You have been driven from public life as a toady, a renegade, an untruthful and dishonest politician; a false friend, a sweating employer, a weak tyrant. Witness the funk you are in now, you whited sepulchre .... Larkin has tamed better, braver, cleaner, and honester foes than you. The gage of the battle is accepted. We will drive you to defeat, or we will break your heart ....[3]

Despite Larkin's threats, Murphy stood firm.

Dermot Keogh has provided a grim account of working conditions on the trams at this time. Pay was twenty-one shillings and sixpence for conductors and twenty-eight shillings for drivers, substantially less than was paid in Belfast or Liverpool. Employees got one day off in ten and worked a day that could last from nine to seventeen hours. Discipline was harsh with punitive fines and punishments. A conductor could lose a day's pay for omitting to collect a fare, allowing a passenger to exceed the distance paid for, or for talking to the passengers, while a driver could lose a day's pay for, among other things, arriving at Nelson's Pillar one minute before time. While training, staff worked for six weeks without pay and then served a probationary period that could last as long as six years. Moreover, all previous attempts at unionisation had been crushed by means of victimisation and sackings.[4] Larkin hoped to change all this.

Obviously, recruiting men into a union under such a regime was difficult, but unrest among the tramwaymen together with the ITGWU's successes elsewhere, led to a determined attempt. If the company could be successfully challenged, if a stand could be made just once, then the expectation was that the overwhelming majority of the workforce would queue up to enlist. Certainly, Murphy was worried. On 19 July 1913, he addressed a meeting of tramwaymen at the Mansion House and actually invited them to form a 'legitimate union' that the company would be pleased to recognise. He announced a shilling a week pay rise and an improvement in the probationers' conditions at the same time as insisting that this had nothing to do with Larkin or with fear of Larkin. He went on to threaten summary dismissal of anyone recruiting for the ITGWU and warned the workers that while a strike on the trams might produce 'turmoil and disorder', they had to consider 'what chance would the men, without funds, have in a contest with a company who could and would spend £100,000 or more to put down the terrorism which is being imported into the labour conditions of the city'.[5] A battle was inevitable, but Larkin hoped to choose the moment, patiently building up the strength of the union so as to give the men a decisive advantage. Murphy struck first.

On 19 August, Murphy sacked all the union members (40 men and 20 boys) working in the despatch department of his *Independent* newspaper. The union responded with a picket and the blacking of the paper. All the city's newsboys refused to sell the paper and workers at Eason's, one of the largest wholesale distributors, walked out rather than handle it. Two days later, he sacked some 200 union members working in the tram company's parcels department. The intention was clear: there was to be a general clear out of union men. This was, of course, not just a disaster for the men concerned, who faced unemployment and the blacklist, but would have been a serious defeat for the union, a defeat that would encourage other employers. In response, the union formalised its demands for thirty shillings a week pay, one day off in every eight and time and a half for Sunday working. The tramway company refused to even meet with any union representatives and at a series of meetings held at Liberty Hall on Saturday, 23 August the decision was taken by an overwhelming majority to strike. There was no walk out on the Monday which seemed to presage the collapse of the tramwaymen's resolve, but at 10 a.m. the following day, 26 August, the second day of the Horse Show, over 200 drivers and conductors abandoned their trams in the street and went on strike. Over 700 men walked out, and while this was less than Larkin had hoped for, the issue had been forced when Murphy began the mass victimisation of union members. Nevertheless, Larkin was still confident of victory, and given the union's strength in the city, had every justification. Once it became clear that the trams could not run, more men would come out and Murphy would be forced into negotiations.

The Law of the Truncheon

What transformed the dispute was the way that the courts and the police threw their weight behind Murphy. On 28 August, Larkin and the rest of the ITGWU leadership were all arrested and charged with seditious libel, seditious conspiracy and unlawful assembly. A union demonstration in O'Connell Street called for Sunday, 31 August was banned. Larkin, however, was no sooner released on bail than he made clear his intention of defying the ban and went into hiding to avoid re-arrest. Already there had been serious clashes in different parts of the city between pickets and the police with people being badly injured. The police had clearly had instructions to drive the union off the streets and were carrying out these orders without restraint. Moreover, the conflict was spreading as other employers joined in. A flour mill dismissed all the union members in its employ and when Jacobs' biscuit factory received a delivery from the firm over 2,000 men and women walked out. At this point, elements on Dublin Trades Council led by William O'Brien began looking for a way out of the fight. They resolved to comply with the ban on Sunday's demonstration in O'Connell Street and to hold a protest rally elsewhere. Larkin repudiated them from hiding.[6]

Police violence reached a peak over the weekend of 30 and 31 August with a general attack on the working class taking place. The workers were to be taught a lesson they would not forget and the state was to make clear its full support for employers who were prepared to resist the union. On Saturday evening there was serious fighting in a number of areas of the city as people defended themselves against police attack. On Burgh Quay and Eden Quay the police beat everyone they could lay their hands on, clubbing two union members, James Byrne and James Nolan, to death. Robert Monteith, at the time, a civil servant, accused the police of 'deliberate murder'. He saw Byrne felled by a truncheon blow, 'without the slightest provocation', by a policeman clearly the worse for drink:

> The horrible crunching sound of the blow was clearly audible fifty yards away. The drunken scoundrel was ably seconded by two of the metropolitan police who, as the man attempted to rise, beat him about the head until his skull was smashed in several places. They then rejoined their patrol leaving the man in his blood. For saying "You damn cowards" I was instantly struck across the jaw and shoulder and knocked to the ground, where I had the good sense to lie quietly until the patrol had passed on.

His fourteen year old daughter, Florence, was out shopping, 'not taking part in any demonstration' but was nonetheless 'clubbed by a policeman in Earl Street, and brought home with her long, golden hair clotted with blood'.[7] In Foley Street, the police invaded Corporation Buildings, a tenement housing nearly 2,000 people, but were forced to retreat at one o'clock in the morning. By this time there were the two men dead and over 200 badly injured.

On the Sunday morning, Larkin was smuggled into the Imperial Hotel in O'Connell Street and made his appearance on a balcony some time after one o'clock. His appearance was taken as a signal by the police to clear the street, which they did with great brutality, clubbing people indiscriminately to the ground. A Liberal MP and industrialist, Handel Booth, in Dublin for the Horse Show subsequently described the Dublin Metropolitan Police as the most brutal constabulary ever let loose on a peaceful assembly. Up and down the road, backwards and forwards, the police rushed like men possessed. Some drove the crowd into the streets to meet other batches of the government's minions wildly striking with truncheons at every one within reach. In escaping many ran the gauntlet until the third or fourth blow knocked them senseless ... kicking the victims when prostrate was a settled part of the police programme.[8]

His testimony was to be an acute embarrassment for the authorities as it could not be dismissed as casually as that of the disaffected populace. Another eye-witness, Count Casimir Markiewicz, the husband of Constance Markiewicz, described the scene:

There was no sign of excitement, no attempt at rescue, and no attempt at a breach of the peace, when a savage and cruel order for the baton charge – unprecedented in such circumstances in any privileged country – was given to the police .... Scores of well-fed metropolitan policemen pursued a handful of men, women and children running for their lives before them. Round the corner of Princes Street, I saw a young man pursued by a huge policeman, knocked down by a baton stroke, and then, whilst bleeding on the ground, batoned and kicked, not only by this po-liceman but by his colleagues .... When the police had finished their bloodthirsty pursuit, they returned down the street batoning the terror-stricken passers-by who had taken refuge in the doorways. It was a complete triumph for the police .... It was, indeed, a bloody Sunday for Ireland.[9]

The *Freeman's Journal* reported how, after the police attacked, a 'broken baton was picked up in the street. It had been split along its whole length'.[10] Within minutes the police had succeeded in injuring over 400 people, many of them seriously.

As news of the police attack spread, so fighting broke out elsewhere in the city with the police coming under attack from angry crowds. Corporation Buildings was once again paid a visit with the police breaking into people's homes, smash-ing up their few possessions and assaulting those who offered fight or were un-able to flee. Men, women and children were punched, kicked and clubbed with one man, John McDonagh, who was confined to bed, being beaten where he lay and subsequently dying in hospital. The police even wrecked the Corpora-tion rent office. At Inchicore, troops were called out to support the police and together they rampaged down Emmet Street, severely beating in the process three labour councillors, William Partridge of the ITGWU, Richard O'Carroll and Thomas O'Hanlon. Sporadic clashes were to continue for the next couple of days. By the end of the proceedings over 500 people had received hospital treat-ment for injuries suffered at the hands of the police with many more nursing their injuries at home.[11]

Early the following year when the Disturbances Commission was meeting to whitewash the police, the Dublin Civic League issued a statement making clear why it was refusing to participate in the proceedings. They condemned the Commission as unrepresentative and regretted 'the breach of the definite undertaking by the Chief Secretary to include on the Commission a representative of the workers'. The statement went on:

> The Civic League is convinced that the body of evidence against the police is so serious and authentic in nature that the fullest and most representative inquiry is absolutely necessary .... The firm of solicitors acting for the Civic League have examined over 500 witnesses. More than one member of the League witnessed the police's wild charge on Sunday, 31st August. A member has inspected houses in Corporation Buildings, Moss Street, Townsend Street and Camden Street, houses that is in three different wards. In these houses were to be seen furniture, windows and fan-lights broken, altars, religious pictures and statues destroyed – in fact the most valued belongings of many workers of good character reduced to a heap of rubbish.

The statement concluded with a demand for a more representative Commission to be established with the power 'to compel the attendance of witnesses, since such is the terror of future persecution from the police that many working people and small traders hesitate to appear'.[12]

The reality of the police terror that was visited on the Dublin working class can hardly be denied. The Dublin Metropolitan Police was already cordially hated throughout much of the city and this hatred was now grown white hot. Looking back on his boyhood, Leon O Broin, a senior civil servant and eminent historian, could fondly recall how during the Lockout he had struck a police inspector with a well-aimed stone during a police attack on a peaceful demonstration of striking tramwaymen.[13] He was far from alone in this sentiment. For others, however, the police were teaching the Larkinites a well-deserved lesson, driving the scum back into the slums and safeguarding religion and property. Archbishop Walsh's secretary, Father Curran, wrote to the Archbishop who was in England at the time, supporting the police. The situation reminded him of 'pictures of the French Revolution'. He told Walsh that this was no longer a tram strike but 'simply the scum of our slums versus the police'. He wished that troops had been deployed and confessed himself amazed at the extent of Larkin's support even among respectable working men: 'The workmen have gone mad over Larkin and will do almost anything for him – even respectable carpenters and bricklayers'. While he acknowledged that the police had been somewhat excessive in O'Connell Street (there were too many well-to-do people batoned to deny otherwise), elsewhere 'any person who got batoned richly deserved it'. Later when the Lockout was underway, Curran wrote to the Archbishop that though the workers were somewhat 'tamed and depressed, they are not sufficiently starved'.[14]

The bloody events of 30-31 August were the result of deliberate collusion between the authorities and Murphy. Evidence of this collusion had already been established on the 28th when Larkin had appeared in court to answer the charges that had been brought against him, charges that included the incitement of 'discontent and hatred between … the working classes of Dublin and the police forces of the Crown'. The police themselves were to quickly surpass any ability Larkin might have had in this regard. At any rate, Larkin personally cross-examined Detective Revelle and the following interesting exchange took place:

Larkin:	Is it true that to your knowledge Murphy was in Dublin Castle?
Revelle:	Am I to answer that question?
Swifte:	Did you ever see Mr Murphy go to Dublin Castle?
(the magistrate)	

Revelle:	I did.
Larkin:	Was it last Tuesday?
Revelle:	It was.
Larkin:	And then you will say that there was no connection between William Martin Murphy and my incarceration?
Revelle:	I cannot answer that.[15]

Of course, collusion between employers and the authorities is hardly new, although considerable efforts are made to disguise the fact. Instead the pretence of impartiality is maintained although we have yet to see the police rampage through an employer's house or rather houses. Nevertheless occasionally the reality breaks through. A recent example where there was clear collusion between government, police and a particularly ruthless employer was the Wapping dispute of 1986 in London. While all those involved deny any collusion as conspiracy theory, in Woodrow Wyatt's diary we have Rupert Murdoch showing him where the police were storing their riot shields days before he finally provoked the print workers into striking.[16] As far as Dublin was concerned the authorities were not only coming to the assistance of Murphy but were sending a message to all of Dublin's employers.

The *Irish Worker* also pointed to the intimate relationships that existed between the employers and the authorities, indeed to a considerable extent they actually overlapped:

Practically the administration is in the hands of the Under Secretary. But is it not strange – or is it strange? – that amongst the shareholders in the Tramway Monopoly we find the name of Mrs Eliza Dougherty, married woman, Under Secretary's Lodge, Phoenix Park, the wife of the man who is bound to be impartial in the dispute with a commercial undertaking in whose prosperity he is financially interested at least indirectly. The meeting on last Sunday was proclaimed by E.G. Swifte. Well, is it not peculiar that the same name should be in the list of shareholders of the Company, E.G. Swifte, 18 Fitzwilliam Square?[17]

The ITGWU was to find formidable forces arrayed against it.

Alerting the British Labour Movement

One consequence of the police terror of 30-31 August was to alert the British labour movement to the situation in Dublin. The *Daily Herald* newspaper played
a vital role in this. While we shall discuss further on its role in the solidarity campaign that was to develop in Britain, it is worth briefly examining its coverage
of the Dublin police riots. Its correspondent, the Dublin socialist and women's
suffrage campaigner, Francis Sheehy-Skeffington, graphically reported on 'an
organised attempt last night on the part of the Crown to bludgeon the strikers
into tame passivity'. The police 'have a look in their eyes I once saw in a dog's ....
To think that any women laboured to give them birth'.[18] He went on:

> I could fill the HERALD with accounts of the fight if time and space would allow.
> For instance, Paddy Kelly, a man of 64 years of age, was coming out of a public
> house knowing nothing of any bother until he found himself in the mad rush
> outside the door, and before he could gather what was the matter he received a
> crack on the skull. The next moment he was being kicked and trampled on by the
> police ....

Skeffington took the injured man to hospital, where he found the nuns dis-
traught at the numbers of injured being brought in. He spoke to a young lad
about 17 years of age who told him:

> 'I saw a man knocked on the skull, saw the police leave him there, and knowing a
> little of first aid, I went with two others to assist him. The four of us were on the
> ground trying to pick him up, when a squad of police, who were hiding, rushed at
> the four of us, and we were all laid out. I have a huge gash on my head, sir, but I
> don't know what become of the others.
> That is his story. P. Broderick, a professional jockey up for the Phoenix Park races,
> was about to leave his hotel on the Quay. 'I had just reached the door when a po-
> liceman struck my skull twice. I fell to the ground and was kicked in the ribs twice'
> is his statement ... J. Duffey, a lad in from Scotland on holiday, was coming out
> of Tara Street station, got to the door, and two police came back and struck him
> twice.

And so on. He saw two policemen at the hospital, escorting an injured prisoner,
whose batons were still 'wet with blood and clotted hair'. The situation was desperate, because 'the scabs on the cars were armed with revolvers' and 'the police
have swords and revolvers'.[19]

At the time, the socialist academic, G.D.H. Cole was writing his *The World of
Labour* where he observed that employers in Britain dare not engage in industrial warfare because it is impossible to just shoot the workers down. He included

a footnote to the effect that events in Dublin 'have a little shaken my faith'.[20] Others were less taken by surprise and rallied to the cause of the Dublin workers. William Partridge crossed over to Manchester to address the Trades Union Congress on 2 September and made clear that they 'were not only struggling for the cause of trade unionism but were defending their very lives'. The employers had 'declared war' on the ITGWU and if they won it would mean 'the destruction of Trade Unionism not only in Dublin but throughout Ireland'.[21] Travelling in the opposite direction, the British Labour leader, Keir Hardie arrived in Dublin the same day and told the press that he regarded what was happening in Dublin 'as the most serious event the Trades Union Movement has had to face for at least a century'. Hardie, as one of his biographer's writes, was always 'instinctively sympathetic to the workers' case'. Following the shooting of the railwaymen at Llanelli in the 1911 strike he had written a savage indictment of the authorities, *Killing No Murder*, which seriously embarrassed his fellow Labour MPs. He was arguably both the first and the last Labour leader of whom it could be said that 'Automatically, his sympathies were wholly with the workers on strike'.[22] While in Dublin he visited Larkin in prison and the following day took part in the funeral of James Nolan who had been beaten to death by the police on 30th August.

The *Freeman's Journal* reported the 'extraordinary demonstration':

> The Transport Union had organised the procession and it was a very remarkable one in many respects. Its length, including carriages was over a mile. In the main it was composed of a mass of men of the labouring class, most of them in their working clothes. It might have numbered up to 10,000 or even more. Features of the procession were 250 tramwaymen in uniform. There were about 1,000 women workers also marching. Some fifty carriages and cars took their place in the procession …. A pathetic sight was the coach containing the widow of the deceased and her five children – one of them a fat little baby …. It was remarkable that not a policeman was to be seen on the streets of that district during the afternoon …. A painful mark of the procession was the number of men, women and even children who had bandaged heads …. The length of the procession as it passed Abbey Street amazed the spectators …. The whole way to Glasnevin Cemetery traffic was altogether discontinued during the time the procession was passing, and in most of the streets the shops were closed and blinds were half-drawn in many houses. The slow and measured march of the cortege and the doleful strains of the funereal music added most impressively to the sad scene.

It was, the paper concluded, 'one of the most solemn and impressive funerals ever seen in Dublin'. The only incident to occur was perhaps indicative: a sudden panic gripped the crowds in O'Connell Street when 'people flew away in all directions under the belief that a baton charge had been ordered … it was a false alarm'.[23]

The Lockout Begins

The Dublin employers met to consider a general lockout on 29 August and agreed in principle. All talk of Conciliation Boards was forgotten as they rallied round Murphy: the ITGWU was to be destroyed. On 30 August, Larkin told readers of the *Irish Worker* that 'the Dublin employers have decided to lock-out all members of the Irish Transport and General Workers Union'. He went on to warn the employers that they were about 'to raise a Frankenstein that will envelop and destroy them all. Time fights on our side'. Murphy, meanwhile, was giving a very different interpretation of events to his fellow employers. On 2 September the *Freeman's Journal* reported a speech he made at a meeting intended to finalise arrangements for the lockout. Murphy noted Larkin's tactic of attacking the employers 'in detail', of concentrating the union's resources against them one at a time and argued that now 'it was time to stop him'. The report went on:

> The fight against Larkin was not after all, Mr Murphy, continued, so difficult; it was much easier than it appeared. He had told workmen over and over again when they were making demands and threatening strikes that the prospect of a strike and anticipation of it had much more terror for the employer than when the actual strike took place .... When the strike actually takes place the employer has got his back to the wall, and the workmen has fired his last cartridge. The employer all the time manages to get three meals a day, but the unfortunate workmen and his family have no resources whatever except submission, and that was what occurred in 99 cases out of a 100. And the difficulty of teaching that lesson to the workingman was extraordinary.

Encouraged by the events of 30-31 August the employers prepared to act.

The Great Lockout began on 2 September when the coal merchants locked out their workers. In the days that followed more and more employers took similar action until by the end of September there were some 25,000 workers, by no means all ITGWU members, locked out by over 400 employers. The workers were required to sign an undertaking not to be a member of the ITGWU and when they refused were promptly locked out: 'I hereby undertake to carry out all instructions given me by or on behalf of my employers and further I agree to immediately resign membership of the ITGWU (if a member) and I further undertake that I will not join or in any way support this union'. As Murphy realised, the union's great strength had been working-class solidarity whereby individual employers found themselves confronting the strength of the whole union, actively mobilised against them. The lockout effectively countered this. The union would no longer meet the employers in detail where they could be defeated one by one, but all together, united against it. Working-class solidarity was to be crushed by employer solidarity. The ITGWU was confronted with a prolonged battle of attrition, designed to bleed away its resources, both financial and moral. It was fighting for its life.

Most accounts of the Dublin Lockout consider it primarily as an event in Irish history, as an episode in the years of struggle that included the Easter Rising, the War of Independence and the Civil War. Consequently they fail to adequately locate it within the context of the great labour revolt that had engulfed Britain as well. While the ITGWU was, as we have seen, staunchly republican and separatist, it also regarded itself as part of a great movement of working-class insurgency that was challenging employers, union leaders and the government in both countries. Larkin identified himself completely with the syndicalists and socialists in Britain, especially those associated with the *Daily Herald* and the Daily Herald League. There was in Britain a layer of working-class activists who were trying to reshape the trade unions as instruments of class war rather than class compromises. This was the constituency to which Larkin appealed, this was the constituency that he was part of. Once the lockout was imposed in Dublin, he quickly realised that the only way the union could escape being ground down in an unequal war of attrition was if the dispute could be spread to Britain. This required British workers taking industrial action in support of their Dublin brothers and sisters and refusing to handle blacked goods. The ITGWU had always extended such assistance to British workers and now that it was fighting for its very survival it demanded that this action should be reciprocated.

Larkin's bad relations with British trade union leaders usually figure as one of the principal criticisms of his conduct of the dispute. He gratuitously alienated the very people who were trying to help him, something that his most severe critics explain psychologically rather than politically. This completely neglects the syndicalist critique of official trade unionism that Larkin had embraced and of which Connolly, moreover, was an important theorist and propagandist. They were both part of an insurgent movement against trade union officialdom, synonymous as far as they were concerned with betrayal and the sell-out, and have to be considered in this context. The problem was that this insurgency had been considerably more successful in Dublin than it had anywhere in Britain, even in South Wales. In Dublin the insurgents had successfully established a militant breakaway union with a mass membership, in Britain they remained a minority in the trade unions, able to challenge but not to overcome the union leaders. But what of the considerable financial and national support that British trade unions were to give to the ITGWU? Certainly, this was vital in allowing the ITGWU to sustain the conflict for as long as it did, but while it allowed the Dublin workers to hold out, it did not promise victory.

A number of factors need to be taken into account when considering the attitude of the British trade union leadership towards the Dublin Lockout. They certainly did not want the employers to win because this would only encourage similar attacks in Britain. Moreover, the failure to provide, at the very least, financial aid for the Dublin workers might well provoke a revolt among their own members. But they were also concerned about Larkinism and the danger that it posed for them. A victory for Larkin would only encourage rank-and-file insurgency in Britain, and would strengthen the syndicalist opposition in their own unions. More generally, their whole approach to industrial relations excluded the idea of victory, it was not part of their strategic thinking. They thought in terms of compromise and saw themselves more as arbitrators than as leaders. In the context of the Dublin Lockout they saw their role as being to curb the excesses of both Larkinism and Murphyism with a view to reaching a compromise acceptable to all men of goodwill. And as far as they were concerned their financial aid not only helped the ITGWU sustain the fight, but also put them in a position to impose such a compromise on Larkin – or so they thought. He, of course, had already had bitter experience of a dispute being sold out from under him in Belfast in 1907 and was determined it should not happen again. More to the point, the Dublin employers would not agree to any compromise; their *minimum* demand was the destruction of the ITGWU. Confronted with the irrelevance of their particular model of trade unionism, the British trade union leadership had no way forward except defeat. The only realistic hope for the ITGWU was a rank-and-file revolt forcing the hands of the British leadership.

Was there any serious prospect of such a revolt? On 16 September railwaymen in Liverpool began to black all Dublin traffic and soon some 13-14,000 men were either locked out or on strike as far afield as Birmingham, Sheffield, Crewe and Derby. The action was completely unofficial, organised by local rank-and-file committees who tried to move towards a national stoppage in support of the Dublin workers. There was a very real possibility of linking the railwaymen's own outstanding grievances with the growing demand for solidarity with IT-GWU. The *Daily Herald* reported enthusiastically on 17 September that there 'are many signs that the Liverpool Railway strike will develop into a national stoppage. Men are out all over that city; and more significant still, Birmingham men are coming out in sympathy …. The situation is critical'. The following day the paper reported that all the railway workers in Birmingham were out and 'all the goods yards in the city were closed'. The strikers 'have forwarded a resolution to London requiring the general secretary and the Executive Committee to declare a national strike in favour of their fellow workers in Ireland and England'. On 20 September, under the headline 'HURRAH FOR THE REBELS', it reported the spread of the strike to Crewe, Derby and Gloucester. In Crewe, men working in the tranship sheds 'struck work yesterday, refusing to handle a wagon of Irish goods …. Between 500 and 600 are out, leaving about a dozen in the tranship sheds, which are the largest in the country'. The Crewe strike, the paper predicted 'will paralyse goods traffic north and south'. But the union leadership was able to secure a return to work despite the fact that 'many branches of the Union are clamouring for a national strike in sympathy with the men of Dublin'.[24]

In his history of the National Union of Railwaymen, Philip Bagwell writes of this period that it was becoming more difficult for the full-time officials 'to keep fully in touch with opinion in the branches where the membership was increasingly influenced by syndicalist doctrines'. He writes that railwaymen 'were less prepared to tolerate the abuses of officialdom, and a series of local incidents that led to unofficial strikes was the result'. He gives three examples which demonstrate the temper of the times. In early December 1912 a driver of the Northern Eastern Railway was demoted after being convicted of drunkenness. Within days over 3,000 men were on strike in his support, closing down docks, mines and steel mills. As far as the men were concerned the charges had been trumped up but even if true the driver was not due on duty for another thirty hours so it was none of the company's business. The situation was serious enough for the Home Secretary, Reginald McKenna, to issue a pardon whereupon he was reinstated at his old rank. In January 1913 a guard on the Midland Railway was ordered to take extra wagons exceeding the load allowed in the company rule book. He refused and was dismissed. The threat of strike action secured his reinstatement. And in July at Leeds, a porter was arrested after removing an egg from a crate of chickens. Within minutes, station staff had walked out on strike until he was released. What these episodes reveal is a degree of general unrest that could be sparked into action by almost any incident.[25]

Even more significant was the Aisgill disaster of 2 September 1913. An overloaded train had stalled and was run into by the train following with three carriages being burned out and sixteen people killed. The driver of the second train, Samuel Caudle, was put on trial for manslaughter, found guilty and sentenced to two months in prison. The general feeling among railwaymen was that he was a scapegoat, and that the company was to blame for the disaster. This has a decidedly contemporary feel to it. There were widespread calls for strike action which were publicised by the *Daily Herald*. On 27 October, the paper reported that 'nearly a thousand rail rebels assembled in fighting mood at St. Pancras Arches' to demand Caudle's release. The call for a national strike 'brought the Arches down'. As well as the release of Caudle, the *Herald* called for the railway directors to be imprisoned instead. Later the paper reported that it could fill 'columns with the resolutions we have received demanding the release of Caudle and calling for a general strike if the Home Office refuses to grant it'.[26] The government was so alarmed that McKenna met with other senior members of the Cabinet (Haldane, Grey, Lloyd George among them) and agreed that Caudle, too, should receive an immediate pardon. The railwaymen's leader, J.H. Thomas, claimed the success as a victory for moderation. This was, of course, so much nonsense. More accurate was the *Daily Herald*'s assessment: 'the railwaymen of Britain will know henceforth that when they want a thing they will get it, not by prayers, petitions, or resolutions, but by putting the fear of a national stoppage of the traffic of this country into the hearts of the State and the forces of Fat'[27] The government was afraid of strike action on the railways at a time when the issue of solidarity with the Dublin workers was very much on the agenda. 'Moderate' union leaders, like Thomas, under savage attack from Larkin and his supporters, had to be helped against the militants. McKenna himself acknowledged that the 'industrial situation' had influenced their quite unprecedented decision.[28] And indeed, the union leaders were able to outmanoeuvre the militants and prevent the revolt spreading.

One defence of Thomas and his colleagues in their role as fire fighters, damping down militancy and putting out unofficial strikes, is that the railwaymen could not afford a policy of sympathetic action. The railways were used by so many firms that the railwaymen would find themselves in dispute continually. This was certainly one of the arguments that Thomas himself used: they would be continually called upon to fight other people's battles. Superficially there does seem something to this. Industrial action should strengthen organisation, not weaken it, and to be involved in constant action in support of other workers' disputes could certainly have undermined the rail unions. It is all a matter of relative strength. Some groups of workers were strong and determined enough to routinely black goods from firms that employed scab labour. Others were not so strong and had to choose more carefully when to make a stand. 1913, when unrest was rife on the railways and when there was one of the great pre-war industrial battles taking place in Dublin, was one of the times to make a stand. This was not just a matter of trade union principle. Victory for the Dublin workers would benefit workers throughout Britain while defeat would be to their detriment. For Thomas and his like there never was a time to make a stand. Only when rank-and-file pressure was irresistible would they fight the employers and then only in order to restore 'normality' as quickly as possible. The *Daily Herald* savaged the NUR leadership for 'their policy of selfishness, inaction and cowardice. They want peace at any price'. But how to respond to this? In the best syndicalist tradition the paper sarcastically urged trade unionists to 'trust' their leaders. The way forward, 'all things considered is for the rank and file to get behind them in a solid body, and to give them to understand that unless they are prepared to lead right ahead they will get run over'.[29]

Wednesday, 17 September, Dublin

Let us look at one issue of the *Freeman's Journal*, not typical, but indicative, that of 18 September reporting events of the previous day. Police at Finglas shot a seventeen-year-old union member, Patrick Daly during an attack on a public house that had served scabs. Large numbers of police, 'all armed with revolvers of the Mauser type' had been drafted into North County Dublin. At Swords, locked out farm labourers had turned out to help a sympathetic farmer get his corn in. At Ballsbridge a demonstration of union members had encountered a tram at some road works and used the debris to wreck it. There were a number of union demonstrations in the city that day (at least three according to the paper). The largest started out from Liberty Hall involving 'thousands of men, women, boys and girls' and 'presented a very orderly and imposing appearance'. They were accompanied by 'a large force of police, mounted and on foot'. At the end of the march, Larkin addressed them:

> The eyes of the whole world was at the present moment centred on the fight that was being waged in Dublin for Trade Unionism. The rank and file of the workers in Liverpool were behind them. He had received wires from Liverpool and Birmingham – there were 5,000 men out in sympathy with them in Birmingham – pledging every support to the men of Dublin …. He advised his hearers to be peaceable and quiet. The police were already responsible for the murder of their comrades, Byrne and Nolan, and only a few hours ago they shot down young Daly in Finglas like a dog. The people should not give any chance to the police who were thirsting to continue their murderous assaults.
> He concluded: 'we have not yet begun to fight'.

The paper gave a very full report of a speech by Father John Condon, attacking the ITGWU for trying to set up a 'tyranny' and warning that Socialism was incompatible with Catholicism. A Catholic who supported Socialism was 'a recreant to his creed and a traitor to the ancient faith for which his fathers bled'. He pronounced Larkin unfit to lead Catholic workers and called for them to establish a new trade union, 'whose aims will be above suspicion, whose methods will be beyond reproach and whose leaders will be men of credit'. We will consider the union reply to this speech further on. Alongside this was a letter from James Connolly where he announced that the ITGWU 'has always desired, and desires now, the establishment of a Conciliation Board'. Such a Board would prevent strikes and this would of itself solve the problem of sympathetic strikes. Nevertheless, he insisted that as a matter of fundamental principle, the union would not give up the sympathy strike:

> For the working class the sympathetic strike is simply an affirmation of brotherhood a recognition that our brother's fight is our fight, our sister's troubles our troubles, that we are all members one of another. This principle is the very lifeblood of the modern Labour movement, one that we cannot possibly relinquish.

That same issue reported that Bewley and Draper, mineral water manufacturers, had locked out some 200 workers and was only prepared 'to consider written applications for reinstatement from workers who shall have severed their connection from the Transport Workers Union'.

Dominating the paper, however, was an article, 'The Idle City', that attempted to provide some sort of overview of Dublin Locked Out:

> What one reads about the strikes and lockouts in the city from day to day conveys only a limited idea of the actual state of affairs. To know that so many quay

labourers, builders' labourers, farm labourers, carters or other workers are idle, that so many more hundreds or thousands are added to the number day by day, that there are disturbances and prosecutions, that negotiations are started and are proved fruitless, that employers and employed seem to be equally irreconcilable – all this is but half the story .... A month ago the congregation of 20 policemen on a street corner in the centre of the city would have created a sensation. It is now a commonplace, which turns nobody's head. Nor does it attract attention when a motor lorry passes with six mounted policemen escorting it as if it were a royal personage .... Take a turn into the Fish and Vegetable Markets. They are deserted .... There are no fish for sale .... The supply of vegetables is curtailed almost to vanishing point .... Potatoes are nearly double in price, and are now 4s 6d per cwt. Cabbages have nearly trebled in price .... Of fruit the supply is very limited .... It is like Sunday along the quays. No labour is about, big lines of berths unoccupied by steamers, not a smoking funnel, save the berths of the City of Dublin Steam Packet Company [not in dispute – JN]; very few carts on the move, a strange quiet everywhere .... The hum of life is concentrated around Liberty Hall. Eden quay, Butt Bridge and Beresford Place are thickly populated all day and practically all night .... The theatres, music halls and picture palaces have suffered by the want of trams .... The pawnbrokers are very busy ....

The following day the *Freeman's Journal* reported boys at the Pro-Cathedral Schools in Rutland Street going on strike in protest against the use of text books supplied by the scab firm, Eason's. On 22 September it carried the story of a crowd trying to rescue a picket from two policemen, but being driven back by a public spirited gentleman, the mace bearer to Trinity College no less, who 'drew a revolver and pointed it at the assailants'. The next day it reported a number of timber yards locking out some 400 workers, bringing 'the ranks of the idle men in the city to the immense figure of 24,000'. And every week produced a lengthening list of union members arrested and imprisoned. On 11 September the paper reported Michael Wade, tramwayman, getting a month for calling Mrs Ellen Kelly 'a scab's wife'. The next day, James Carmody got three months for intimidation. On 16 September it was reported that Florence MacAuley had been given a month for intimidation, Joseph McDonald two months for throwing a brick at a tram and Michael Warnock a month for assaulting a scab. How many of those imprisoned were convicted on the basis of perjured police evidence is, of course, impossible to know, although anyone with a practical knowledge of demonstrations or picketing will be familiar with the phenomenon. What we do know is that on 12 September the *Freeman's Journal* reported the acquittal of Christopher Reilly, charged with throwing stones at the police. Two officers, 124D and 144D gave identification evidence against him, but unfortunately he was already in Mountjoy Jail when the offence was committed. This, one suspects, was the only alibi likely to secure the acquittal of a working-class defendant, man or woman, during these times.

A Prospect of Peace

On 24 September, the Board of Trade announced that Sir George Askwith was to conduct an inquiry into the dispute. The ITGWU welcomed the news and Larkin issued a statement:

> The Irish Transport Workers' Union has never offered any objection to mediation, nor is it true that they have refused to carry out their obligations. The Dublin Tramway Company never brought any charge against the 200 men who were dismissed for belonging to the union, but simply picked out the active members of the union, and as everyone in Dublin knows, it was the refusal to reinstate these men, guilty of no wrong act, that let to all the trouble.
>
> In its essence the dispute is very similar to that which gave rise to the omnibus trouble in London, now satisfactorily settled. Dublin tram men were refused what was recognised as a reasonable condition for the London busmen. If the busmen had struck it is doubtful whether the metropolitan police would have been turned loose in the streets to baton every striker they saw. But in Dublin things are different. I want to make clear that we do not object to mediation, but we will never forego the right of the men to belong to the Transport Workers' Union.[30]

The inquiry opened on the 29th with both union and employer representatives giving evidence.

Inevitably, the exchanges were acrimonious, with Larkin making it clear that the terrible poverty in Dublin was the responsibility of the employers, both collectively and individually. They positively boasted that they controlled 'the means of life; then the responsibility rests with them'. The capitalist system was brutally murdering men and women in Dublin, 'the greatest Church-going city, he believed, in the world'. 'We are determined', Larkin declared, 'that this shall no longer go on; we are determined the system shall stop; we are determined that Christ will not be crucified in Dublin by these men'. More immediately, he proposed a settlement that involved the reinstatement of all locked out workers, the withdrawal of the employers' ban on ITGWU membership and the establishment of a Conciliation Board, with all those firms affiliated being exempted from sympathy strikes for two years. The employers would have none of this. When the Askwith tribunal recommended terms very close to Larkin's: the withdrawal of the employers' ban, an end to sympathy strikes and the establishment of conciliation boards, they rejected it out of hand. On 14 October they announced their own terms: the ITGWU would have to be reorganised with a new leadership appointed that was acceptable to the employers, and the locked out workers would only be re-employed as vacancies occurred. Larkinism had to be destroyed and the Dublin working class broken.[31] The best comment on the employers' terms was provided on 16 October when thousands of ITGWU members once again marched through the city. One of them was carrying a placard which read: 'We are prepared to recognise the Employers' Association provided it is completely reorganised and they get a new set of officials'.[32]

This was a public relations disaster for the employers. The union had unreservedly accepted the Askwith proposals, while the employers had quite summarily rejected them. A considerable body of Dublin middle-class opinion, associated with the Dublin Industrial Peace Committee (its members included Joseph Plunkett and Thomas MacDonagh, for example) had expected Askwith's intervention to resolve the dispute and was outraged by the employers' attitude. The *Freeman's Journal*, while routinely condemning Larkin, nevertheless laid into the employers, telling them that the days 'for suppression had gone by' and that 'it is impossible to destroy the Transport Workers' Union'. Indeed, the paper blamed the greed and intransigence of the employers for having caused Larkinism in the first place. 'It is not denied', it pointed out, 'that wages have been extensively and substantially raised in consequence of Mr Larkin's agitation, which means that employers have refused to give terms they could well afford until they were compelled'. This had played into the hands of the agitator.[33]

Most devastating, however, was the letter sent to the *Irish Times* by the writer, George Russell, better known as AE, the editor of the cooperative journal, *Irish Homestead* and a member of the Dublin Industrial Peace Committee. Addressed to 'the Masters of Dublin', it appeared on 7 October and attacked the employers in the most vitriolic terms:

> Your insolence and ignorance of the rights conceded to workers universally in the modern world were incredible, and as great as your inhumanity. If you had between you collectively a portion of human soul as large as a threepenny bit, you would have sat night and day with the representatives of labour, trying this or that solution of the trouble, mindful of the women and children, who at least were innocent of wrong against you. But no! You reminded labour you could always have your three square meals a day while it went hungry. You went into conference again with representatives of the State, because dull as you are, you know public opinion would not stand your holding out … and then when an award was made by men who have an experience in industrial matters a thousand times transcending you, who have settled disputes in industries so great that the sum of your petty enterprises would not equal them, you withdraw again, and will not agree to accept their solution, and fall back upon your devilish policy of starvation. Cry aloud to heaven for new souls! The souls you have got cast upon the screen of publicity appear like the horrid and writhing creatures enlarged from the insect world, and revealed to us by the cinematograph.[34]

Murphy and the other employers were unmoved. The lockout would continue regardless. And while it was very useful for the ITGWU to at least momentarily have 'public opinion' on its side, public opinion did not win disputes and in this as in other industrial battles was no substitute for solidarity action.

The Hibernians and the Priests

When, at the very start of the Lockout, Murphy had urged the tramwaymen to form a 'loyal' union which the company would recognise, the man who obliged was the secretary of the Ancient Order of Hibernians, John Nugent. The Hibernians part in setting up Murphy's sham 'yellow' union was to be the first blow in their protracted campaign against the ITGWU. Nugent himself was a Dublin businessman and city councillor, a man of some influence in the United Irish League, where the sectarian Hibernian organisation made itself useful to the leadership, undertaking those jobs that Redmond and company did not want to dirty their hands with. Now Nugent allied himself with Murphy and the Hibernians launched a vicious sectarian war on Larkin and his followers. It is almost certain that the anti-Larkinite newspaper, *The Liberator*, that was launched on 23 August, was the creation of the Hibernians, with funds provided by Murphy and others. It started out purporting to be the voice of moderate, decent trade unionism, attacking Larkinism for being anti-Catholic and anti-Irish, but once the Lockout had begun, came out openly in support of the employers. In its pages, Larkin was subjected to a weekly torrent of abuse and slander. His name was always printed '£arkin' and he was regularly accused of embezzling funds, of living in luxury while his members starved. On one occasion he was denounced as an atheist with the fact that he sent his son to St. Enda's, Padraic Pearse's school, rather than to a Christian Brothers establishment as evidence. Pearse actually wrote to the newspaper to assure it that St. Enda's was 'a purely Catholic school, and that the teaching of the Catholic religion holds first place in its programme'. This did not let Larkin off the hook, because for *The Liberator* socialism was ample proof of atheism. The paper denounced all talk of compromise warning that there could be 'no conciliation, no agreement, no truce while the Transport Union is under the domination of the present Syndicalist clique'. It was unfortunate if the workers had to be starved back to work, 'but it would be even worse for themselves and for Ireland if Larkinism and Syndicalism were allowed to grow unchecked'. According to *The Liberator*, 'the Devil it was who sent Larkin to Ireland, that our people might be led away from honour, from self-respect, from obedience to God's commands, and stray into the trap set by the Devil's Missioner – the Socialist'.[35]

More damaging were the attacks mounted on the union by members of the priesthood. These were bitterly resented. We have already referred to the attack on Larkin by Father John Condon that was reported in the *Freeman's Journal* and elsewhere on 18 September. Larkin penned a devastating reply:

Reverend Father – I feel that I should be shirking a manifest duty if I allowed your insidious attack on the working class of this city to pass without comment as you were careful to explain you were not speaking as a Priest, but as an ordinary man .... May I point out to you, sir, that you forgot to explain that you were also speaking as a shareholder in a commercial undertaking, which is affected by the present deplorable dispute which you correctly described as economic war ... what of the seventy odd priests who are shareholders in the Dublin United Tramway Company and who are responsible along with that other pillar of the Church, William 'Murder' Murphy, for the terrible bloodshed and tragedy of death? Have you no word of condemnation for them? Is it because you yourself are a shareholder, taking profits from a trade of which one cannot find words adequate to describe the horrors caused by its continuance. I refer to the drink traffic .... You have never had time to protest about the lot of the working class, but you found time to attack their efforts to improve their lot .... Thank God, that there are others who dignify the high and holy calling; who instead of attacking the working class, sympathise with their efforts, and realise the urgent need for improvement.[36]

Murphy's *Irish Catholic* magazine replied with a quite straight-faced editorial, 'Satanism and Socialism' in which it was argued that Larkin's words were themselves proof 'that Socialism is essentially Satanic in its nature, origin and purpose'.[37] What is interesting, of course, is that far from being a Satanist, Larkin was a sincere Catholic, outraged by priests taking the side of the employers in the struggle, the side, as he saw it, of Mammon.

William Partridge continued the assault on Father Condon in a later issue of the *Irish Worker*:

May I suggest to the Rev. gentlemen who from the pulpit from which the attack on the late Charles Stewart Parnell was first begun in Dublin has now assailed our Chief, that if his object was not to deliver the working classes of Dublin back into bondage, he might without damage to his case, have postponed the assault till the Transport Workers' Union had first dealt with the modern assassins. And may I remind him that the Union led by Larkin is the only organisation of workers in Ireland that provides a Christmas feast for the poor and homeless of our city in celebration of our Saviour's birth; that the Union led by Larkin is the only organisation of workers I know of whose members make special provision for sending subscriptions to the Roman Catholic Church. Its members working on coal boats and others subscribe 2d per man per boat to the City Quay or Ringsend Chapels, and that in all its club houses collecting boxes are exhibited for charitable institutions; and I have read a letter of thanks from a Rev. Father praying for Larkin and the members of his Union for the generous donations made.

It was the union's sensitivity to the Catholic faith of its members that made the sense of betrayal at the hands of the clergy now that it was fighting for its life all the greater. And moreover, as Partridge pointed out, this same Father Condon, who had the temerity to criticise Larkin was a shareholder in the Guinness brewery, another non-union firm.[38]

The attack on the clergy continued in a front page article by 'Shellback' that appeared in mid-October. He argued that the employers' greatest crime was their attempt 'to dragoon the Catholic church and its clergy into their service and against the people'. A few priests had gone along with this and he went on to address them:

> The Rev. gentlemen who have taken the side of money and batons in the present crisis, may be under the impression that it is their duty to, at all times, condemn the poor and put obstacles in the way of their emancipation, otherwise they would have spoken just as loud, or louder, against the poverty-manufacturing conditions of industrial Dublin, that obtained before the day of Jim Larkin, or they would have discovered that the greater part of their congregations lived under conditions far below that of an ordinary dog, who at least has a kennel to himself … it proves conclusively the absolute indifference of those priests of Ireland in the past to the needs and requirements of the people in her capital city, who just now appear to be so anxious to obstruct the advance of Socialism, under whose rule such horrible stinking conditions could not possibly exist.

He continued:

> Still I don't blame them for what do they know of the lives of the common people? They visit them on their sick bed; they christen them; they marry them and they bury them, and they do all these things with the best and most holy intentions, but what do they know of the horrors of their daily life? What do they know of that fearful anxiety for the future? What do they know of the horrible pain caused by the children's cry for food? I don't blame them, for their daily experience offers them small opportunity to learn anything of the actual living conditions of the common people and their principal tutors in matters connected with the social conditions of the workers, are generally members of the very class who are now depending on the wailing of hungry infants to give them the power to continue their unholy subjection of the wealth-producers of Dublin.[39]

However, the test of the ITGWU's resolve in the face of clerical condemnation was still to come.

Notes

1 *Irish Worker* 7 June 1913.
2 For Murphy see in particular Thomas Morrissey SJ, *William Martin Murphy*, Dundalk 1997; Andy Bilenberg, 'Entrepreneurship, Power and Public Opinion in Ireland: the Career of William Martin Murphy', *Irish Economic and Social History* XVII, 2000; and Dermot Keogh, 'William Martin Murphy and the Origins of the 1913 Lock-out', *Saother* 4 1978.
3 *Irish Worker* 26 July 1913.
4 Keogh, op cit, pp. 20-21. For an interesting discussion of labour relations at Jacobs' biscuit factory see Michael Rowlinson, 'Quaker Employers', *Historical Studies in Industrial Relations*, 6, 1998.
5 Ibid, p. 22.

6   In his *The Rise of the Irish Working Class*, Belfast 1982, Keogh argues that the tram-
    way strike was on the verge of collapse when police brutality gave it a new lease of
    life and that O'Brien's decision to abide by the O'Connell Street ban demonstrates
    the essential moderation of the Dublin labour movement with the exception, of
    course, of Larkin. He completely misunderstands the situation. The police action
    on 30-31 August was a calculated effort to drive the union and its supporters off
    the streets and thereby prevent the picketing of the trams, picketing that would
    have inevitably closed them down. While there were certainly elements on Dublin
    Trades Council who would have liked to avoid a fight and reach an accommodation
    with the employers, they were rendered impotent by the employers determination
    to destroy the ITGWU. (pp. 193-199).

7   Robert Monteith, *Casement's Last Adventure*, Dublin 1953, p. 6. L. Monteith went
    on to join the underground Irish Republican Brotherhood (IRB) and was to be sent
    as an envoy to Germany during the War.

8   Keogh, *Rise of the Irish Working Class*, op cit, p. 202.

9   *Freeman's Journal*, 1 September 1913.

10 Ibid.

11 The best account of these events is in Padraig Yeates, *Lockout: Dublin 1913*, Dublin
    2000, pp. 64-98.

12 *Freeman's Journal* 15 January 1914.

13 Leon O Broin, *Just Like Yesterday*, Dublin 1987, p. 2. For an excellent discussion of
    the long-standing hostility of the Dublin working class to the DMP see Brian Grif-
    fin's unfortunately unpublished PhD thesis, 'The Irish Police 1836-1914: A Social
    History' (Loyola University of Chicago 1990).

14 Thomas J. Morrissey SJ, *William J. Walsh, Archbishop of Dublin 1841-1921*, Dublin
    2000, pp. 246-247.

15 *Freeman's Journal* 29 August 1913.

16 Sarah Curtis, ed, *The Journals of Woodrow Wyatt* 1, London 1998, p. 59.

17 *Irish Worker*, 6 September 1913.

18 *Daily Herald*, 1 September 1913. For Francis Sheehy-Skeffington see Leah Leven-
    son, *With Wooden Sword*, Dublin 1983.

19 *Daily Herald*, 2 September 1913.

20 G.D.H. Cole, *The World of Labour*, London 1913, p. 289.

21 *Freeman's Journal*, 3 September 1913.

22 Kenneth Morgan, *Keir Hardie: Radical and Socialist*, London 1975, pp. 242-244.
    Hardie was involved in a fierce exchange over Larkinism with Philip Snowden in
    the *Labour Leader* newspaper in which he defended strikes: 'It is the experience
    gained by the strike which ultimately filters into the consciousness of the working
    class and makes political action as triumphant reality' (p. 248). Nevertheless, he re-
    mained an opponent of syndicalism as a strategy and a supporter of parliamentary
    socialism.

23 *Freeman's Journal*, 4 September 1913.

24 *Daily Herald*, 17, 18, 20 September 1913.

25 Philip S. Bagwell, *The Railwaymen: The History of the National Union of Railway-
    men*, London 1963, pp. 337-340.

26 *Daily Herald*, 27, 31 October 1913. For the disaster see L.T.C. Rolt, *Red for Danger*,

London 1955, pp. 198-202. The inquiry into this accident recommended 'automatic train stops as introduced on London's Underground'.

27 *Daily Herald*, 1 November 1913.

28 David Howell, *Respectable Radicals: Studies in the politics of railway trade unionism*, Aldershot 1999, pp. 136-149.

29 *Daily Herald*, 22 September 1913.

30 *Freeman's Journal*, 25 September 1913. For their part it is clear that the employers had no intention of reaching a settlement. Only days before the inquiry opened, T.M. Healy, the employers' legal representative, wrote to his brother that 'the strike will continue until the men are exhausted'. He thought that a deal was possible with the British union leaders but Larkin had sabotaged it. See Frank Callanan, *T.M. Healy*, Cork 1996, pp. 488-489.

31 *Freeman's Journal*, 6 October, 7 October, 15 October 1913.

32 *Freeman's Journal*, 17 October 1913. The paper reported: 'One of the biggest strike processions held since the industrial crisis is the city became acute took place through the streets yesterday. The display was designed by the strike leaders as "an answer to the employers' ultimatum" of Tuesday last'. At the subsequent meeting, Connolly 'asked the audience to uncover as a mark of sympathy with the widows and orphans caused by the Welsh colliery disaster. The whole meeting reverently uncovered for some moments'.

33 *Freeman's Journal*, 9 October 1913.

34 Nevin, op cit, pp. 212-214. See also Henry Summerfield, *That Myriad-Minded Man: a biography of George William Russell*, Gerrards Cross 1975, pp. 161-162. For a more recent study of Russell see Nicholas Allen, *George Russell and the New Ireland*, Dublin 2003.

35 *The Liberator*, 6, 13, 27 September, 18, 25 October 1913. See also my '"The Devil It Was Who Sent Larkin To Ireland": *The Liberator*, Larkinism and the Dublin Lockout of 1913', *Saothar* 18, 1993.

36 *Irish Worker*, 20 September 1913.

37 Callanan, op cit, p. 487.

38 *Irish Worker*, 27 September 1913.

39 *Irish Worker*, 18 October 1913.

Chapter IV
The Lockout: Free Larkin

The employers had decisively lost the battle for public support in the first phase of the Lockout. Their refusal to negotiate, the brutality of the police and the union's publicising of its case had all contributed to this. To complete the job a British socialist feminist associated with the *Daily Herald*, Dora Montefiore, proposed the children's holiday scheme where sympathetic families in Britain would provide holidays for the children of the locked out workers. As well as providing welcome relief for the hardpressed Dublin workers, it would also be a public relations coup that would complete the employers' isolation by demonstrating the extent to which their strategy required the starvation of children. It could be expected to attract considerable favourable publicity and hopefully emulate the success of similar schemes in Belgium, Italy, France, and, more especially during the great Lawrence textile strike in the United States the previous year. This was not an unreasonable expectation. Dora Montefiore, it is worth emphasising, was not some sort of naïve do-gooder who was to find herself out of her depth in Dublin.[1] She was a remarkably tough and intelligent woman, with considerable experience of the suffrage and labour movements in a number of countries. She was a respected socialist propagandist, both in print and on the platform, who knew both Clara Zetkin and Rosa Luxemburg. Her later career saw her go on to be one of the key speakers at the Leeds Convention in June 1917 where she urged delegates 'to do what the Russians had done'. In 1920 she was a founder member of the Communist Party of Great Britain and was elected onto its executive (the only woman member). Later, in 1924, she was a delegate to the Fifth Congress of the Communist International, representing the Communist Party of Australia. She was to find herself travelling to the congress with another delegate, Jim Larkin.[2] Moreover, the scheme was organised under the auspices of the *Daily Herald* and through the Daily Herald Leagues that were playing a heroic role in supporting the locked out workers.

In his biography of James Connolly, C. Desmond Greaves remarks of the scheme that 'it is surprising that Mrs Montefiore ... did not fear a repetition of the sectarian repercussions which wrecked it in America'.[3] This is a complete travesty because at Lawrence, while the scheme had to overcome immense difficulties, it had played an important part in the strike's eventual victory. Here the scheme had been organised by Elizabeth Gurley Flynn, an Irish-American IWW leader. She later recalled the despatch of the first group of 150 children to New York as 'a happy episode in a series of sombre, tragic situations in the Lawrence strike of 1912'. The attempt a week later to send children to Philadelphia was not so fortunate. On 24 February forty children together with parents and friends assembled at the Lawrence railroad station:

> just as they were ready to board the train they were surrounded by police. Troops surrounded the station outside to keep others out. Children were clubbed and torn away from their parents and a wild scene of brutal disorder took place. Thirty-five frantic women and children were arrested, thrown screaming and fighting into patrol wagons. They were beaten into submission and taken to the police station. There the woman were charged with "neglect" and improper guardianship and the frightened children were taken to the Lawrence Poor Farm. The police station was besieged by enraged strikers.[4]

The conduct of the police caused an outcry throughout the United States and abroad. The episode highlighted both the plight of the children and the brutality of the police. As Flynn's biographer observes, the children's holiday scheme proved 'a brilliant stroke ... liberal journalists began to pour into the city'.[5]

The two standard histories of the IWW endorse this. According to Philip Foner, the 'children's affair helped to change public opinion from hostility to sympathy towards the strikers ... the picture of the near-starvation state of the Lawrence children and the accounts of the brutality of the authorities brought the real facts of the strike to the attention of the American people and their sympathy was now definitely with the strikers'.[6] While for Melvyn Dubosfsky, the children's holiday scheme and the authorities' response 'proved to be the strike's turning point' and made 'the entire nation witness to the arrogance, stupidity and brutality of Lawrence's employers and public officials'.[7] And Dora Montefiore herself made the very same point at the time: 'The Socialist's care of the kiddies put heart into the Lawrence Strikers ... and brought great sympathy and practical support to the strikers'. What she looked forward to was the establishment of 'some permanent, not red cross, but red flag organisation ... to take care of the dependent non-combatants', in today's 'industrial warfare'. Make no mistake, she warned 'the industrial rebellion is on right now' and we 'must strengthen our forces at every point'.[8]

According to Montefiore, through the good offices of the *Daily Herald*, some 300 'responsible homes' were offered and a large consignment of children's' clothes was collected, 'which the girls on strike at Burn and Co's factory at Hatton Garden first overhauled and mended'. She emphasises that the scheme had the active support of a wide section of the labour movement with help being volunteered by trades councils, union branches, socialist and labour organisations and, of course, the Daily Herald League. The Shop Workers, Gasworkers and Firemen's and Sailors' Unions all promised 'dozens of homes'. This needed emphasis 'in order to refute the accusation that our mission to Dublin was an irresponsible one'.[9] Once satisfactory arrangements were made to receive the children, she went to Dublin to arrange their transportation. There was every expectation of a great practical and propaganda success. No one expected the police to behave as the Lawrence police had. What they had miscalculated was the response of the Catholic Church.

On 21 October 1913, William Walsh, Archbishop of Dublin, published a letter in the press condemning the scheme, and asking the mothers if they had 'abandoned their faith'. They were accused of sending 'away their children to be cared for in a strange land without security of any kind that those to whom the poor children are to be handed over are Catholics, or indeed, are persons of any faith at all'[10] Whether wittingly or not, this gave a green light to the Hibernians and a number of anti-socialist priests to confront the union with the full support of the Dublin press. The children were being kidnapped and deported to England to be proselytised or worse. This was printed as fact in the Dublin press, all denials were ignored, and the clergy were urged to save the day. Crowds of Hibernians led by priests picketed the docks and the railway stations to physically prevent any children leaving with the police standing by watching. Montefiore described one episode:

> The scene of confusion was indescribable; some of the women were "answering back" to the priests and reminding them how they had been refused bread by the representatives of the Church, and how, now that they had a chance of getting their children properly cared for, the priests were preventing the kiddies from going. Other women worked upon by the violent speeches of the priest were wailing and calling on the saints to forgive them.

She wrote to Walsh the day his letter appeared in the press to explain the situation and assure him that the children's spiritual needs were being looked after, but to no effect. His letter in reply made clear that he would 'give neither countenance nor support to any scheme of deportation' and referred to 'some sinister rumours' that had come to his attention. Montefiore concluded that 'it was no use wasting time on this obtuse prelate, and I determined to go ahead with our work, regardless of the action of clericals, capitalists and their Hibernian tools'. She did, however, take great exception to Walsh's mention of 'sinister rumours'. These 'were rumours set about purposely by the priests and Hibernians that we three women [herself, Lucille Rand and Grace Neal – JN] were agents of the

While Slave Traffic'. They were accused of this in the street and received hate-mail to the same effect at their hotel.

The union made one last attempt to defuse the situation by sending a group of children to stay with Catholic families in Belfast. There could surely be on objection to this. More than any other episode this demonstrates the extent to which the furore was got up by the priests to do down Larkin. Montefiore went to the station to see them off and

> was there witness of a scene which I should not have thought possible in any part of the United Kingdom. At one end of the platform, in front of the compartment into which the parents were attempting to get their children, there was a compact, shouting, gesticulating, fighting crowd of Hibernians. In the centre of this crowd was the little party of children and parents, and scattered among them the priests, who were talking, uttering threats against the parents, and forbidding them to send their children to Protestant homes. Some of the women were upbraiding the priests for allowing the children to starve in Dublin; and according to an American paper, whose correspondent was on the platform, 'one women slapped the face of a priest who was attempting to interfere'.

Eventually, the police intervened, not to allow the children to board the train, but to prevent them.[11] Montefiore and a number of her helpers were arrested for kidnapping with the priests intimidating some parents into giving perjured evidence against them.[12] The charges were eventually dropped, but they had done their work.

There is no doubt that Larkin's enemies felt that they had at last found the means of destroying the union, of turning its members against it. The London *Times* gloated that the priests 'have reasserted their authority over the women of the working classes, and it is no longer certain that Mr. Larkin enjoys the unquestioning obedience of the men'.[13] Arnold Wright, in his account of the Lockout, described these events as 'one of the most remarkable and significant uprisings of Catholics that Dublin had witnessed for many a long day'.[14] The new Hibernian scab newspaper, *The Toiler*, which revealed that the children were to be handed over to the Mormons and shipped to Utah, proclaimed that 'the Larkinite conspiracy has been unmasked'.[15] While Augustine Birrell, the Liberal Chief Secretary for Ireland, optimistically concluded that 'it has broken the strike'.[16] But while the union was shaken by this manifestation of clerical hostility, the rank and file remained solid. Larkin met the clerical challenge with indignant outrage: 'I am not frightened by the Archbishop or the priests … I say the priest who says I would allow a child to be proselytised is a liar in his heart'.[17] His involvement was temporarily ended, however, when on 28 October a hand-picked jury found him guilty of sedition and he was sentenced to seven months imprisonment. William Partridge attempted to put as generous construction on Walsh's actions as possible by acknowledging his intervention as 'reasonable' but complaining that it 'has been made an excuse for the most undeserved and injudicious display of unreasonable bigotry ever seen in a city hitherto famed for its tolerance'. The union, he made clear, would 'remove any child from a home in England not approved by the local priest there and undertake to place it in any home selected by him'.[18] Walsh was unmoved.

Fighting Back

On 1 November, the *Irish Worker* published a ferocious letter from the poet, W.B. Yeats protesting against the way the Dublin press was 'deliberately arousing religious passion to break up the organisation of the workingman, appealing to mob law day after day, with publishing the names of the workingmen and their wives for the purposes of intimidation'. He demanded to know why the Hibernians had been allowed to take control of the railway stations 'like a foreign army' without any interference from the police. By what right were the Hibernians 'permitted to drag children from their parents' arms, and by what right one woman was compelled to open her box and show a marriage certificate'. There was clear evidence of a conspiracy to condone mob violence against the ITGWU ('Prime Ministers have fallen and Ministers of State have been impeached for less than this'). Those responsible for these disgraceful scenes were attempting to 'turn the religion of Him who thought it hard for a rich man to enter into the Kingdom of Heaven into an oppression of the poor'.[19]

With Larkin in prison, Connolly had taken over the running of the union and abandoned the children's holiday scheme. His response to clerical attack had two aspects to it. On the one hand, he very deliberately put the Church on the spot. As the priests were claiming that there was no need to send children to England because charities in Dublin could cope with their relief, Connolly suspended all free dinners at Liberty Hall for a week and told people to go to the Church. According to the official history of the union, which scrupulously avoids any criticism of the Church, this brought home the magnitude of the problem and 'Archbishop Walsh joined those calling for a settlement'.[20] This account completely fails to take on board the intensity of clerical hostility to ITGWU and seriously distorts the historical record. The *Irish Worker*, edited by Connolly at this point, presents a considerably less sympathetic view of the Church's response to the suspension of dinners than appears in the official history:

> Owing to the publicity given to the statements that his Grace the Archbishop and the Dublin clergy were ready to deal with all cases of distress in this city, and that therefore there was no need for sending children abroad, the free dinners which have been a feature at Liberty Hall for some weeks were discontinued on Tuesday night, in order to prevent the possibility of overlapping, and the women and children told to present themselves at the Archbishop's palace or at the presbyteries of the various chapels in the city.
> On Wednesday some of the women went to the palace of the Archbishop and told

the footman that they were sent from Liberty Hall for the dinners. The footman said the dinners were not for Larkin's people, but he would send the secretary to them. The Archbishop's secretary told them that there was nothing for them or the children of the workers on strike, or locked out, that there was going to be a collection made at all the churches on Sunday, and that the proceeds of the collection were going to be handed over to St Vincent de Paul's Society to buy clothes for poor children, but that those belonging to the workers engaged in the dispute were not to receive any such benefit.[21]

At the very same time, he published an article in the Glasgow *Forward* that made clear that he had always been sceptical about the scheme, defended those involved in it and laid into the priests who had slandered them in the most uncompromising terms. He then went on to solicit Walsh's intervention in the dispute in terms that even given the difficulties of the time seem somewhat compromised. While some of his priests might have behaved badly Walsh was 'a gentleman' with 'his own high sense of honour' who had never impugned the motives of Montefiore and her co-workers. She would certainly not have agreed. And this is to say nothing of his slander of working-class mothers. In effect, he apologised for Walsh's disgraceful conduct, but then went on:

> But if your Grace is as solicitous about the poor bodies of those children as we know you to be about their souls, or even if you are but one tenth part as solicitous, may we suggest to you or your laymen that your duty is plain. See to it that the force of public opinion, that the power of the press, that all the engines at your command are brought to bear upon the inhuman monsters who control the means of employment in Dublin to make them realise their duties to the rest of the community. We have done our part, we have told the Dublin Industrial Pence Committee, that we are ready to negotiate … To you we repeat our offer: we are willing to accept the mediation of any party …. This is our offer to you …. If the employers reject your offer of mediation and still declare their contempt for any public opinion they cannot rig in advance, then it is your manifest duty to organise public support for the workers to defeat their soulless employers.[22]

This quite remarkable call for and expectation of a Catholic Archbishop taking up the workers' cause was, as we have seen, very much part of Connolly's analysis of the Catholic Church. He believed that the time would come when the Church would side with the workers, that just as it had rallied to the farmers during the Land War so it would rally to the workers during the Industrial war.

Walsh, needless to say, did not take on the task of organising 'public support for the workers'. How could Connolly mistake him in this way? Walsh was a staunch nationalist, indeed the British government had done its best to prevent his appointment to the post of Archbishop. He had supported the farmers in the Land War and was to go on to support Sinn Féin and the revolutionary Dail Eireann in 1918. On a number of occasions in 1889 and 1890 he had mediated in industrial disputes to the satisfaction of the workers involved. There is no doubt that he had considerable sympathy for the plight of the poor, but as objects of charity, not as a political and industrial force out to change society. While initially he had thought the workers' grievances justified, by the time of the children's holiday scheme, he had come to regard Larkinism as a threat that had to be destroyed. His sympathy for the poor was to be sacrificed to the harsh necessities of class war. As he told a meeting of the Society of St. Vincent de Paul on 27 October, while 'the sight of poor ill-clad children makes a powerful appeal to the hearts of our charitable people', they had to 'harden their hearts' and only give to the charities which helped the respectable and respectful poor. He went on to make clear his objection to the children's holiday scheme: 'It will but make them discontented with the poor homes to which they will sooner or later return, that is to say, those of them who will return at all'.[23] To defeat this scheme, he allowed his priests to lie and slander, to whip up sectarian hatred and prejudice and to organise vigilante mobs. His responsibility for this cannot seriously be denied. When the Dublin Labour Party was defeated in the city elections in January 1914, Walsh congratulated the Lord Mayor, Lorcan Sherlock, on his 'notable victory' over those who 'in addition to the havoc they have wrought in the industrial world of Dublin, have done no little harm in ... deadening the moral and religious sense of not a few amongst the working population'.[24] In effect, he gave his support to a party of slum landlords and corrupt placemen, who had fought a campaign of lies and slander dressed up as religion and condemned Larkin, of all people, for deadening the moral and religious sense of the working class.[25]

What is interesting, of course, is the working-class response to the Church's stance. There was to be no Dublin equivalent of the 1909 Barcelona riots when working-class crowds destroyed twelve churches and forty convents and other religious buildings.[26] Dublin in 1913 was not Lawrence in 1912, where the anarchist and ferocious anti-clerical Carlo Tresca had led Italian IWW members behind a banner that read 'Arise! Slaves of the World! No God! No Master! One for All and All For One!'.[27] The Irish response was very different. But what has to be remembered is that while the Dublin working class did not turn on the Catholic Church, the Catholic Church could not break the ITGWU. Larkin perhaps summed up the children's holiday scheme best as 'The finest tactical error ever made ... the Dublin workers have withstood the shock of the priestly attack and now they know their friends'.[28]

With the imprisonment of Larkin on 28 October 1913, Jim Connolly took over as acting general-secretary of the ITGWU. He immediately launched a campaign to free Larkin, exploiting the remarkable contrast between the vindictive prosecution of Larkin and the failure to prosecute the Unionist leaders, Sir Edward Carson and James Craig, who were openly organising rebellion against the Crown in Ulster. The contrast was so stark, the unfairness so blatant, that even Labour moderates were outraged and a number of Liberal ministers were alarmed. As Lloyd George observed: 'No amount of argument could persuade the British workman that the difference in treatment accorded to Larkin as compared with that meted out to Carson is anything but pure class distinction'.[29] Christopher Addison, a Liberal MP, wrote to Lloyd George, warning him that Larkin's imprisonment 'arouses the greatest possible resentment amongst many quite moderate working men'. While he agreed with the policy of not prosecuting Carson, 'no amount of argument will convince the average man that we are acting fairly, if, at the same time, we put Larkin in jail'.[30] What was intended as a fatal blow against Larkinism, in fact proved to be a disaster for the authorities.

On Sunday 1 November a great rally to demand Larkin's release was held at the Albert Hall in London. The *Freeman's Journal* reported that the 10,000 strong audience was 'distinctly Socialist in character' with a large number of women present, 'many of whom wore Suffrage badges and sashes.[31] Another 20,000 people were turned away. Among the speakers were George Bernard Shaw, Dora Montefiore, George Lansbury, George Russell, Delia Larkin and Connolly himself. Shaw proceeded to apologise on behalf of 'the priests of Dublin ... very ignorant and simple men' and lamented 'the great Church to which they belong being made a catspaw of a gentleman like Murphy'. He called on all 'respectable citizens' to arm themselves so as to 'put a decisive stop to the proceedings of the police' and urged the Liberal government to prosecute him for his seditious remarks.[32] Sylvia Pankhurst, on the run from the police herself, received a tremendous reception when she spoke and was one of a number of speakers who linked Larkin's situation to that of the suffragette prisoners being forcibly fed at that very moment.[33] Connolly called on British workers to vote against the Liberal government in forthcoming by-elections to secure Larkin's release. But arguably the bravest speech, certainly the speech that attracted the most attention back in Ireland, was George Russell's. This was at once a savage attack on the Catholic Church, a tremendous indictment of the Dublin employers and a great celebration of Larkin and the Dublin working class. He condemned the priests for their disgraceful conduct over the children's holiday scheme and noted that 'a very holy man' had warned that if Dublin children were allowed to receive proper meals in England they

> might be so inconsiderate as to ask for them all their lives. They might destroy the very interesting experiment carried on in Dublin for generations to find out how closely human beings can be packed together, on how little a human being can live, and what is the minimum wage his employer need pay him. James Larkin interrupted these interesting experiments towards the evolution of the underman, and he is in jail,

He went on:

This labour uprising in Ireland is the despairing effort of humanity to raise itself out of a dismal swamp of disease and poverty. James Larkin may have been an indiscreet leader. He may have committed blunders, but I believe in the sight of Heaven the crimes are all on the other side. If our Courts of Justice were courts of humanity, the masters of Dublin would be in the dock charged with criminal conspiracy, their crime that they tried to starve out one-third of the people of Dublin, to break their hearts and degrade their manhood, for the greatest crime against humanity is its own degradation.

'You have no idea', he told his audience, 'what labour in Ireland, which fights for the bare of means of human support, is up against'. Despite all the odds, the battle for 'the cooperative commonwealth' was underway and by the time it was over, 'Democratic control of industry will replace the autocracy which exists today'. He praised the workers for rejecting the employers' document, observing that 'real manhood' is generally found only among those earning 'from five to twenty-five shillings per week'. Above that limit of wealth, the men who will sacrifice anything for a principle 'get rarer and rarer'. The working class, he concluded

are the true heroes of Ireland today, they are the descendants of Oscar, Cuculain , the heroes of our ancient stories .... It is in the workers in the towns and in the men in the cabins in the country that the hope of Ireland lies .... I am a literary man and not a manual worker. I am but a voice, while they are the deed and the being, but I would be ashamed ever in my life again to speak of an ideal if I did not stand by these men and say of them what I hold to be true. If you back them up today they will be able to fight their own battles tomorrow, and perhaps to give you an example. I beseech you not to forsake these men.

Russell returned to a storm in Dublin where the press rounded on him and the Hibernians organised an attempt to close down the *Irish Homestead* and drive him out of the cooperative movement. He responded with a letter of 11 November which none of the Dublin newspapers would carry, but which was distributed as a leaflet. Here he condemned the Dublin press for being 'manifestly biased on the side of the employers' and responded to the abuse that had been heaped upon him personally. He was not against religion, far from it, but he was an enemy of the 'deity of the infuriated bigot' who was in reality 'the old Adversary' in disguise. The 'hooligans of religion in Dublin' were no better than 'the hooligans of religion in Belfast'. He warned that if the authorities were deliberately intent on turning Dublin into another Barcelona where the labour war was conducted by means of assassination and bombings, then 'they could not devise a policy more certain to bring about the result'.[34] He withdrew nothing and rode out the controversy.

The consequences for another speaker at the rally, Sylvia Pankhurst, were more severe. Her participation precipitated her expulsion from the suffragette organisation, the Women's Social and Political Union (WSPU). The WSPU leadership, in reality her mother, Emmeline, and her sister, Christabel, rejected any alliance with the labour movement, even with such staunch supporters of women's suffrage as Larkin, Connolly and Lansbury. Sylvia's working-class East London Federation of Suffragettes was soon cut adrift. This split prefigured the sharp rightward turn that Emmeline and Christabel were to make, enthusiastically supporting the British war effort in 1914 and campaigning both during and after the war against the left. Indeed, Emmeline was to eventually stand as a Conservative candidate for Parliament in the aftermath of the General Strike. Sylvia's trajectory was very different: determined opposition to the war, support for the Russian Revolution, a shortlived embrace of Communism and the championing of the cause of Abyssinia in the 1930s.[35]

The Albert Hall rally was a great success, but more important was the demand for a general strike to secure Larkin's release that was taken up by tens of thousands of British workers, railwaymen and miners, urged on by the *Daily Herald*. In an editorial, 'For a National Strike', on 5 November, the paper urged that 'the rank-and-filers in the Trade Unions generally should get down fair and square to the question of a general strike on behalf of their brethren in Dublin'. This was followed a couple of days later by another editorial, 'Now For the Greater Unionism!', that proclaimed that 'One of the supreme tests and trial-stages of Trade Unionism has come'. It went on:

> The vital matter of national action rests really with the rank and file. It is they, not officialism, that make the Greater Unionism …. Thousands of them – miners, railwaymen, transporters in general – have spoken out unmistakably for the national strike. They should press the matter home …. There is no use in playing at revolution. It is foolish to imagine that the freedom of the workers will come without struggle and sacrifice …. The Dublin workers have fought the fight of Trade Unionism against the bosses and the Castle for the long weeks. The rank-and-filers of Britain could win the battle for them and deal capitalism a staggering blow in less than a week.[36]

At the same time, Connolly's call for British workers to vote against the Liberal government in by-elections began to have an impact. The Liberals lost Reading and only held Linlithgow with a considerably reduced majority. Lloyd George acknowledged that while these results had various explanations, 'the most prominent … is probably Jim Larkin'.[37] In the circumstances, the Cabinet, despite the opposition of Irish Chief Secretary, Augustine Birrell decided to retreat. Asquith told the King that Birrell had defended Larkin's imprisonment as necessary 'in view of the dangerous condition of affairs at that time in Dublin', but that other ministers, particularly Lloyd George, were very critical of 'the manner in which the jury was "packed" and on the tone of the prosecution'. After some debate, the Cabinet had decided unanimously on Larkin's immediate release. This was a tremendous victory for the ITGWU and its British supporters. Later, when Birrell tried to justify his conduct, at a rowdy meeting in his Bristol constituency, he was somewhat appropriately struck by a well-aimed dead cat.[38]

Larkin's release after serving only seventeen days of his seven-month sentence was a great victory and was celebrated as such in Dublin. Speaking at Liberty Hall on 13 November, Larkin demanded the release of all the men and women imprisoned for Lockout offences. He attacked Nugent and the Hibernians ('unhung hooligans'), repudiated their latest slander that he was the son of Carey the Informer and appealed to the non-sectarian tradition of the United Irishmen. The employers, he promised, were going 'to sup sorrow with a long spoon'. He was going to carry the fight across the water and 'light a fiery cross in England, Scotland and Wales'. The fight was to be stepped up.

Later that evening Larkin was too unwell to attend the demonstrations and the rally held to welcome his release. As the marchers assembled, 'a rocket blazed up into the sky from the roof of Liberty Hall and loud cheers were raised'. For half an hour the growing crowd 'was delighted with ... rockets and fireworks, the burning of red and green fire, and the sputtering of a fiery star on the roof'. Then two bands led the march, 'an unusually noisy one' with the women and girls singing union songs including 'We Are Going To Join Jim Larkin's Union' and 'I am One of the Horrible Larkinites'. Some of the young men on the march carried large staves for protection from the police who were loudly booed. At the end of the march, Connolly proclaimed Larkin's release 'their first great victory', a victory that proved 'they were stronger than any Government'. He warned his audience that he was 'going to talk sedition' and went on to announce the formation of the Irish Citizen Army and the closing of the port of Dublin, both responses to the employers importation of scabs into the city.[39]

The question of the imprisonment of growing numbers of union members and sympathisers was a cause of great concern to the union leadership. Every week saw men and women receiving prison sentences for often minor offences. The Dublin working class seemed to have had its civil liberties suspended with strikers jailed for calling a strikebreaker a scab, while scabs who brandished and fired revolvers in the street were fined. One union official, James Byrne, had died from pneumonia contracted while he was on hunger strike in protest against his imprisonment. He was given a union funeral, his coffin followed by thousands of men and women through Kingstown on 4 November. On 20 November, at another rally at the Albert Hall, Larkin asked his audience not to 'forget that there were over 300 men lying in gaol in Dublin ... and over 57 mothers and daughters – girls of 16 up to women of 60'. He went on to single out one particular case, that of Mary Ellen Murphy, a sixteen year old, 'pure, clean-minded, clean-souled', who was serving her time in 'a home for fallen women – the Magdalen Institution'. She had been sentence to a month in prison for assaulting a scab and was sent to the High Park Convent Reformatory which also housed a

Magdalen asylum for prostitutes. The union objected to the inadequate segregation of girls like her from 'those who had forgotten their race, their sex and their soul'.[40] This seems to have been a rather opportunistic attempt to wrong-foot the Church, to put the clergy on the defensive, and it undoubtedly caused the Church some embarrassment although the Dublin press absolutely predictably used the occasion to attack the union for its anti-clericalism. The union was certainly representing the concerns of the family, with Mary Ellen's father, Patrick Murphy, issuing a statement to the press complaining that during Retreat only a partition separated his daughter from the prostitutes and commenting that 'I would rather see my daughter in Siberia than in such a place'.[41] Nevertheless, the episode does provide an instance where the union's Catholicism can be seen as positively disabling. It condemned the Magdalen women, one of the most oppressed and exploited groups in Ireland, when it should have championed their cause. The Church had even secured their exemption from the protection of the 1895 Factory and Workshop Act. To support these women, moral outcasts, was just not possible in Ireland at this time.[42]

Throughout November the ITGWU held demonstrations demanding the release of the Lockout prisoners. On 30 November thousands of men and women assembled at Liberty Hall and marched to Corydon Park where they watched 250 Citizen Army men being drilled by Captain Jack White. They marched back to Liberty Hall where speakers addressed them. This, Connolly told the crowd to great laughter was 'what a strike looked like when it was fizzling out'. He reiterated the union's stand on the Mary Ellen Murphy case and ended by making clear their willingness to negotiate. 'They were not', he said, 'expecting the social revolution before Christmas, nor did they intend to put Jim Larkin in the Vice regal Lodge before New Year's Day, but they were now as always ready to accept any reasonable proposal to bring about a settlement'.[43] Among the other speakers was the American IWW leader, Big Bill Haywood, who later remembered reviewing the Citizen Army at Corydon Park and the subsequent meeting at Liberty Hall where he led the booing of the police. Inside Liberty Hall, he was struck by a big sign with the letters IWW on it, only to learn that this was for the 'Irish Women Workers'. Haywood spoke in support of the Dublin workers in Belfast, London, Liverpool and elsewhere, and remembered how, on the train travelling between meetings, Larkin read Rabelais.[44]

The Importation of Scabs

Towards the end of September, Connolly had expressed concern about rumours that the Shipping Federation was preparing to import scabs into Dublin. 'Moderate as I am', he proclaimed, on the day that a ship carrying scabs puts into the Liffey, 'the streets of Dublin will run with the blood of the working classes ....
On that day it will be war and war to the knife'.[45] The threat did not materialise on this occasion. Later when Larkin was imprisoned, it became a reality. On 29 October some fifty scabs arrived from Manchester to work in the timber yards.

With strong police protection ('eight or nine mounted policeman, and as many more constables on cars or on foot'), they began making deliveries.[46] Many of them were armed with pistols. On 6 November, another 160 scabs arrived on board the Shipping Federation's steamer, *Ella*, from Liverpool with the promise of more to follow. The next day, Connolly had the city placarded with a rallying call to the union membership.

Importation v. Deportation
It is a crime to deport Dublin children in order to feed, clothe and house them better than ever they were before.
All the newspapers are against it.
It is not a crime to import English scabs to take the bread out of the mouths of Dublin men, women and children, and to reduce them to slavery.
The newspaper are overjoyed at this.
Fellow-workers All this collection of hypocrites and sweaters who paraded our docks and railway stations a few days ago and prostituted the name of religion to suit the base ends of those who for generations have grown fat by grinding the faces of the poor are silent as the grave in the face of importation of English scabs. They poured insults, lies and calumny upon the English Labour men and women who offered our children the shelter and comfort of their homes on the day of our trial, but they allow English blacklegs to enter Dublin without a word of protest. Will you allow this?
You must rally and fight as you never fought before, beginning Monday 10 November. All individual picketing is abolished and all persons or strike or locked out must attend a mass picket outside the doors or gates of their former employment at the usual hours of labour, commencing at the hour of opening in the morning
…
Fellow-workers, the employers are determined to starve you into submission, and, if you resist, to club you, jail you and kill you. We defy them.
If they think they can carry on their industries without you we will, in the words of the Ulstermen, take steps to prevent it.
It is your duty to find the ways and means. Be men now, or be for ever slaves.
James Connolly

This certainly recognised the gravity of the situation. With the importation of scabs, the employers had seized the initiative.

Being on strike or locked out involved great hardship, but while the job was closed down the workers knew that their employers were also being hurt. The battle involved a trial of strength where the workers could be confident that if they could hold out long enough, the hurt they were inflicting would in the end bring the employers to terms. Once the employers were able to begin moving goods and replacing large numbers of their workers with scabs then the nature of the conflict had changed. The situation of the employers had improved with the pain they were suffering starting to lessen, while the position of the workers had deteriorated with the inevitable decline in morale as their jobs disappeared.

Once large numbers of scabs were brought in the battle of attrition became increasingly one-sided with defeat becoming a serious prospect. Connolly's immediate response to this situation was, as we have seen to call for mass picketing. This was not to work.

Dublin was filled with police and troops. The police had already demonstrated that they were prepared to baton the workers off the streets and pursue them into their homes if necessary. Two workers had already been beaten to death and hundreds more injured. And while the police had acted with impunity, hundreds of workers had been imprisoned, overwhelmingly on the evidence of these same policemen. Moreover, if the police were not capable of protecting the scabs, then troops were readily available to do the job. Connolly's call for mass pickets went unheeded. Dublin was, as the *Daily Herald* put it, under 'the Iron Heel' with three companies of troops called out to protect just the scabs at Jacobs. The authorities were engaged in 'a deadly attack on picketing' and were attempting 'to terrorise the workers'. 'For all practical purposes', the paper editorialised, 'martial law has been proclaimed in Dublin in the desire to bend and break Trade Unionism'.[47] In these circumstances the workers had not the confidence to take on police and troops in pitched battles outside the factory or yard gates. The problem they faced was demonstrated by a report that appeared in the *Freeman's Journal* on 8 November regarding an incident on Wood Quay. A lorry carrying wooden frames was surrounded by a crowd of workers who were intent on upsetting the load. It was guarded by a number of scabs who, when the crowd got close, produced revolvers. One of them fired a warning shot into the air and the crowd were driven back. On a number of occasions, the courts had already made quite clear that they condoned the use of firearms by scabs. In such circumstances, all that was possible was a guerrilla war against the scabs, a war that had its successes, but could not turn the tide. On another occasion, the paper reported how a scab cart carrying sugar, flour, hams and other provisions was ambushed on City Quay. The pickets unyoked the horse, scattered the goods over the road, tipped the cart into the Liffey and dispersed. They were replaced by a large crowd of women and children who looted what remained of the load. The driver, in the paper's rather plaintive words, 'was left ultimately with nothing but his horse'.[48] This was not enough to turn the tide.

The ITGWU responded to the failure of mass picketing in a number of ways. On 13 November, Connolly had announced the formation of the Citizen Army, a disciplined force of union members, armed with wooden staves, who would protect the pickets from police attack. More controversial was the decision to close the port of Dublin by calling out on strike those dockers whose employers had not joined the lockout. This decision, taken without a vote of the men involved, was bitterly resented by many dockers who called for Connolly's removal. Larkin stood by his lieutenant and the men came out on strike. Decisive, however, was Larkin's decision to carry the fight to Britain. While acknowledg-

ing the part that financial assistance from the British labour movement had
played in sustaining the Dublin workers, Larkin had always believed that solidarity action would settle the dispute. With the successful importation of scabs,
the ITGWU had to secure the blacking of Dublin traffic or face the prospect of
defeat. The balance of forces in Dublin could only be tipped in the ITGWU's
favour if British workers actively enlisted on their side. Solidarity action was an
urgent necessity and no sooner was Larkin released from prison than he set out
to carry his 'fiery cross' through England, Scotland and Wales. The success the
movement had in securing his release gave him every confidence that the employers latest move could be trumped.

The Irish Volunteers

Before proceeding to a discussion of the solidarity movement in Britain, let us
first look at the attitude of the republican movement in Dublin towards the
lockout. According to Desmond Greaves, by this stage of the dispute, 'the republicans, the Irish-Irelanders and the Liberal intelligentsia' had all rallied to the
ITGWU. Certainly many had, but that is not the whole story by any means, and
what Greaves leaves out of his account is, in many ways, more significant than
what he includes. The fact is that while many individual republicans sympa-
thised with the union, the largest and most important republican organisation,
the Irish Republican Brotherhood, refused to take sides. Tom Clarke's biographer makes the point that he was 'a staunch supporter of trade unionism' and
was 'unreservedly sympathetic to the working class'. Nevertheless, for Clarke,
'labour and its mighty struggle in the 1913 lock-out was but a sectional fight
when considered a relation to the whole movement for national freedom'.[49] This
attitude was inevitably to bring the republicans into the conflict with the Larkinites for whom the labour struggle and the national struggle were inseparable.

At the start of the Great Lockout, Sean O'Casey was a staunch Irish-Irelander,
an active member of the IRB and a member of the ITGWU. He had long argued within the union that the workers had no need of socialist politics, but
should rally to the republican movement for their salvation. With the start of
the Lockout and the brutal police attacks on the workers, O'Casey urged that
the IRB should declare itself for the union, should side, as he saw it, in the manner of Wolfe Tone and John Mitchel, with 'the men of no property'. He was
told instead that the IRB could not get involved in a sectional dispute, but that
individual members could support the locked out workers if they wished. He
was to later put this stance down to the fact that the IRB 'appealed only to clerks
and artisans – the great body of workers were set aside'. There was, he recalled
hardly 'a man of them knew how to use a hack or shovel'.[50] For the time being,
however, he accepted the decision and continued to be active in both the IRB
and the ITGWU where he was joint secretary of the Relief Fund Committee.
He was involved in the establishment of the Citizen Army and was all the more
outraged when, towards the end of November, the IRB was instrumental in es-

tablishing the Irish Volunteers. The decision to launch the Volunteers was taken in response to the formation of the Ulster Volunteer Force by the Unionists. For O'Casey, however, it 'was one of the most effective blows which the Irish Citizen Army received'.[51] Even worse was the fact that while a number of Home Rule organisations were invited to participate in the founding of the Volunteers, the ITGWU was not. As far as O'Casey was concerned, having refused to ally itself with the locked out workers, the IRB now proceeded to ally itself with the representatives and supporters of the employers. The most prominent members of the Volunteer Executive were 'men who had done all they could to snatch from the workers the right to join the Trades Union of their choice'. There were men involved in establishing the Volunteers who 'had locked out their employees because they had ventured to assert the first principles of Trades Unionism'.[52]

Why was the ITGWU not invited to participate in the founding of the Irish Volunteers, O'Casey asked?

> Will the officials of the Volunteers explain why, that while every national body society and club, UII, BOE, GAA, Sinn Féin, received invitations to attend the initial meeting, held to start the movement, the Transport Union, the largest union of unskilled workers in Ireland was ignored? That in a celebrated article, entitled 'The Coming Revolution', contributed to *An Claidheamh*, before the founding of the Volunteers, P.H. Pearse expressed the wish to see every member of Sinn Féin, BOE, UIL, and the Transport Union armed; that subsequently, dealing with the Volunteers in *Irish Freedom*, he mentions all these organizations but omits the Transport Union ... why is it that in the official organ reference was made in the speeches reported or articles contributed to every organization in Irish National life save and except the Labour movement?[53]

The answer is clear. To have invited the participation of the ITGWU would have meant that the more respectable participants would have refused to be involved. As far as the IRB leadership was concerned, Larkin was not acceptable on the platform because his very presence would have disrupted the alliance they were trying to construct. Despite the real sympathy some of the IRB leadership had with the workers (Bulmer Hobson, the architect of the Volunteer initiative, was deeply critical of police conduct, for example), and the open republican commitment of the ITGWU, the union was an embarrassment. In the conditions of class war that prevailed in Dublin in November 1913 the IRB had to in effect choose between the ITGWU and the Home Rulers, and they chose the latter.

This did not go unchallenged. The Irish Volunteers were launched at a rally at the Rotunda Rink in Dublin on 25 November. The hall was packed and overflow meetings were held outside. However, when Laurence Kettle, the joint secretary of the Volunteer provisional committee, rose to speak, an organised attempt was made to disrupt the proceedings. Kettle was well-known for his own anti-trade union views, and, at that very time, his father, one of Parnell's old lieutenants, had locked out union members employed on his farm, imported blacklegs and actually boasted of it in the press. A large contingent of ITGWU men had infiltrated the hall and drowned out his voice with heckling and cat-calls. Scuffles broke out between the hecklers and stewards. At the same time, another body of union men tried to invade the hall but were kept out by stewards armed with hurley bats. The disturbance was successfully contained, and at the end of the meeting some 3,500 men were enrolled in the Irish Volunteers. Among them were many workers who might otherwise have joined the Citizen Army. Later in his history of the Citizen Army, O'Casey explained this anomaly as deriving from 'the undeveloped comprehension by the workers of the deeper meaning of the Labour movement' so that 'the call of the National Tribe appealed to them more strongly than the call of the Tribe of Labour'. Neither 'the fierce teachings of Jim Larkin' or 'the quiet but equally effective reasoning of Jim Connolly' could withstand the call of the Nation.[54]

O'Casey described his own break with the IRB in a letter he wrote to Horace Reynolds twenty-five years later. At a general meeting of the IRB in Dublin he criticised the organisation's stand and was howled down. In the heat of the moment, Bulmer Hobson drew a revolver and threatened the dissidents. After this experience, O'Casey and some others withdrew from the IRB and threw themselves into the labour movement. This, as far as he was concerned, did not involve any abandonment of republicanism. Indeed, what he now argued was that the interests of the Irish working class had to be the touchstone of Irish republicanism and he rejected those like the IRB who would not accept this. The ITGWU remained a republican organisation, while the IRB had compromised itself by its embrace of the Home Rulers.[55] This was to be the source of a continuing conflict into 1914.

Notes

1   Emmet Larkin, for example, refers to Dora Montefiore as a 'well-known social worker': Emmet Larkin, *James Larkin*, London 1968, p. 124.

2   For Montefiore see Karen Hunt, 'Journeying Through Suffrage: The Politics of Dora Montefiore', in Claire Eustance, Joan Ryan and Laura Ugolini, eds, *A Suffrage Reader*, London 2000 and 'Dora Montefiore: A Different Communist' in John McIlroy, Kevin Morgan and Alan Campbell, eds, *Party People, Communist Lives*, London 2001. Karen Hunt's biography of Dora Montefiore is eagerly awaited. See also Montefiore's autobiography, *From a Victorian To a Modern*, London 1927.

3   C. Desmond Greaves, *The Life and Times of James Connolly*, London 1961, p. 319. It is a mystery as to why the extremely knowledgeable Greaves chose to be so misleading here. The most likely explanation is that it is part of his habit of doing down Larkin and elevating Connolly: Larkin was enthusiastic about the children's holiday scheme, Connolly was sceptical.

4   Elizabeth Gurley Flynn, *The Rebel Girl*, New York 1979, p. 138. Connolly had

stayed with the Flynns' during his time in the United States and members of the family had been involved in the Irish Socialist Federation with him in New York.

5   Helen C. Camp, *Iron In Her Soul: Elizabeth Gurley Flynn and the American Left*, Pullman 1995, p. 32.

6   Philip S. Foner, *History of the Labor Movement in the United States: The Industrial Workers of the World 1905-1917*, New York 1965, pp. 326-327.

7   Melvyn Dubofsky, *We Shall Be All: A History of the Industrial Workers of the World*, Urbana 2000, pp. 146-147.

8   *Daily Herald*, 16 October 1913.

9   Montefiore, op cit, pp. 157, 159.

10 Thomas J. Morrissey, *William J. Walsh Archbishop of Dublin 1841-1892*, Dublin 2000, p. 249.

11 Montefiore, op cit, pp. 165-167, 170-171.

12 Quite astonishingly even today Thomas Morrissey's biography of Walsh continues to give credibility to these charges. See Morrissey, op cit, p. 251.

13 *The Times* 24 October 1913.

14 Arnold Wright, *Disturbed Dublin*, London 1914, p. 3.

15 *The Toiler* 1 November 1913.

16 Leon O Broin, *The Chief Secretary*, London 1969, p. 77.

17 Emmet Larkin, *James Larkin*, London 1968, p. 125.

18 *Irish Worker*, 1 November 1913.

19 According to Roy Foster, Yeats was at this time urging the Abbey Theatre 'to put on a polemical play about drunken policemen "while the strike is on"': R.F. Foster, *W.B. Yeats: A Life* 1, Oxford 1998, p. 501.

20 C. Desmond Greaves, *The Irish Transport and General Workers Union: The Formative Years*, Dublin 1982, pp. 107-108.

21 *Irish Worker* 1 November 1913.

22 *Forward* 1 November 1913. See also Morrissey, op cit, p. 255 where he writes of Connolly's 'striking tribute' to the Archbishop.

23 *Daily Herald*, 29 October 1913. The paper reported Walsh's speech under the headline, 'The Cat Out of The Bag'. On a number of other occasions the paper editorialised against the conduct of the Dublin clergy: 'Theologians and Slum Sanctity' (23 October 1913) and 'Priests and Proletariat' (24 October 1913). These scorching attacks were written by the paper's deputy editor, W.P. Ryan, himself an Irish Catholic and a longstanding opponent of Irish clericalism. The Dublin priests, he argued, 'do practically no slum work' and, buy and large, 'accept the present order, with its extremes of vulgar riches, often ill-got riches and sheer degrading poverty'. Many priests were 'the friends and upholders of the master class', some of them were men of wealth, even shareholders 'in Murphy's tramway company'. He observed that while the clergy condemned the children's holiday scheme, 'there is never any outcry against the sending of youths and girls from the west and northwest for months of the year to harvest-fields, etc., of Scotland and Britain'.

24 Morrissey, op cit, p. 264.

25 On 24 January 19114 the *Irish Worker* responded to Walsh's letter: 'There was a time when the Archbishop of Dublin was reputed to be a friend of the people who, through struggling for justice, became victims of the self-same system of law-and-

order. His congratulations to Lorcan Sherlock indicate that he is now opposed to the victims of law-and-order in the struggle for justice'. The article nevertheless concluded 'by expressing a hope that the old spirit of mutual help and goodwill which bound priests and people of Ireland together like bands of steel will again be revived and the spectacle of ministers of the Gospel of the poor Man of Nazareth standing by the oppressors of the poor will disappear from the fair face of Innis-fail'.

26   For an account of this episode see Joan Connolly Ullman, *The Tragic Week*, Cambridge MA 1968.

27   Camp, op cit, p. 35.

28   *Daily Herald*, 28 October 1913.

29   C. J. Wrigley, *David Lloyd George and the British Labour Movement*, Brighton 1976, p. 46.

30   Padraig Yeates, *Lockout: Dublin 1913*, Dublin 2000, p. 388.

31   *Freeman's Journal* 3 November 1913

32   Ibid; Shaw's Albert Hall militancy is completely missing from Michael Holroyd's multi-volume biography, in particular volume 2, *Bernard Shaw: The Pursuit of Power 1898-1918*, London 1989, and perhaps more surprisingly from Gareth Griffith, *Socialism and Superior Brains: The Political Thought of Bernard Shaw*, London 1993.

33   Barbara Winslow, *Sylvia Pankhurst: Sexual Politics and Political Activism*, London 1996, p. 64. See also Mary Davis, *Sylvia Pankhurst: A Life in Radical Politics*, London 1999.

34   Donal Nevin, ed. *James Larkin: Lion of the Fold*, Dublin 1998, pp. 216-222.

35   Winslow, op cit, pp. 64-67. On the Pankhursts more generally see Martin Pugh, *The Pankhursts*, London 2001.

36   *Daily Herald*, 5, 7 November 1913.

37   Larkin, op cit, p. 127.

38   O Broin, op cit, pp. 78-79.

39   *Freeman's Journal* 14 November 1913

40   *Freeman's Journal* 21 November 1913

41   *Freeman's Journal* 1 December 1913. See also Peter Murray, 'A Militant Among the Magdalens? Mary Ellen Murphy's Incarceration in High Park Convent During The 1913 Lockout', *Saothar* 20, 1995.

42   In her fine study of the Magdalen Asylums, *Do Penance or Perish*, Piltdown 2001, Frances Finnegan makes the point that these institutions survived into the 1970s. They were finally closed down not because of protests from the labour movement or the women's movement but because the increasing ownership of domestic washing machines made their laundries unprofitable.

43   *Freeman's Journal* 26 September 1913

44   William D. Haywood, *Bill Haywood's Book*, New York 1929, pp. 273-274.

45   *Freeman's Journal* 26 September 1913.

46   *Freeman's Journal* 31 October 1913.

47   *Daily Herald*, 12, 14 November 1913.

48   *Freeman's Journal* 23 November 1913

49   Louis N. Le Roux, *Tom Clarke and the Irish Freedom Movement*, Dublin 1936, pp.

84, 122-123.

50 David Krause, *The Letters of Sean O'Casey* 1, London 1975, p697.

51 P. O. Cathasaigh, *The Story of the Irish Citizen Army*, Dublin 1919, p. 9.

52 Ibid, p. 10.

53 *Irish Worker* 7 March 1914

54 O Cathasaigh, op cit, p. 10. For the founding meeting of the Irish Volunteers see F. X. Martin, ed, *The Irish Volunteers*, Dublin 1963, p. 105-110.

55 Krause 1, op cit, p. 697.

Chapter V
The Lockout: Solidarity, Betrayal and Defeat

The movement of solidarity with the Dublin workers that was built in Britain was one of the most remarkable in British labour history. Providing the backbone for this movement was the *Daily Herald* newspaper. This was hardly surprising considering its origins. As George Lansbury later recalled:

> Early in 1911 there was a strike and lock-out of printers. In London they were demanding a 50 hour week to lead on to 48. The men were very determined .... As usual during strikes, the Press grossly misinformed the public as to what the struggle was about, in order to controvert the lies which were poured out each day, the strike committee decided to bring out the *Daily Herald*.

The first issue appeared on 25 January 1911. In the course of the dispute it developed into a labour newspaper but once victory had been achieved it lost momentum and ceased publication at the end of April. Soon after a committee was established to resurrect it as a radical labour paper with Lansbury playing a key role. As he observes:

> It was in the natural order of things that the *Daily Herald*, being the successor of a strike sheet, always found itself supporting workers who were out on strike, no matter what section they may have belonged to. Writing a week after its first issue, Ben Tillett said: 'The Daily Herald is the expression of the entirely revolutionary phase of British Labour'. From this time up till the war broke out, the *Daily Herald* was known as the rebel paper and its supporters as the rebels.

'The policy of the paper', Lansbury wrote, 'was not merely unofficial, it was assuredly anti-official'.[1]

The *Daily Herald* showed what it was made of in its coverage of the sinking of the *Titanic* on 15 April 1912, the same day that the paper was re-launched.

While other newspapers lamented the loss of life, the *Herald* analysed the figures, showing that working-class passengers in steerage had been left to drown. Out of 255 steerage class women and children, 134 drowned, while out of 266 first and second class women and children, only twenty drowned. The headlines said it all: 'Women and Children Last', 'Profits First – Passengers Afterwards' and 'Thirty Per Cent for Shareholders and 53 Steerage Children Drowned'.[2] This outrage at the inequalities and injustices of class society informed every page of the paper, but just as important was its celebration of resistance. On 4 October 1913 in an editorial, 'Hail To The Rebels' the paper made clear where it stood:

> The capitalist critics and alarmists want to restrict or silence or delude the rebel elements. Strikes to them spell disease and danger. We on the contrary want to enlarge the infected areas and intensify disaffection here, there and everywhere. If all industrial Britain and Ireland were to seethe with revolt next week, and decide absolutely to hold up the whole business of the three kingdoms we would rejoice exceedingly .... The hope of Britain lies in revolt, more revolt, universal revolt.

Under the editorship of the syndicalist, Charles Lapworth, the paper routinely supported and encouraged strikes and attacked those trade union and Labour Party leaders who opposed them. Philip Snowden, a Labour leader who would be perfectly at home with New Labour today, came in for particularly, well-deserved, abuse, as a man whose ideas 'we have to fight to the death'.[3] The paper gave its support to workers in disputes both large and small with special mention here of the Tonbridge cricket-ball makers who went on strike to secure their first pay rise in seventeen years. Mention must also be made of the *Herald*'s Australian cartoonist, Will Dyson, whose artwork filled the front page every day. His savaging of the ruling class ('the Fat') and its accomplices was tremendously popular throughout the labour movement and his cartoons were sold as postcards ('Dysonian Fat – frighteners') and projected at meetings and rallies.[4] With a circulation of between 50,000 and 100,000 copies a day, the *Daily Herald* was read by and circulated among a significant proportion of the most advanced section of the British working class.

From the very beginning of the Lockout, the paper, as we have seen, gave enthusiastic support to the ITGWU, supporting solidarity action, criticising those union and Labour Party leaders unsympathetic to Larkin, and calling for a general strike in support of the Dublin workers. The paper sponsored meetings in support of the ITGWU throughout the country and had played a crucial role in organising the children's holiday scheme. The key figure in orchestrating this solidarity was W.P. Ryan, the Irish socialist, who was the paper's deputy editor and one of its main leader writers. The efforts of the paper were supported by those of the Herald Leagues that had been established during the winter of 1912-13, primarily to help keep the paper afloat, but that became central to rank and file activity. Lansbury described the character of the Herald Leagues:

In our ranks are to be found Socialists and Anarchists, Syndicalists and Suffragists, Trade Unionists and others. We have been united by an idea and not by a programme, that idea being that our first step towards revolution – nay, even reform – is the awakening of the people. In this we have been most successful, wherever there has been a strike or a lock-out, a Labour fight or a Suffrage fight, the Daily Herald Leaguers have rushed into the turmoil.[5]

They were given a great boost in the campaign to support the Dublin workers, raising funds, organising Larkin's 'fiery cross' crusade, calling for solidarity action. Such was the paper's impact that a Herald League was even formed in Dublin by Bob Wigzell, a railwayman. At the peak of its activity it had over 400 members including Delia Larkin and Francis Sheehy-Skeffington, and played a vital role in sustaining the workers' resistance.

While the unofficial movement rallied behind the Dublin workers, what of the official movement? These can be no doubt that the locked out workers were sustained in their struggle by the financial assistance provided by the British trade union movement. This was of considerable moral as well as material comfort. The British food ship, the *Hare*, which arrived on 27 September, not only carried a £5,000 cargo of food, but was also a potent symbol of international solidarity. The Dublin workers did not stand alone. Other ships were to follow. The British relief effort, organised under the auspices of the Trades Union Congress, provided over £13,000 in food shipments in October, over £16,000 in November, and nearly £21,000 in December. Even in January 1914, with relations between the ITGWU and the British TUC at their lowest ebb, over £11,000 in food was shipped to Dublin. The food relief was accompanied by substantial financial assistance, paid over to the Dublin Trades Council and other bodies. The Miners' Federation gave £14,000 to assist the locked out workers, with many local associations giving more. The Amalgamated Society of Engineers (ASE) gave newly £4,000, Sexton's NUDL £500 and the National Union of Teachers (NUT) £1,000. The Cooperative movement made substantial donations as did many trade councils, union branches and political organisations. Money was collected at meetings and rallies, door-to-door and in street collections. The socialist press, in particular the *Daily Herald*, raised substantial sums.[6] Many individuals and groups sent donations ranging from the stokers on HMS *Duke of Edinburgh* who raised 10s, to the socialist and poet, Rupert Brooke, who sent 2 guineas.[7] According to one estimate the British labour movement raised around £150,000 for the relief of Dublin – in today's money some £10,000,000.[8]

The *Daily Herald* carried reports of rank-and-file fund-raising activities, usually under the auspices of the Herald Leagues. On Sunday 19 October 1913, for example, there was

a big demonstration to collect money for the Dublin strikers ... in Finsbury Park.

Ted Leggatt (London Carmen) sold by auction a number of flowers which had been given for the purpose, and also a walking stick and other articles, given by a lady. A diamond ring, a silver brooch, a keyless watch, a lady's handbag and several other objects were also given.

The day before

some North London members of the DAILY HERALD League went out with barrel organs to collect for the Dublin strike Fund. There was no trouble with the authorities until the YMCA, Tottenham Court Road was reached, when the collectors were moved on by the police. Outside the London Pavilion Music Hall they were all run in together with the barrel organ.

As the paper reported, the summonses served on the four men were among the items auctioned in Finsbury Park the next day, fetching '2s each'.[9] When George Lansbury spoke at a meeting at Bow Baths on the Monday, another auction was held, with a captured police truncheon featuring among its items. It sold for one guinea.[10] This effort was replicated throughout the country.

There is no doubt that the provision of this financial assistance was driven by the rank and file, by socialists and syndicalists, by the militants within the labour movement, with many union leaders recognising that to do anything less would provoke rebellion in their own ranks. Nevertheless, they also hoped to be able to use this assistance as leverage to secure a compromise settlement, that the Dublin workers' financial dependence would force them to accept terms negotiated by British officials. Larkin, of course, already had first-hand experience of this in Belfast in 1907. He was under no illusion that the British union leaders would have accepted a settlement that would have left the ITGWU seriously weakened and many of its members victimised. That he was able to resist such a settlement derived partly from the resolve of his members, but also from the fact that the Dublin employers did not want to merely inflict a defeat on the ITGWU, but to completely destroy it. Larkinism had to be rooted out. They wanted to roll back trade unionism in Dublin and were just not prepared to accept the sort of compromise settlement that the British union leaders were accustomed to concluding.

Given that this was the reality of the situation, financial assistance, no matter how generous, was never going to win the dispute. This had been clear from the outset, from the very moment the employers' document had made its appearance, but now that the employers had begun importing large numbers of scabs it had become a question of considerable urgency. To defeat the Dublin employers, the ITGWU needed solidarity action in Britain and while the *Daily Herald* called for a general strike, Larkin crossed to Britain to campaign for the blacking of Dublin traffic. His 'fiery cross' crusade through Britain was a remarkable attempt to raise up an irresistible rank-and-file demand for solidarity that would force the official union leadership into action. This was an absolutely realistic and balanced assessment of the situation. The only alternative to solidarity action was defeat.[11]

Fiery Cross Crusade

The first great meeting of Larkin's syndicalist crusade was held at the Free Trade Hall in Manchester on 16 November. The venue was filled, with thousands turned away. The meeting had originally been called to demand Larkin's release, but was instead turned into a demand for solidarity. Larkin proclaimed himself 'the official mouthpiece, the ambassador from the working classes of Ireland'. He described the social conditions in Dublin, condemned Home rule as inadequate ('when people say, "We want Home Rule because we want to be members of the Empire", I say, "Damn the Empire"') and demanded the release of all the lockout prisoners. While in prison he had been given first class treatment because he was in the limelight, the other working-class prisoners were given third class treatment, although he had a warder spit in his face. He denied that he was calling for a general strike and remarked sarcastically that he would never tell the 'wise men from the East of English Trade Unionism what to do'. It was for the rank and file to decide the course of action. He went on:

> You have sent money and moral assistance. You have got me out of jail. You can get those out of jail who are still in, and get the scabs out of Dublin, and you can get us what we are fighting for – the right to combine. You can do it, and men and women like you …. We want to carry out the fundamentals and ethics of Trade Unionism, so don't 'scab' us. Are you going to allow us in Dublin to be offered up as a sacrifice. If not send a message to your leaders and tell them that the employing class in Dublin will not get any help from this side of the water.

Money was not enough, they had to 'resolve to stand by the men and women of Dublin till death'.[12]

Ben Tillett spoke, calling on the workers to arm and challenging the Home Secretary, McKenna, to come out at the head of the police after which 'there would be no more McKenna'.[13] Connolly, who also spoke at the meeting was sufficiently impressed to write in the *Irish Worker* that it 'went far to wipe out the evil memories of the past', when the Manchester mob had celebrated the execution of the Manchester Martyrs in 1867.[14] This was to be the first blow in the decisive battle. The only way to win the struggle in Dublin was by securing solidarity action in Britain, by securing the blacking of Dublin traffic. If the employers could bring in scabs, many of them imported from Britain, the British workers had to treat everything they touched as 'tainted goods'. In this way, the importation of scabs would be defeated, rendered an expensive luxury, rather than a decisive blow. This was the case, 'the fundamentals and ethics of Trade Unionism', that Larkin, Connolly and their supporters argued. Trade unionists should not handle goods touched by imported scabs brought in not just to break a strike but to destroy a union. The message met with a tremendous response.

Larkin spoke a number of times at massive meetings in London, Bristol, Sheffield, Liverpool and Leeds, urging solidarity action and, on a number of occasions, attacking British trade union and Labour Party leaders, the likes of J.H. Thomas and Havelock Wilson, Ramsay Macdonald and Philip Snowden. According to R.M. Fox, his '"fiery cross" speeches ... stirred militancy to life in Britain'. He remembered feeling 'that here at last was a voice giving adequate expression to my feelings of revolt, and in all the workshops young men felt the same'. Dublin had become 'a beacon burning on the horizon and Larkin was the man with the torch spreading the flames'.[15] Jack Murphy, who was to become one of the leaders of the shop stewards' movement during the World War and of the Communist Party afterwards, heard Larkin speak in Sheffield and later recalled his impact:

> Six-foot Jim Larkin with his powerful, torrentially passionate eloquence swept the audience off its feet. He finished his speech with a rendering of William Morris's *The Day is Coming.*
> I had never heard an orator of this calibre before, nor seen an audience so roused to demonstrative enthusiasm .... Here was the fighting leader, bearing in his person all the marks of battle, who would storm hell itself.

This meeting was a decisive moment for Murphy because it led to his visiting Dublin where he met Connolly, whose arguments won him over to 'Syndicalist Socialism'. Larkin and Connolly, he later wrote, were 'the tornado and the lighthouse'.[16] Murphy's future wife, the suffragette, Molly Morris, who was also at the Sheffield meeting, remembered Larkin as 'a human tornado challenging civilisation itself to give all that it had got to give to aid them to win out against the tyrants of Dublin. I have never heard a man speak as this man spoke'. It was at this meeting that she decided the time had come to declare herself a socialist.[17]

The *Daily Herald* cheered Larkin's crusade on. As early as 10 November 1913 it reported that over 130 NUR branches had called for joint action with the transport workers and miners to aid the Dublin workers. This demand had been taken up by workers in many other industries. The paper quoted a member of the NUR's London District Council: 'I have never seen enthusiasm as there is among our men in the London branches. They are ready for anything in the way of sympathetic action'. The only obstacle was the union leadership, but he thought it likely that 'the whole of our forces' will be 'ranged behind the men of Dublin before many days are over'.[18] As the Herald editorialised:

> At this stage more than ever the rank and filers are the determining factors in the situation. They have brought about the release of Larkin and on them devolves the

work of following up the victory … The spirit of the rank and file has been stirred to an unprecedented degree. The evidence on that point is striking. Make it more so; make it overwhelming … there is absolutely no hope of bringing the powers that be to their senses, and of avoiding utter horror and chaos in Dublin, except through decisive action on this side of the Irish Sea.[19]

The response to the 'fiery cross' crusade included a second wave of unofficial strike action in support of the Dublin workers. In South Wales, two ASLEF members, Driver James and Driver Reynolds, were sacked for refusing to move tainted goods. Some 30,000 railwaymen were soon out on unofficial strike in their support and in support of a demand for the eight hour day. Other groups of workers showed sympathy. On one occasion, steelworkers stopped a train, forcing the driver and fireman to join the strike. The union leaders, in particular J.H. Thomas intervened to secure a return to work without the reinstatement of the two drivers. To force ASLEF to accept the settlement, Thomas threatened to instruct NUR members to do their work. As the NUR's semi-official history puts it, 'Mr J.H. Thomas went down and turned the tables on the malcontents'.[20] Another, more radical, history observes that there was 'for some time afterwards considerable anger in South Wales against Mr J.H. Thomas'.[21] As Larkin remarked at the time, the ITGWU 'could have settled the Dublin strike thirteen weeks ago if we had allowed the employers to victimise their men'.[22] The good work Thomas did at this time, suppressing rank-and-file unrest, began to convince the railway companies that it would be to their advantage to recognise someone like him rather than find themselves confronting the likes of Larkin. In March 1914 Thomas received his first offer of formal recognition from the railway companies.[23]

There was considerable support for the Dublin workers on the docks, with one official, Harry Orbell, finding it increasingly difficult to keep London dockers at work:

> In all my experience I have never known a time when there has been manifested a desire to help any union in dispute as there is among dockers both in London and the provincial ports towards their Dublin comrades. We have had to rearrange the whole of our paid officials in London, placing them in certain centres with the express purpose of preventing any disorganised move …. It has been with the greatest trouble – and some of us have received rather strong words – that we have so far been able to hold the men in check …. Should it come to a stoppage I think it will be of such a magnitude as has never been equalled in any previous dispute.

On Merseyside, where Peter Larkin was active, officials had difficulty keeping their members at work.[24]

There was considerable sympathy with the Dublin workers and, together with the unrest produced by domestic grievances, this posed a challenge to the trade union leaders. The socialists and syndicalists, the 'malcontents', had to be constrained and outmanoeuvred. To this end, on 18 November the Parliamentary Committee of the TUC took the unprecedented step of calling a special conference of the TUC to consider the Dublin situation. The news was announced the next day to the audience at another great Herald League rally held at the Albert Hall in London. The news that the TUC had reached a decision was greeted with derision, that the decision was to call a special conference with cheers and that it was to be held in three weeks with 'fierce groans and hisses'. The chairman, T.E. Naylor said, to loud cheers, that 'if the Trade Union leaders were in earnest', the conference 'should have been called in three days'. Larkin, Ben Tillett, Big Bill Haywood, Will Dyson and others all spoke at the rally. Dyson was enthusiastically cheered when he made the point that as far as the leaders of the Labour movement were concerned, the punishment 'for inciting rebellion was gaol' whereas the punishment 'for inciting submission was Parliament'.[25]

The pressure from the rank and file had been great enough to force the TUC to call a special conference (a remarkable achievement in itself), but now the promise of official action in the future became an argument against unofficial action now. To keep control of the situation, the union leaders promised official action without any intention of coming to the aid of Dublin. Larkin himself fell for this stratagem, trusting the promises of Ben Tillett and other left-wing union leaders, instead of campaigning for unofficial action. He told the readers of the *Irish Worker* that 'The fight is here in Britain at the present .... Remember the 9th of December is the fateful day'.[26] The great rank-and-file leader, instead of placing himself at the head of a movement of revolt, put his faith in the TUC. Instead of calling for unofficial action, he called on his supporters to put pressure on their leaders to support the Dublin workers on 9 December. This was a terrible mistake.

On 22 November, the *Daily Herald* published a manifesto drawn up by Larkin that appealed directly to the British rank and file to bring their recalcitrant leaders to heel. It is worth quoting at length:

Comrades in the British Labour Movement.
Giving every credit to your leaders of the best of intentions with reference to the accomplishment of our work in Dublin, I feel that something more might have been done .... Your leaders suggest, not in words, that you of the rank and file are not with us in the struggle in Dublin, that the magnificent spirit of human brotherhood that has manifested itself in all sections of the working class and of the intelligent middle class is of no moment, that you of the rank and file are apathetic and though you subscribe your shillings you are not willing and never intended to give us of yourselves, that you are prepared to back up your sympathy only in word and money value, but not in deeds. If that were correct one might feel dispirited.
If the voice of the leaders rings true, you are humbugging yourselves, you are

humbugging your leaders, and, what would be far worse, you are humbugging the women, the children, and the big-hearted heroes who are fighting this struggle in Dublin. I have suggested to those in command that you have only got to be asked the question, 'Are you workers, you of the common people, prepared to stand by your brothers in Dublin in the truest sense, that you do not intend to mislead us, that you are always with us, and that we are one and indivisible as a class?' I have told your leaders that they have but to put this question to you, and they will get an answer in no uncertain tone that this is not a mouth sympathy, that you mean as you always mean, you men of the rank and file, to do things. Not diplomacy, not expediency, is the watchword of the men and women who work …. I claim on your behalf that you meant, and still mean, to put your whole body and soul into this fight in Dublin, and if your leaders have not up to now realised the vital issue at stake you men of toil do understand, and understanding, are prepared to act.

He went on to warn that the union leaders were preparing a settlement of the Lockout over the heads of Dublin workers, a settlement inimical to trade union principles:

But you and I of the rank and file, we love trade unionism. We are not prepared to accept the employers' definition of what trade unionism means; we are not prepared to accept advice and instructions from the employing class as to what a trade union should do. We intend to carry out to its fullest and highest the spirit of trade unionism which is embodied in the well-worn phrase, 'An injury to one is an injury to all'. We say that your leaders have come far short of this gospel of human brotherhood. They seem to have no vision. They seem to speak and act as though trade unionism was meant to be used as a salve for the sore of poverty, ill-usage, long hours and low wages. We say trade unionism is a root remedy, and by industrial action we can accomplish great things.

We are not willing to say that trade unionism shall be used either by Industrial Commissioners, Conciliation Boards or by Cabinets to chloroform the workers, and to persuade them to remain as dumb-driven dogs. Some of the leaders have forgotten that they worked at the bench, in or out of the factory, on the docks, or in the stokehole. They have forgotten the footplate and the engine; they have forgotten the laborious work of the goods yard; they seem to think that round tables, conferences, nice language, beautiful phrases, that fall trippingly from the tongue, conciliation boards, and agreements are the be-all and end-all of life.

Man does not live by agreements. Man does not live by contracts drawn up by employers' hirelings. Man lives by bread. To get bread one must work, and if one works one is entitled to say under what conditions one will work, and when working what shall be the rate of pay. While the accursed wage system lasts, let us see to it that we shall get the highest wages we can force from the employers; let us see that we compel them to reorganise the best possible conditions; let us forget that we are sectionalised; let us forget our craft lines of demarcation; let us also forget sex distinctions in the workshop, and live according to the truest spirit within us …. Therefore, we ask you that from now until the meeting of December 9th be not weary in well-doing. Be earnest in the fight. We need not insult you by saying send us the wherewithal to exist in the meantime. We feel assured of that. Send resolutions, send instructions and demands to your leaders that they shall strike a true and honest note, that they shall lead from the front and not from the rear, that they shall give voice to the beliefs of the rank and file. Tell them that you are heartily in sympathy with the victims of capitalism, whether it be in Dublin, Johannesburg, New Zealand or any part of the globe; that what you can do you will do.

When you give instructions to those you have elected you mean that they must carry them out; that you, as organised workers, will no longer blackleg on your fellow workers, no matter what Conciliation Boards may say, no matter what contracts may bind you to. There is no clause in any contract, there is no rule laid down by any Conciliation Board that I know of, which compels a man to be a scab. A Trade Union, when it makes an agreement with an employer, makes agreements on the understanding that they are dealing with men who can carry out a bargain made. They do not arrange things for non-union men, but they arrange as union men to work under union conditions and to insist that to blackleg is against the very basic principles of Trade Unionism. Therefore, tell your leaders now and every day until December 9th, and raise your voice upon that date to tell them that they are not there as apologists for the shortcomings of the capitalist system, that they are not there to assist the employers in helping to defeat any such section of workers striving to live, nor to act as a break on the wheel of progress. Tell them that this bloody warfare in Dublin must come to an end, this sacrificing of men, women and children must cease, and if they are not prepared to bring it to an end, then you of the rank and file will see to it that 'finis' shall be written. I leave the cause of Dublin workers in your strong hands, knowing that your heart and brain will direct them to do the work that is required to lift us from the morass of poverty and degradation, in full confidence that you at long last are realising your powers and that you mean to exercise your powers, and as in the beginning, so we shall continue. Let us make 1913 the year in a new industrial epoch. The greater unionism gives us something to live for.

Yours Fraternally

Jim Larkin

This manifesto, one of the most remarkable documents in trade union history, in many ways, captures the essence of Larkinism: its powerful call for solidarity, for the refusal to handle 'tainted' goods, its indictment of the compromises and betrayals of the trade union leaders, its uncompromising anti-capitalism, its celebration of militancy, and its faith in the rank and file. The problem, however, was that while Larkin and his supporters were well aware of the limitations of the trade union leadership, their strategy consisted of trying to compel them to act against their nature by means of resolutions, instructions and demands. They had to be *made* to lead from the front. This was, of course, tantamount to asking a dog to talk or a cat to live under water. It was not going to happen. The only realistic hope of forcing the trade union leaders to black Dublin traffic would have been if, by 9 December, they were confronted by a powerful unofficial movement, outside of their control, acting independently, a movement spreading across the country, carried from city to city, from port to port. The union leaders would have been forced to take steps to put themselves at the head of such a movement, to attempt to bring it under control, and in such circumstances active support for Dublin, the blacking of Dublin traffic, would have been agreed for fear of something worse. The union leaders would have been carried along by the momentum of the movement, most reluctantly, some willingly, but the battle in Dublin would have been won.

Instead of working to create such a movement, Larkin was sidetracked into regarding the TUC special conference as decisive, into arguing for resolutions for future official action rather than for immediate unofficial action. This begs the question of whether or not a rank and file revolt in support of the Dublin workers was actually possible. The evidence suggests that feeling was strong enough and that when combined with domestic grievances and local unrest, such a movement could have been raised up on the docks and on the railways with the potential to spread throughout the country. The difficulty that union officials had keeping their members at work is a good indication of the potential. The problem was that the networks of syndicalists, socialists and militants within industry were not well-organised enough to overcome this opposition. Whether Larkin's intervention would have made enough of a difference we have no way of knowing. What is clear, however, is that only a rank-and-file revolt offered any hope of success. In the context of the Great Labour Unrest such a revolt was very much within the realm of possibility.[27]

Most criticism of Larkin's conduct of the Lockout identifies his attacks on British union leaders as his most serious error of judgement, needlessly alienating his friends and providing ammunition for his enemies.[28] Certainly, Larkin was free with his abuse, on one occasion describing Ramsay Macdonald and Philip Snowden as 'serpents', who should not be allowed 'to raise their foul heads and spit their poison any longer', and Havelock Wilson and Jimmy Thomas as men with 'neither a soul to be saved nor a body to be kicked'.[29] This was very much part of his repertoire. He was criticised for it at the time. Bob Williams, for example, one of the leaders of the National Transport Workers Federation, who had shared a platform with Larkin and was wholeheartedly committed to the cause of the Dublin workers, nevertheless condemned Larkin's attacks as a mistake. What is interesting though is that Williams thought Larkin's attacks mistaken because he was confident that the TUC special conference would take action to support the ITGWU on 9 December. This is an important point. When he criticised Larkin in the *Daily Citizen*, he went on to make clear that, in his opinion, financial support on its own had failed to win the dispute and that consequently '(s)omething much bigger and more far-reaching must now be undertaken'. He went on to warn, quite correctly as it turned out, that 'If the Dublin workers are allowed to have their spirits crushed in consequence of the importation of scab labour, then none is free from this constantly threatening menace to our industrial rights and privileges'.[30] Williams's expectations of the TUC special conference were seriously mistaken, indeed, as one of Larkin's advocates, he was actually refused credentials by means of procedural duplicity, something that suggests Larkin's understanding of the British trade union leadership was more acute than his own.

What of the men upon whom Larkin concentrated his fire? An overwhelming case can be made that Macdonald, Snowden, Wilson and Thomas were indeed four of the greatest traitors in the history of the British labour movement. Only Wilson had any credentials as a militant and 1913 was the year he handed them in to be replaced by those of a class collaborator, running the seamen's union in an unholy alliance with the shipping companies. The other three were, of course, all to defect to the Conservatives in 1931, making official something that had long been apparent, and becoming leading members of the National Government. When he spoke in Hull during his 'fiery cross' crusade, Larkin had warned against Thomas and other union leaders of his kind:

> These men who wore tall hats and frock coats in London and bowler hats when among the boys were getting too big. They should be wary of a man whom the capitalists patted on the back. They should also be suspicious of a man who dined and wined with those who caused the Dublin trouble.[31]

This was a warning that should have been heeded. Thomas was one of the best trade union leaders that the British capitalist class has ever had and there is plenty of competition.[32] Larkin's attacks on these men were not the problem, they were going to betray the Dublin workers whatever he said. On the contrary, the problem was the failure of rank-and-file revolt to force the hand of the TUC special conference on 9 December.

9 December 1913

The TUC special conference settled the fate of the Dublin workers. It met in the aftermath of an abortive peace conference between unions and employers that took place in Dublin from 4 to 7 December. British officials, including one of the leaders of the Labour Party, Arthur Henderson, met with the employers in private before bringing the two sides together. Writing in the *Irish Worker*, Larkin warned of a sell-out: 'well disposed gentlemen that you and I have a bitter experience of are prepared to settle the present difficulty by hook or crook – mostly crook'. If allowed to, they would abandon many of the locked workers in return for a paper settlement.[33] He was absolutely right. What the British officials were after was a withdrawal of the ban on the ITGWU in return for the abandonment of the sympathetic strike. The most that Connolly, who was in charge of negotiations for the ITGWU, would agree to was a two year moratorium on sympathetic action for those firms who were part of a conciliation scheme. While the employers would never have accepted this, talks actually broke down on the question of the reinstatement of the locked out men and women. The employers refused to give any guarantees and made clear that they would take back workers at their discretion, when and if they could. In these circumstances, the withdrawal of the ban on the ITGWU would have been any empty gesture, because its activists and militants would have been subject to wholesale victimisation.

It was with the break down of these talks that the TUC special conference met. Larkin and Connolly found themselves confronted not by a conference of rank-and-file delegates, but by a conference of full-time officials. As R.M. Fox remarked, while the conference was ostensibly 'to decide what was to be done about Dublin ... (in reality) it was to decide what was to be done about Larkin'.[34] The conference was packed against him: according to Bill Moran there was not one delegate who had been formally elected or mandated for the occasion, instead they were all either appointed by their executives or chosen from the delegation to the annual TUC.[35] Even worse, as Bob Williams of NTWF subsequently complained, even though critical of Larkin, he was kept out of the conference 'because his views were not satisfactory to the members of the Parliamentary Committee' of the TUC. The spurious grounds for his exclusion was that he was an official of a federation of unions and not of any particular union, and yet 'this happened at a Conference where Mr. W.C. Anderson, who joined in the scurrilous abuse of Larkin, boasted that he was not a Trade Union official, and was not in any way connected with a Trade Union'. One of the resolutions proposed was 'moved and seconded by two middle-class members of the Fabian Society, who could not claim the slightest association with a Trade Union'.[36] The game, the outcome of which was never seriously in doubt, was rigged anyway.

What did take Larkin by surprise, however, was the ownership of the hand that wielded the knife that stuck the fatal blow: Ben Tillett! He proposed a motion condemning Larkin's attacks on the leaders of the British trade union movement and opened the floodgates for a score of attacks on the ITGWU leader. Tillett, one of the most prominent 'left' trade union leaders, had appeared on the platform with Larkin on a number of occasions, had made the most incendiary speeches and, moreover, had freely abused the leadership of the Labour Party. As his biographer points out, however, 'he played a double game throughout'. Tillett talked militant right up until the moment action was required only to then reveal that he was following a different agenda altogether. His position as a left trade union leader was founded on a militant rhetoric that was all the more extreme the less practical consequences that followed. Once his rhetoric was put to the test, he was revealed as someone who put his relationship with his fellow trade union leaders before any commitment to the rank and file. What is interesting, of course, is that he did not just retire into the background once action was required, but stepped forward to assume the role of Judas without any apparent shame or embarrassment.[37] His resolution provoked uproar with Larkin defending himself in the most uncompromising fashion:

> Neither you nor these gentlemen on the platform can settle this Dublin dispute. I challenge you to try it. I know, however, that the rank and file of the British trade unionists will support the Dublin workers in their battle, and if we do not get that support we will do what we have done before – fight it out. This is a game of war; it is not a game of beggar-my-neighbour. I know the men we have to deal with. All they want to do is to delay the negotiations in order that they may weed the men out. The ban against the union has not been withdrawn. The employers of Dublin are neither truthful nor honest, and the only way to deal with them is to deal with them with a strong hand. We have always been able to do that.

He made absolutely clear that ITGWU members would never handle 'tainted' goods and that he expected the same from the British trade union movement. He went on:

> We say all your money is useful, but money never won a strike. Money can't win a strike. Discipline, solidarity, knowledge of the position and the strength to carry out your will – these are the things.
> They could win the Dublin strike tomorrow if they wanted it, and if they didn't mean it they should shut up or put up. If the Union men of this country wanted to win the strike all they had to say was that Dublin should be a self-contained town just now; that she would live upon herself, with the exception that food would be taken in to the men, women and children in the trenches. All the money and all the leaders would not beat the men they were fighting. He had said hard things, and they had said harder and more bitter things against him. He had done according to his lights. He did not get any thousand a year or any five hundred a year. He had worked in the limelight and the dark and had given service that he made no apology to any man there for. He was told coming there that they were going to pass a resolution condemning Larkin and telling him to get out of the road, and that they would settle the strike. You try that on, Larkin will not get out of the road. Larkin will go down fighting.[38]

Tillett's Judas' resolution was carried almost unanimously with only six delegates voting against it.

The more substantive resolution proposed by J.W. Kelly offered no further help to the ITGWU but instead authorised the reopening of negotiations with the Dublin employers. Instead of the blacking of Dublin traffic, the British officials were to return to Dublin and agree the terms of the ITGWU's surrender. An amendment was moved by Jack Jones of the Gasworkers proposing a levy in support of the ITGWU and that an ultimatum be presented to the employers threatening the refusal to handle tainted goods if a settlement on satisfactory terms were not concluded. This would have given the British negotiators some muscle and Larkin believed would have won the dispute. The amendment was defeated with 203,000 for and 2,280,000 against. It was voted down not just by the right wing of the trade union leadership, but by the left wing as well. Larkin had no doubt as to what the real agenda was. He told the *Daily Herald* that it was 'a gathering of paid officials who had come together to whitewash their black sheep'. One of the delegates had assured him that 'ninety-nine delegates out of every hundred had come to that Conference to settle Larkin'. 'They were out for blood'. Larkin joked, 'and if the courage of some of these self-appointed delegates had been equal to their hate, I would have been distributed in the form of souvenirs of meat, bone and muscle'.[39] The *Daily Herald* condemned the conference and, once awareness dawned of Tillett's role, carried letter after letter condemning his treachery. It was all too late however.

The movement for solidarity action was crushed and the Dublin workers were isolated. In Connolly's words:

> We asked … that the working class of Britain should help us to prevent the Dublin capitalists carrying on their business without us. We asked for the isolation of the capitalists of Dublin, and for answer the leaders of the British labour movement proceeded calmly to isolate the working class of Dublin …. And so we Irish workers must go down into Hell, bow our backs to the lash of the slave driver, let out hearts be seared by the iron of hatred, and instead of the sacramental wafer of brotherhood and common sacrifice, eat the dust of defeat and betrayal.[40]

Defeat

After the British TUC's betrayal defeat was inevitable although the ITGWU struggled on. On 10 December, Larkin spoke in Glasgow to an enthusiastic audience of over 4,000 people and continued with his 'fiery cross' crusade. Enthusiasm, however, was no substitute for organisation. Back in Dublin, on 14 December the union gave secret advice to its members to return to work if they could secure suitable terms from their employers. Some began to go back, but for most the lockout continued. British officials arrived once again to attempt a settlement, but talks broke down on the issue of reinstatement on 20 December. The union continued the struggle through the Christmas period and on 1 January 1914 issued a new Manifesto:

> The Dublin newspapers are excelling themselves in this festive season as liars of the first order, and if they are not accomplishing the purpose they aim at, they are, at least, adding considerably to the gaiety of nations. Every day the placards announce 'More men renewing work', 'Strikers rushing back', and so on, until one is inclined to wonder if there are really any men left out.
> The sole basis for all this romancing has been that a few small firms have agreed to resume work under Union conditions, and by agreement with the Union officials. But all this is carefully distorted by the capitalist Press, and the impression is sought to be conveyed that each body of men who have gone back have broken

away from the Union.

This was far from the case and the Manifesto insisted that even 'at this juncture' it was clear that 'a little sane Trades Union action in support of the Transport men ... would win a decisive victory'. Instead, British unions, and in particular Havelock Wilson's Seamen's and Firemen's Union, were scabbing on the Dublin workers. The Manifesto continued:

> the Seamen's and Firemen's Union has singled itself by its open and persistent violation of every code of honour among Trade Unions in the transport industry. Practically every boat in Dublin worked by scab Labour is manned by men of that Union .... The National Union of Dock Labourers, which pledged itself to support the Dublin fighters is cheerfully working every scab boat trading between Dublin and British ports .... Add to this that the National Union of Railwaymen, whose officials made such a show at the London Conference, had in their pocket at the time a resolution declaring their intention to re-open the port of Dublin as soon as the Conference was over. This they did by starting the London and North Western boat from Dublin on the very day following the Conference; proving that arrangements had already been made ... before the Conference met.

This 'wholesale scabbing' had dire consequences not just for the Dublin workers but for British workers as well. 'We in Dublin', the Manifesto continued,

> consider that the threatened general lock-out in the building trade in London is a direct result of the treacherous action of the Havelock Wilsons, Thomases and other Union officials, who have so loudly denounced the sympathetic strike and proclaimed the right of one Union to scab upon another.
> Cheered by the vindication of the authors of such sentiments by the London Conference, the employers are following up the retreat of Labour by the telling blow of a general lock-out in London. Thus the truth of the contention is enforced that every blow at Labour in Dublin allowed to pass unchallenged in Great Britain would soon be copied, and repeated with added force, in that country.

It was signed by both Larkin and Connolly.[41]

With the Dublin employers continuing to import scabs throughout December, the situation on the city's streets became increasingly dangerous and embittered. There was an almost daily catalogue of clashes between union members, scabs (many of them armed) and the police. On 11 December an armed scab fired at a hostile crowd but hit the Vice-Chairman of the Port and Docks Board, Mr Joseph Holloway. Connolly made the point that if a prominent businessman were shot 'by a member of the Transport Workers' Union, not only the man who fired it, but all the officials of the Union would have been arrested'.[42] The gunman was eventually found guilty of grievous bodily harm, but was set free. On 15 December another scab was actually fined two pounds for discharge his revolver in public without due cause (presumably there were no union members in range) and that same day, as a nice contrast, George Bergin, an ITGWU member, was jailed for a month for calling a working tramwayman a scab.[43] With the use of firearms condoned by the courts, tragedy was inevitable. On 18 December an armed scab shot a sixteen year old girl, Alice Brady, on picket duty; she died on 2 January 1914. Her funeral was to be 'the occasion of an impressive demonstration of sympathy with the relatives of the deceased on the part of the Irish Transport Workers' Union with the women's section of which she had been associated'.[44] Her killer was freed on bail and, even more incredibly, when brought to trial, a handpicked jury found he had no case to answer and he walked free.

The scabs did not have it all their own way. On 17 January the *Freeman's Journal* reported that the previous day some 600 union members had attacked scab vehicles in Lower Abbey Street. Some of the 'free labourers were roughly handled' and inevitably a revolver was fired 'in the melee' although no one was hit. The paper reported that after the battle one of the vehicles, together with its horse, had disappeared. On 18 January there were a number of serious clashes in different parts of the city. One incident involved two scabs, both armed with revolvers, who were overpowered and beaten – one of them, Thomas Harten, kicked to death.[45] One of the union's picket organisers, Thomas Daly, an unsung hero of the Lockout was to be arrested and charged with the murder on 26 January. He had possession of Harten's revolver. He was eventually found not guilty, and although he certainly knew those responsible, never informed on them. He was sentenced to two years for other lockout offences. Harten's death did not calm the situation. On 23 January, the *Freeman's Journal* reported 'a revolver duel' between scabs and pickets in Townsend Street the previous day, with the police arresting nineteen men, all union members of course, who were subsequently imprisoned. This violence was too late in the day, however; the product of bitterness and despair, rather than a means of achieving victory. By now the issue was no longer in doubt. The return to work had begun.

The Dublin labour movement suffered another blow in January in the city's municipal elections. The Dublin Labour Party contested thirteen seats (out of eighty) but won only two. In the contested wards the DLP polled 10,377 votes against its Home Rule opponents 13,777. Although the labour candidates were denounced as 'Larkinites' in the press, only two of them were, in fact, ITGWU members (Thomas Foran and P.T. Daly) with most of the others members of craft unions. This was certainly a setback and yet another serious blow to morale, but it was hardly decisive. The result was certainly not a measure of working-class support for the ITGWU or for Larkinism as less than half of working-class men actually had a vote in local elections.[46] It certainly did not affect the outcome of the Lockout. Larkin's opinion was very much the other way round, that it was the setbacks the ITGWU had suffered that produced the poor electoral showing. Indeed, he argued that if the elections had taken place in November the previous year then 'far from holding our own … we would have had the satisfaction of chronicling not less than eight victories'.[47] This would have been a great boost to morale, but in practical terms would hardly have dented Home Rule domination of the council.

At last the union recognised the inevitable. On 18 January the ITGWU finally gave instructions for the members to return on what conditions they could secure.[48] The return to work began immediately, but there were still serious clashes with scabs and police as the workers met with victimisation and the blacklist. By the middle of February there were still some 5,000 workers locked out and the last to accept defeat were the women of Jacob's biscuits who did not go back until mid-March. Hundreds of men and women fell victim to the blacklist, while those who got their jobs back returned on humiliating terms. Connolly described the situation at Jacobs in the *Irish Worker*:

> When the girls apply for re-employment this manager after brutally insulting them before the scabs whom he brings in in order that he may parade the applicants before them, compels them to submit to his examination of their clothes, their hats, skirts and blouses, to submit while he pinches their arms, and examines their physical condition and that all through his degrading examination he keeps up a running fire of insulting remarks of which the following are a fair example:- 'So you had to come back when you were starving' …

He reported that of the 672 union men at Jacobs, only a hundred had been taken back and that these had had their wages cut by between 2 and 4 shillings a week.[49]

What is the significance of the ITGWU's defeat? According to Greaves in his biography of Connolly, it was not a defeat at all. Rather it was 'a draw'. There were no sackings, he claimed, and the pledge to leave the union was 'reduced to a scrap of paper'.[50] When we turn to his later official history of the ITGWU he acknowledges the victimisation that took place, the bankruptcy of the union and its dramatic loss of membership, but argues that the dispute was not 'lost, won or drawn. It was all three'.[51] He is pretty well sure to be at least partly right. In fact the dispute ended in a crushing defeat and it is idle to pretend otherwise. The ITGWU, which had appeared to have Dublin in its grasp in the early summer of 1913, had been broken by the employers and the state. The union survived as an organisation, but the movement of working-class revolt had been defeated. The apparently irresistible tide of Larkinism had been turned back.

How did Larkin himself assess the situation? He denied that the employers had beaten the ITGWU. They had successfully withstood 'all the forces of reaction combined; priests, Press, publicans, police, plutocrats – all of whom are but sections of the capitalist forces, backed up by a Government which will go down in history as the disgrace of the century.' What had defeated them was not the employers, but the 'insidious conspiracy … of the alleged British labour Lead-

ers.' It was not 'Murphyism' that had defeated them, but 'the political expediency of the McDonald-Snowden type.' It was 'the foulness and treachery of our
own class gave us pause', but he promised 'we are getting our second breath, and
then we will make the pace a hot one'.[52] On a number of occasions, he acknowledged that the ITGWU had 'had to retreat to our base', but he still insisted that
the building of the one big union was the way forward, 'the only sound logical
method and the only way that makes for success.' This was a sound assessment
of the state of the union, but recovery, when it came, was to come without his
help and in the very different context of war and revolution.

What of the solidarity movement in Britain? In the aftermath of the special
TUC conference of 9 December 1913, Charles Lapworth was dismissed as editor of the *Daily Herald*. His attacks on the leadership of the Labour Party had
finally proved too much for the paper's directors, who wished to keep channels
to the likes of Macdonald and Snowden open. Lansbury replaced him as editor,
although for the time being W.P. Ryan was effectively in charge. The change
of editor did not compromise the paper's support for strikes. It continued its
support for the Dublin workers to the very end and subsequently campaigned
ferociously on behalf of the locked out London building workers. As Raymond
Postgate observed, the master builders fancied 'themselves already in the position of Murphy', and, encouraged by his victory in Dublin, sought 'to emulate
his union-smashing' in London.[53] While the *Daily Herald* was to oppose the
outbreak of war and later support the Russian Revolution, it became the paper
of the Labour left rather than of the rebel movement.

More generally, the defeat of the ITGWU in the Lockout was a crushing blow
to the Dublin labour movement although wartime conditions were to allow a
remarkable recovery from 1917 onwards. The Lockout was also a serious blow to
the 'syndicalist' left in Britain that had done its best to come to the assistance of
the Dublin workers, but had failed to overcome the union leadership's opposition to solidarity action. Once again the outbreak of war was to radically trans-
form conditions, with the Russian Revolution and the triumph of Bolshevism
providing a revolutionary alterative to the politics of syndicalism.

The Scab's Testimony

One interesting question is how much support Larkinism retained among the
Dublin working class in the face of defeat. This is, of course, difficult to estimate,
but we have available one witness, Patrick McIntyre, the editor of *The Toiler*,
a man who could certainly not be accused of any bias in Larkin's favour. *The
Toiler* was another Hibernian scab newspaper, aimed at a working-class readership, that first appeared on 13 September 1913. Its predecessor, *The Liberator*,
which we have already noticed, had folded at the end of November, leaving *The
Toiler* as the lone voice of the Dublin scab. The paper had savagely abused the
Larkinites ('the Kidnap Party') over the children's holiday scheme, enthusiastically praised Murphy for liberating the working class from tyranny, and most

famously attacked Larkin for being the son of James Carey, the informer who had betrayed the republican perpetrators of the Phoenix Park assassinations in 1882. Indeed, in the pages of *The Toiler*, the Larkinites became the 'Careyites'. The abuse continued week after week, a relentless torrent of lies and slander, to which Larkin was, on a number of occasions, provoked to respond.[54] *The Toiler* advocated the use of violence against the Larkinites. Prison was no deterrent for 'a Larkinite corner boy'; they only understood 'a good beating'. Indeed, the paper recommended even more extreme measures: ' the only effective remedy is the use of firearms. The sight of these little death messengers sends shivers into the cowardly souls of the guttersnipe Careyite corner boys'.[55] The courts, as we have seen, effectively endorsed this position.

As the defeated workers began returning to work, *The Toiler* carried a regular column denouncing Larkin's rank-and-file supporters by name, serving as a blacklist. A sample gives something of the flavour:

Big Mary, formerly of Tramway Terrace, is now living in more congenial surroundings in Fitzroy Lane. When the strike began she brought eggs to throw at the men who remained at their posts. Now she would be glad to have them to eat.

Little hunch back Ryan, the grocer's porter is very much down in spirits, owing to Jim's defeat. The lower Jim gets the bigger the hunch is getting.

Shaun Casey, (Sean O'Casey-Jn), head of Larkin's souper pipers' band, Seville Place. Well, Shaun, my Irish-speaking bowsie, you were afraid of the Toiler scout to bring the band to the runaway army's Swords march out. How much of the collection did you collar.

We hear that McEvenue of the Joinery Department of the Guinness Brewery is a red-hot Larkinite or Careyite .... Take a friend's tip McEvenue of the Joinery Department, keep your Careyite views to yourself, for the Brewery scout has you under observation.

We have a big corner boy named Brown – another Larkinite. This clown during the strike beat the decent men from working. Now my bowsey, the police are on your track, and keep quiet, I know you for a long time, you corner boy.

Doyle, Ballybough road .... This foul-mouthed Larkinite blackguard toils in the Ballybough manure works and is always talking of the fine rise in his wages Larkin got him .... Does the manager of the works know the way you are trying to corrupt the men .... Take warning if he finds you out he will kick you out.

Jimmy Finnegan, Clarence Street. This drunken little sot toils in Smith and Pearson's. Ossory road .... Well will wonders never cease [my] half starved Larkinite pup .... Bowsie take warning, keep yourself quiet.

Little Jimmy Byrne, the vulgar-spoken rag seller is blaming people in Winetavern Street for putting him in the Toiler .... If Jimmy kept his gob shut and not be praising Larkin he would not be in the Toiler today.

We have Tommy Keenan. This dying clown is another great Larkinite, and came out on strike in Perry's row, and was glad to crawl back. Now Tommy, you will let the decent men alone. Now keep quiet you mongrel.[56]

This, in itself, is a useful testimony to the extent of continued support for Larkin, evidence of how deeply rooted Larkinism was in the Dublin working class. More significant, though, is McIntyre's acknowledgement that, despite everything, including his own efforts, the workers remained loyal to Larkin. As late as October 1914 he complained 'of the chasms of hate, mistrust and ill-will that at the present moment exists between employer and worker in Dublin' and lamented the failure of the workers to free themselves from Larkin's influence. The workers had an attitude to Larkin that 'almost amounted to reverence' so that, as far as he was concerned, 'the outlook is not promising. Capital and labour in our city are at daggers drawn and there is no responsive cord between them'. The workers had still to free themselves from 'the incubus' of Larkinism.[57] This is a remarkable testimony from one of Larkin's sworn enemies.

The last issue of *The Toiler* appeared on 19 December 1914 and McIntyre pursued his journalistic career elsewhere. At the time of the Easter Rising, he was editing a newsheet, the *Eye-Opener*. He was one of the men arrested (the others were the socialist Francis Sheehy-Skellington and a Unionist journalist, Thomas Dickson) by British troops under the command of Captain Bowen Colthurst and summarily executed on his orders on 25 April 1916.[58]

Notes

1   George Lansbury, *The Miracle of Fleet Street*, pp. 34, 44, 48. The most recent history of the *Daily Herald*: Huw Richards, *The Bloody Circus: The Daily Herald and the Left*, London 1997, unfortunately only devotes fourteen pages to the years of the Great Labour Unrest.

2   Raymond Postgate, *The Life of George Lansbury*, London 1951, p. 144. For Lansbury see also John Shepherd, *George Lansbury: At The Heart Of Old Labour*, Oxford 2002.

3   *Daily Herald*, 23 September 1913.

4   For Will Dyson see Ross McMullin, *Will Dyson: Cartoonist, Etcher and Australia's Finest War Artist*, Sydney 1984.

5   Keith Harding, 'The Cooperative Commonwealth: Ireland, Larkin and the *Daily Herald*' in Stephen Yeo, ed, *New Views of Cooperation*, London 1988, pp. 91-92.

6   Padraig Yeates, *Lockout: Dublin 1913*, Dublin 2000, pp. 321-323.

7   Nigel Jones, *Rupert Brooke*, London 1999, p. 346. Although best remembered for his patriotism and untimely death during the Great War, Brooke was a socialist and member of the Fabian Society. He wrote to his mother on 7 January 1914 that 'I feel wild about Dublin. I always feel in strikes that "the men are always right .... Of course, the poor are always right against the rich .... But Dublin seems to be one of the clearest cases on record'.

8   Donal Nevin, ed, *James Larkin: Lion of the Fold*, Dublin 1998, p. 471.

9   *Daily Herald*, 20 October 1913.

10   *Daily Herald*, 21 October 1913.

11   There are remarkable similarities between the situation of the Dublin workers in 1913 and British coal miners in 1984-85.

12   *Freeman's Journal* 17 November 1913.

13   Jonathan Schneer, *Ben Tillett*, Beckenham 1982, pp. 168-169.

14   *Irish Worker* 22 November 1913.

15   R. M. Fox, *Smoky Crusade*, London 1938, pp. 175-176.

16   J.T. Murphy, *New Horizons*, London 1941, pp. 38-41. Murphy considered Con-
     nolly the greater man, 'a Communist before there was a Communist movement'.
     'The only other man who affected me in the same way was Lenin', he was to
     recall. For an interesting discussion of Murphy, one of the British working class
     movement's 'most prominent intellectuals of the twentieth century', see Ralph
     Darlington, *The Political Trajectory of J. T. Murphy*, Liverpool 1998, (p. 2).

17   Molly Murphy, *Molly Murphy: Suffragette and Socialist*, Salford 1998, p. 28.

18   *Daily Herald*, 10 November 1913.

19   *Daily Herald*, 15 November 1913.

20   G.W. Alcock, *Fifty years of Railway Trade Unionism*, London 1922, p. 475.

21   G.D.H. Cole and R. Page Arnot, *Trade Unionism on the Railways*, London 1917,
     p. 35.

22   Yeates, op cit, p. 464.

23   Ken Coates and Tony Topham, *The Making of the Labour Movement: The Forma-
     tion of the Transport and General Workers' Union 1870-1922*, Nottingham 1994, p.
     485.

24   Bob Holton, *British Syndicalism 1900-1914*, London 1976, p. 193.

25   *Daily Herald*, 20 November 1913.

26   *Irish Worker* 22 November 1913.

27   A useful comparison can be made with the unofficial action taken by British
     dockers in 1972. The imprisonment of five dockers led to a wave of strike ac-
     tion that forced the TUC to call a general strike. See Ralph Darlington and Dave
     Lyddon, *Glorious Summer: Class Struggle in Britain, 1972*, London 2001, pp. 141-
     177.

28   Yeates, op cit, pp. 434-435.

29   *Freeman's Journal* 1 December 1913.

30   *Freeman's Journal* 27 November 1913.

31   *Freeman's Journal* 1 December 1913.

32   For Thomas see Gregory Blaxland, *J.H. Thomas: A Life for Unity*, London 1964. It
     is surprising in these New Labour times that Thomas has not attracted a revision-
     ist biographer to argue the case for the man who kept the trains running during
     the War and prevented revolution afterwards (two of his boasts). In a recent ar-
     ticle, Martin Pugh has suggested the lines such a biography might take: he was 'a
     bridge linking the labour movement and the political establishment, a position
     that exposed him to accusations of treachery, but made him an asset to a party
     now aspiring to office': Martin Pugh, 'The Rise of Labour and the Political Cul-
     ture of Conservatism 1890-1945', *History*, 2002, p. 520. Thomas was, of course,
     to be sacked from the National Government for leaking budget secrets to one of
     his wealthy friends in 1935. Earlier in 1931 he had appealed to the NUR confer-
     ence for a special pension and been voted down by 75 votes to 5. There was some
     justice, but not enough.

33   *Irish Worker* 6 December 1913.

34   Fox, op cit, p. 172.

35	Bill Moran, '1913, Jim Larkin and the British Labour Movement', *Saother* 4, 1978, p. 44.

36	*Daily Herald*, 13 December 1913.

37	Schneer, op cit, pp. 168-171. According to Schneer, Tillett was only posing as a revolutionary in 1913, but with the outbreak of War in 1914 emerged into the open as 'an industrial conservative and political moderate.' Even while a Labour MP after the War, he privately approached the Conservative Party for money (pp. 197, 218-219). Tillett's own memoirs are silent on his betrayal of Larkin. See Ben Tillett, *Memories and Reflections*, London 1931.

38	*Freeman's Journal* 10 December 1913

39	*Daily Herald* 10 December 1913

40	*Forward* 9 February 1914

41	*Daily Herald* 1 January 1914. According to one history of the building trades unions, it was Murphy's defeat of the ITGWU which spurred the London building employers 'to emulate his union-smashing': Raymond Postgate, *The Builders' History*, London 1923, p. 415. The London building workers lockout began on 24 January 1914 and lasted into July before the unions were finally defeated. See also Richard Price, *Masters, Unions and Men*, Cambridge 1980. Only the outbreak of war in August prevented massive confrontation between employers and unions on a scale greater than anything that had gone before.

42	*Freeman's Journal* 12 December 1913

43	*Freeman's Journal* 16 December 1913

44	*Freeman's Journal* 5 January 1914

45	*Freeman's Journal* 19 January 1914

46	Peter Murray, 'Electoral Politics and the Dublin Working Class before the First World War', *Saothar* 6, 1980.

47	*Irish Worker* 17 January 1914

48	In his account of this meeting, Greaves has Larkin speaking against a return to work, urging his members to hold out for another year, and being received in absolute silence. This seems part of his systematic denigration of the man: C. Desmond Greaves, *The Irish Transport and General Workers Union: The Formative Years 1909-1923*, Dublin 1982, pp. 118-119.

49	*Irish Worker* 14 March 1914.

50	C. Desmond Greaves, *The Life and Times of James Connolly*, London 1960, p. 338.

51	Greaves, *Irish Transport and General Workers Union*, op cit, p. 121.

52	*Irish Worker* 7 February 1914.

53	Raymond Postgate, *The Builders' History*, London 1923, pp. 415, 417. See also Richard Price, *Masters, Unions and Men*, Cambridge 1980, for the lockout.

54	*Irish Worker* 31 January and 7 February 1914.

55	*The Toiler* 27 June 1914.

56	*The Toiler* 17 January, 21 March, 4 and 18 April, 9 and 16 May, 6 and 27 June 1914.

57	*The Toiler* 10 October 1914.

58	For McIntyre see my "The Curse of Larkinism": Patrick McIntyre, *The Toiler* and the Dublin Lockout of 1913', *Eire-Ireland* 1995

PART TWO

Chapter VI
The Road to Easter Week

The *Irish Worker* maintained a consistently hostile attitude towards the Irish Volunteer organisation that had been founded in Dublin in November 1913 and had then spread throughout the country. The organisation was a rival for working-class support to the ITGWU's own militia, the Irish Citizen Army, and, moreover included in its leadership men who were clearly aligned with the employers in the Great Lockout. The main spokesman for this hostility was Sean O'Casey. He attacked the Volunteers on two fronts: first, they were hostile to the working class movement, and second, they had betrayed republican principles. By joining with Home Rulers to establish the Volunteers and excluding the ITGWU, the IRB had accepted both that the working class had to be kept down and Home Rule. This was a double betrayal as far as O'Casey was concerned.

At the end of January 1914, the *Irish Worker* published O'Casey's 'An Open Letter To Workers In The Volunteers'. Here he castigated those workers misguided enough to enlist:

> Many of you have been tempted to join this much talked of movement by the wild impulse of genuine enthusiasm. You have again allowed yourselves to be led away by words – words – words! You have momentarily forgotten that there can be no interests outside of those identified with your own class. That every worker must separate himself from every party – every movement that does not tend towards the development of the faith that all power springs from and is invested in the people …. Workers, do you not think it is high time to awake from your sleep and yielded allegiance to no movement that does not avow the ultimate destiny of the workers …. Workers, ye are fools to train and drill for anything less than complete enfranchisement, for the utter alteration of the present social system, for liberty to ensure that natural and absolute development of every Irish-born man and woman …. Workers, this movement is built on a reactionary basis, that of Grattan's Tinsel Volunteers. Are you going to be satisfied with a crowd of chattering well-fed

aristocrats and commercial bugs coming in and going out of College Green? Are
you going to rope Ireland's poor outside the boundaries of the nation? Do you
know what Mitchel said of Grattan's precious Parliament? This: 'This Parliament
is a very fine thing to talk or sing about; it has association of a theatrical sort, but
no Irish workman or peasant will every draw a trigger to restore it'.[1]

This contribution drew a reply from James MacGowan, himself a member
of the ICA, who favoured close links with the Volunteers. He argued that the
Volunteers were not modelled on Grattan's Volunteers of 1782, but drew their
inspiration from the 'spirit that animated the '98 men, the spirit that caused the
revolution of '48 to rise from the pauper graves of the Famine years, the spirit
that served the Fenians'. The Volunteers were generating 'a spirit of comradeship, a spirit of brotherhood among all Irishmen'. As far as he was concerned
the very presence of men like Pearse, Macken and Tom Kelly in the Volunteer
leadership 'is sufficient guarantee that the interests of the workers shall not be
trampled upon'. He accused O'Casey of doing the job of the British government
in attacking the Volunteers and challenged his right to appeal to the memory of
John Mitchel.[2]

O'Casey would have none of this and replied with a contribution that made
the Larkinite position absolutely clear:

> I am chided for using the name Mitchel. I quote Mitchel because I am a republican
> in principle and practise; because he denounced tyranny everywhere he found it …
> because he stood for the Irish worker against the English Lord and Irish aristocrat,
> because tho' present-day ranting extreme Nationalists conjure with his sacred
> name they ignore, I believe they deliberately ignore, the fact that he stood for, and
> fought for, the class they elect to despise and pass by.

The only brotherhood that O'Casey was prepared to acknowledge was that
'engendered by a common heritage of pain, oppression and wage-slavery' and
he warned against following well-to-do leaders 'in efforts that are bound to leave
the workers' last state equally bad as their first'. As for the claim that the Volunteers embodied the spirit of '48 and the Fenians, he poured scorn on it: 'Fancy
John McNeill and Laurence Kettle claiming kinship with the Fenians!' Appeals
to the credibility of Pearse, Macken and Tom Kelly left him unconvinced: 'How
is it that while Honest Tom Kelly held a high position on the Sinn Féin Executive, the official organ slashed unmercifully at the workers in the throes of an
industrial struggle?' And as for Pearse: 'This leader of democratic opinion consistently used the trams on every possible occasion, though the controller of the
Dublin tramway system was the man who declared the workers could submit or
starve'. 'Personally'. He went on,

> I hold the workers are beside themselves with foolishness to support any

movement that does not stand to make the workers supreme, for these are the people, and without them there can be no life nor power …. Not in the shouts of the deluded wage-slave Volunteers, but in the hunger-cry of the nation's poor is heard the voice of Ireland.[3]

The argument between the two men continued in a further three issues of the *Irish Worker*. At the same time, O'Casey was in the process of taking over as secretary of the ICA and was urging that it should be reorganised, so as to become a more effective alternative pole of attraction to the Volunteers.

With the crumbling away of working-class resistance to the Lockout in the early months of 1914, the ICA appeared about to founder. It had been established to provide protection for union members during the dispute and now appeared to have lost its *raison d'être*. O'Casey proposed, with Larkin's support, that it should be reorganised into 'a systematic unit of Labour' with a proper constitution and elected officers. Steps had to be taken 'to improve and strengthen the condition and widen the scope of the Irish Citizen Army'. The intention was for the working class to make an intervention in nationalist politics and establish the ICA as a credible alternative to the Volunteers. So much was made clear by O'Casey's exchanges with James MacGowan. To this end, it was agreed to hold a general meeting of the ICA at Liberty Hall on 22 March.

At the meeting, O'Casey read out the proposed Constitution:

1.   That the first and last principle of the Irish Citizen Army is the avowal that the ownership of Ireland, moral and material, is vested of right in the people of Ireland.
2.   That the Irish Citizen Army shall stand for the absolute unity of Irish nationhood, and shall support the rights and liberties of the democracies of all nations.
3.   That one of its objects shall be to sink all differences of birth, property and creed under the common name of the Irish people.
4.   That the Citizen Army shall be open to all who accept the principle of equal rights and opportunities for the Irish People.

Larkin then urged that a fifth clause be added and Countess Markiewicz duly proposed it from the floor:

Before being enrolled, every applicant must, if eligible, be a member of his Trades Union, such Union to be recognised by the Irish Trades Union Congress.

After the acceptance of the Constitution by the meeting, the Army Council was elected. Even though Larkin had earlier warned against those who would try 'to influence or capture their organisation, or to wean it from its first attachment of Labour ideals', the Council included a strong party in favour of closer cooperation with the Volunteers. This party included Captain Jack White, the

ICA chairman, Countess Markiewicz, and O'Casey's erstwhile antagonist, James MacGowan. Connolly, it is worth noticing, was not at this time a member.[4]

Hostilities between the ICA and the Volunteers continued regardless, reaching a crescendo in May 1914. On the 9th the paper printed a letter from 'E.K', drawing attention to a recent statement by Colonel Maurice Moore, one of the Volunteer leaders, in the *Irish Times*. Here, Moore made clear that in the event of public disorder, 'the Irish Volunteers are expected to assist the police in maintaining peace'. 'E.K' denounced any idea of cooperation with the police, with 'the murderous ruffians who, during the recent labour dispute in Dublin butchered two of our fellow citizens, and maimed hundreds of others and spared neither women nor children', and called upon those workers who had misguidedly enlisted in the Volunteers to 'instantly repudiate Moore's statement in no uncertain way'. In the same issue of the paper, Larkin joined in with a savage attack on the Volunteers leadership:

> We are informed from a source that we must appreciate that the record of names, addresses, antecedents and movements of every boy and man who has been gulled into enrolling in the alleged 'Irish National Volunteers' has been furnished to the Government; that an undertaking has been given by the creatures controlling the machinery of the organisation at headquarters that no ammunition will be issued at any time without the sanction of the Government; that on the part of certain of the leaders that they have given a sworn declaration to the government that they will at all costs support the British Government; that they have no sympathy with any movement outside Ireland; that they are good, loyal men; that if any attempt is made by the Republican section to capture the organisation, they will immediately inform the government and hand over all monies, equipment, arms, etc., to the Government ... that in case of any disturbances they will try and persuade the Volunteers to undertake police work and protect property .... Comrades of the working class, we appeal to you not to associate with your known enemies in the industrial field. Join your own army – the army of the dispossessed – the army of the houseless, homeless, countryless, Irish working class. Join the Citizen Army.[5]

And the attack was pressed home a fortnight later with a challenge to the Volunteers executive from Sean O'Casey on behalf of the ICA to debate the legitimacy of the Volunteers leadership's 'appeal for the sympathy and support of the Irish working class'.[6]

The matter was not left there. The next issue of the paper carried a front page article accusing the Volunteers of acting as 'a sort of auxiliary force, so that in the event of the national or city police not being strong enough to cope with locked-out or striking workers, they will be available, and in sufficient strength to, as it were, turn the tide of battle'. The Volunteers were roundly condemned as 'a scab military institution, and like all such will be ever ready to assist, no matter how dirty the work may be'. Larkin himself, once again weighed in and in an editorial condemned the Volunteers as 'a Castle-controlled organisation' that would 'if given the opportunity, attack, baton, shoot and massacre the organized working class'. This fear that the Volunteers were a potential strike-breaking force, an extension of the Hibernians, was strongly felt. And indeed, there was no doubt that the Volunteers leadership did include men who would have been quite happy to participate in the suppression of working-class unrest. Larkin was worried that this would be their role in a Home Rule Ireland. It made the strengthening of the ICA all the more urgent.[7]

Redmond Takes Over

Events in June seemed to bear out Larkin's strictures. On 6 June 1914 John Redmond demanded that the Volunteer Provisional Committee be expanded to include a majority nominated by him or he would split the organisation. The *Irish Worker* urged the Volunteer to 'let the politicians go hang themselves if necessary'. It was not to be. On 16 June a majority of the Provisional Committee voted to capitulate to Redmond and accept his nominees. 'On Your Knees! Provisional Committee: You Half-Baked Rebels', editorialised the *Irish Worker*. And one of the renegades, the paper reported, was actually 'to deliver the oration of Bodenstown on Sunday. Poor Tone – it is enough to make him turn in his grave'.[8] Behind the scenes, however, the voting on the Provisional Committee had been split, with a hardcore of IRB members (even the IRB was not united) voting to defy Redmond. Outmanoeuvred by the Home Rulers, this hardcore turned to the Irish Citizen Army for support, for allies. On 21 June, at the insistence of Tom Clarke, the ICA was allowed to participate in the annual pilgrimage to Wolfe Tone's grave in Bodenstown cemetery and was invited to form part of the guard of honour. The occasion was a great success and seemed to herald closer relations between the ICA and at least a section of the Volunteers. Nevertheless, the following day in a speech to ITGWU members, Larkin went out of his way to urge them to join the Citizen Army, 'the only army that would do Ireland any good ... if they were in any other army they would be false to their class'. There were, Larkin emphasised, 'no scabs in the Citizen Army's ranks'. The working class had never betrayed Ireland whereas all that could expected 'of the middle and so-called upper class (was) treachery'.[9]

Clearly there were serious differences within the Citizen Army leadership over relations with the Volunteers. As far as O'Casey was concerned, the Bodenstown pilgrimage changed nothing. The republicans should have broken away from the Volunteers and thrown in their lot with the ICA. In his report of the Bodenstown pilgrimage in the *Irish Worker*, he wrote that:

> Today Republicanism in Ireland is mouldering .... Even in the assembly that looked reverently at the unpretentious tomb, how many were there that entered into the man's buried life or understood his principles. I would venture to say that to very many in that crowd Wolfe Tone had died in vain .... Even some of those whom we were called upon to trust as Republican leaders have announced

by their votes on the Provisional Committee of the National Volunteers that it is expedient to believe that John Redmond is the fountain-head of Ireland's hope .... Would to God Wolfe Tone were here today! In his day he abandoned Grattan, his scintillating Volunteers, and his property-protecting Parliament, and linked his fortunes with the oppressed people of Ireland .... Today we have a miniature Grattan in John Redmond. Who is going to take the place of a Wolfe Tone in the vanguard of an oppressed people that we may fight again the battle for an Irish Republic?

He warned that Redmond intended to use the Volunteers 'to break up democratic progress even as some of the Volunteers of '82 hunted down the followers of Wolfe Tone in glorious '98'. Trying to create 'a union of all classes is impossible', he wrote, and urged the republicans to recognise that

all workers are, through the force of necessity potential rebels. Wolfe Tone held no foolish hopes of the union of all classes. He hated the aristocracy and thoroughly despised the propertied class and the merchants .... Today the only possible union that Republicans can hope for is a union between themselves and the workers, whose principles are practically identical with their own.

In effect, he was appealing for those republicans who were disillusioned with the Volunteers to come over to the ICA.[10]

This article was O'Casey's last contribution to the *Irish Worker*. Soon after it appeared, he resigned as secretary of the ICA and drifted out of the organisation. The reason for this was the failure of his attempt to prohibit joint membership of the ICA and the Volunteers. He had never agreed with this and now with Redmond actually in control of the Volunteers he felt the time had come to put a stop to it. To this end, at a meeting of the Army Council he proposed a resolution that confronted one of the main culprits, Countess Markiewicz, with a choice between the ICA and the Volunteers:

Seeing that Madame Markiewicz was, through Cumann na mBan, attached to the Volunteers, and on intimate terms with may of the Volunteers leaders, and as the Volunteers' Association was, in its methods and aims, inimical to the first interests of Labour, it could not be expected that Madame could retain the confidence of the Council; and that she be now asked to sever her connection with either the Volunteers or the Irish Citizen Army.

The resolution was lost and a vote of confidence in the Countess was carried by one vote. The Council called upon O'Casey to apologise to her and taking this as a vote of no confidence in himself, he promptly resigned as secretary. There can be no doubt that O'Casey's resolution was motivated at least in part by personal animosity: quite unfairly, he always regarded Markiewicz as a revolutionary tourist. This probably lost him the vote. He was particularly put out by

Larkin's failure to support him.[11]

Meanwhile, one unlikely group of conspirators led by Sir Roger Casement and Erskine Childers, both enthusiastic supporters of the Irish Volunteers, had organised the landing in Ireland of a large quantity of weapons. On 26 July 1914, 900 rifles were landed from the yacht *Asgard* at Howth and a large contingent of Volunteers marched out to take public possession of them. On their return march to Dublin, an attempt was made to disarm them by soldiers of the King's Own Scottish Borderers, but they successfully dispersed, losing some of their weapons to the ICA in the process. On their return to Dublin the British troops were taunted and jeered by hostile crowds and some stones were thrown. At Bachelor's Walk in the city the troops finally retaliated, firing into the crowd, killing three people and wounding thirty-eight, one of whom subsequently died.[12] This was a stark contrast to the uninterrupted importation of much larger quantities of weapons by the Ulster Volunteer Force at Larne in April 1914. Indeed, Connolly had actually pointed out at the time that if Nationalists or Labour men had dared behave like the Unionists, there would have been 'at least 1000 arrests made ... the next morning'. The Bachelor's Walk shootings proved the point.[13]

The *Irish Worker* used the episode to point out the consequences of the republicans not uniting with the working class during the Lockout. The troops had been transported to Howth in William Martin Murphy's trams: 'he turned the passengers out of his cars and replaced them by the armed murderers of the King's Scottish Borderers'. They were 'driven and conducted by the scabs who took the place of the men locked-out last August'. If the ITGWU had emerged victorious from the lockout and 'if the former employees, members of the Irish Transport and General Workers' Union had been in charge of the cars neither soldier nor police would have been taken'. The point was well made. The republicans should have seen working-class victory in the lockout as something strengthening the national cause, not as a diversion from it. Moreover of the four people shot dead at Bachelor's Walk, one was an ITGWU member and lockout veteran and another was the wife of an ITGWU member and lockout veteran.[14]

Partition

Before we consider the ITGWU's response to the outbreak of war, it is worth briefly considering the stand that it took over the proposed partition of Ireland, the 'compromise' that was being worked out by Redmond, Carson and Asquith. On 14 March 1914 Connolly had warned in the *Irish Worker* that Redmond was preparing 'to sacrifice to the bigoted enemy the unity of the nation and took with it the lives, liberties and hopes of that portion of the nation which in the midst of the most hostile surroundings have fought to keep the faith in things national and progressive'. He went on to insist with quite remarkable prescience that partition would 'mean a carnival of reaction both North and South, would set back the wheels of progress, and destroy the oncoming unity of the Irish Labour movement, and would paralyse all advanced movements, whilst it endured'. To prevent partition, he concluded, 'Labour in Ulster should fight even to the death'.[15] A week later in the Glasgow *Forward* he argued that partition 'should be resisted with armed force in necessary' and that the working class 'would much rather see the Home Rule Bill defeated than see it carried out with Ulster or any part of Ulster left out'.[16]

The assault on Redmond's betrayal was kept up. On 21 March 1914, the *Irish Worker* carried a front page article, 'The Irish Party and the Betrayal of Ulster' that lamented the absence of Parnell and savaged Redmond and the Home Rule leadership as 'a set of pigmy statesmen who strut the political stage after the manner of the fabled jackdaw in peacock's feathers'. They were prepared 'to acquiesce in the determination of the British Government to stereotype, by Act of Parliament, two distinct Irelands'. More than that, it was the sectarianism of the Hibernians that was responsible for the current crisis, for reviving the fortunes of the Orange Order. If it were not for the Hibernians, the Orange Order would have disappeared long ago and it is 'to Brother Devlin and not to Brother Carson (that) is mainly due to the progress of the Covenanter movement in Ulster'. It was the activities of the Hibernians that had placed

> such a effective check upon the fusion of Orange and Green that was rapidly taking place amongst the workers of Ulster. In resurrecting the old religious quarrels new opportunities were given to English statesmen, and the result is today beheld in the lopping off of sufficient territory as will ensure for generations to come that Irish energy, wit and enterprise will be spent in faction-fighting between two avaricious bodies in Ireland rather than in a combined effort to lift the toilers of all creeds to a position of affluence in the land of their birth.

While one might quarrel with this particular understanding of developments in the North, the *Irish Worker's* uncompromising condemnation of Catholic sectarianism is particularly impressive. And in that same issue of the paper, Larkin editorialised against partition, calling instead for 'a united Ireland, the Ireland of Tone, Emmet and McCracken', three Protestants.[17]

On 30 May 1914 the *Irish Worker* published an 'Address' to delegates to the Irish Trades Union Congress that assembled in Dublin the following day. Written by Connolly, the article ended with a powerful statement on partition:

> The Ulster Volunteers may be able to frighten a Liberal Government willing to be frightened but were a Labour Movement able to call out the Textile Operatives of Belfast, or even its spinners, and to keep them out until Ulster threw in her lot with Ireland, the paralysis of industry and loss of profit to Belfast capitalists would frighten the guns out of the hands of the Carsonite army without the shedding of a single drop of blood.

In conclusion, we say to fellow delegates with all solemnity that there are no real Nationalists in Ireland outside of the Irish Labour movement. All others merely reject one part of another of the British Conquest, the Labour Movement alone rejects it in its entirety, and sets itself to the Reconquest of Ireland as its aim.[18]

The Congress carried a motion condemning partition, that was proposed by Connolly, by 84 votes to 2.

The Outbreak of War

Larkin responded to the outbreak of war on 4 August 1914 with a ferocious editorial in the *Irish Worker*:

If England wants an empire let her hold the empire. What have we to do with her murderous, grasping, thieving work? Surely Ireland's sons can see the game that is being played with them? We are told Ireland's hope was in her Volunteers. God help her then. For what we prophesied … has come to pass. 1782 is to be re-enacted again, and the Chalice of Liberty is to be dashed from the lips of Kathleen ni Houlihan by her own unworthy sons. Out of every port in Munster, Leinster and Connaught is pouring our best blood to fight for a people who are unable to fight for themselves. Bands are playing, knaves are cheering them, but what of their women and children left behind. Britain will not even provide them with work-houses … oh, Irishmen, dear countrymen, take heed of what we say for if you do England's dirty work you will surely rue the day. Stop at home. Arm for Ireland. Fight for Ireland …. Remember by taking Britain's side in this unholy war you are giving up your claim that Ireland is a nation.

This was a war for the British Empire and Ireland's war was at home. In the same issue, Connolly hammered home the point. As far as he was concerned should a German army land in Ireland tomorrow they should be perfectly justified in joining it if by doing so they could rid this country once and for all from its connection with Brigand Empire …

Should the working class of Europe rather than slaughter each other for the benefit of kings and financiers, proceed tomorrow to erect barricades all over Europe, to break up bridges and destroy transport services that war might be abolished, we should be perfectly justified in following such a glorious example.

However, 'pending either of our consummations it is our manifest duty to save the poor from the horrors this war has in store …. We must consider at once whether it will not be out duty to refuse to allow agricultural produce to leave Ireland'. This would involve not just strike action but 'armed battling in the streets'. Such a policy might yet see Ireland 'set the torch to a European con-flagration that will not burn out until the last throne and the last capitalist bond and debenture will be shrivelled on the funeral pyre of the last warlord'.[19]

Even before the war broke out, the two men had been developing a strategy to capture the leadership of the Volunteers from the Home Rulers. They had hoped to overthrow Redmond and to pull the republicans within the Volunteer movement into their orbit by means of their intransigent opposition to partition. Now, with Redmond committing Ireland to support the British war effort the time seemed ripe. To this end, Connolly argued that the very existence of the Volunteers 'even without arms, could have made the adhesion of Ireland to either side or even the real neutrality of Ireland, of so much importance that great and substantial national advantage would have been offered her'. The failure to take advantage of the situation had plunged the Irish people to 'the lowest depths as a race'. While Redmond's conduct was predictable, what of the republicans 'who in their cowardly fear of an ignorant newspaper – rigged public opinion surrendered the control of the Volunteers to the Redmondite wire-pullers'. They had to break with the arch-collaborator Redmond and join with the Citizen Army to extort independence from the British.[20]

Redmond's support for the British Empire and call for Irish Volunteers to enlist provoked a torrent of abuse. In an editorial entitled 'The Irish Judas', Larkin asked, 'Is there no man to provide a rope for this twentieth century Judas, who not even as clever as his predecessor, failed to receive the thirty pieces of silver'.[21] A fortnight later in another editorial he urged Irish men and women to enlist, but 'into the Volunteers or the Citizen Army at once .... You know not the hour when the voice of Liberty may summon you'.[22] And a week later a further editorial entitled 'Redmond Eats His Own Vomit' hammered the same points home'.[22] Clearly Larkin's earlier hostility towards the Volunteers was changing and by now he and Connolly shared the same perspective.

By now Redmond's stand had succeeded in alienating many of the original founders of the Irish Volunteers, including Eoin MacNeill. With the IRB working in the background they proceeded to break away. This development was welcomed by Connolly as a great victory that 'sent a thrill of joy through the heart of every true man and woman in the country'. It had dealt 'a staggering blow' to 'the insidious attempt to betray the Volunteers into the clutch of the Empire'. 'Never', he wrote, 'was the peril of Irish Nationality greater, never were the forces of national and social freedom more in danger of death from moral asphyxiation than at the outset of the Redmond-Asquith conspiracy'. Redmond's attempts to 'bully, seduce or confuse the Volunteers into an en masse enrolment as soldiers in the British Army' was, according to Connolly, 'the most gigantic, deep-laid and loathsome attempt in history to betray the soul of a people'. He pledged his full support to the breakaway committee whose 'Napoleon-like stroke ... in resuming control at the psychological moment saved the situation for the country at large'. A 'fight to the finish' was starting, he warned:

For some of us the finish may be on the scaffold, for some in the prison cell, for others more fortunate upon the battlefields of an Ireland in arms for a real republican liberty .... We shall show the world that though Redmond may sell Ireland he cannot deliver the goods.[24]

The following week Connolly urged the breakaway Volunteers to follow the Citizen Army in adopting a 'forward policy' which would enable them to complete the rout of 'Messrs Redmond and Devlin'. They had to recognise that their fight is a struggle to the death,

> that the prize at stake is the soul of a Nation, and therefore every ounce of energy, every bright coinage of the brain, must be flung at once into the struggle. The volunteers must realise that against the shamelessly vile methods of the politician there is but on effective weapon – the daring appeal of the Revolutionist ... the Provisional Committee must attack aggressively, resolutely, openly, or they and their followers will be wiped out of existence. Aggressive action will convert the waverers better than a thousand speeches, or a hundred printed proclamations.

He urged them to adopt two pledges which would without doubt win 'the adhesion of everyone worth their salt in Ireland':

> Pledge the Irish Volunteers to remain in armed service in Ireland for Ireland and to resist all attempts of any other nation to deprive Ireland of their services.
> Pledge the services of their armed forces to Ireland to enforce the repeal of all clauses in the Home Rule Act denying to Ireland powers of self-government now enjoyed by South Africa, Australia or Canada.[25]

What he envisaged was a mass Volunteer movement extracting these concessions by the threat of rebellion, and if that failed, by rebellion itself.

Connolly's articles at this time show him desperately trying to work out a revolutionary strategy in a situation where working-class opposition to war across Europe had never materialised. In these circumstances he adopted the rhetoric of Irish nationalism ['the soul of the nation'] not of working-class internationalism. Moreover, his 'daring appeal of the Revolutionist' involved being prepared to fight to the death not for a republic, let alone a workers' republic, but for the degree 'of self-government now enjoyed by South Africa, Australia or Canada,' that is for something very like the Free State that was to be finally established in January 1922. How can we explain this confusion? In order to consolidate the split in the Volunteers, Connolly, with Larkin's support, moved to the right. They were determined not to alienate the moderates in the breakaway leadership and if a turn to the right was necessary to bring about the establishment of a mass volunteer movement opposed to both the Home Rulers and to the British government, then so be it. However, Connolly was still advocating revolutionary methods if only to achieve moderate demands. British refusal to make concessions would in turn inevitably pull the breakaway Volunteers to the left.

It was not to be. It was not Redmond who was to be isolated and marginalised, but the Citizen Army and the breakaway Volunteers. They were swept aside as the overwhelming majority of the Volunteer rank and file rallied to Redmond and the British Empire. Instead of a mass movement all that was left was a rump and moreover a rump that rejected closer cooperation with the Citizen Army. On 25 October 1914 the breakaway volunteers held a convention at the Abbey Theatre in Dublin. Connolly attended the convention and asked that the Citizen Army be allowed to affiliate and to have two representatives on the new executive committee. The request was refused because the committee feared that this would drive even more people over to Redmond.[26]

Meanwhile, Larkin had left for the United States. He had set sail on 14 October 1914, leaving Connolly as acting general-secretary of the ITGWU. Originally, Larkin had intended leaving P.T. Daly in charge, but there had been vigorous objections because, as Connolly put it, this would 'jeopardise our understanding with nationalists'.[27] Why did Larkin go? Ostensibly, it was to raise funds for the union, but it has also been suggested that he was exhausted and that he had given up on Ireland. It seems most likely that it was his intention to return with funds raised in America in a matter of months. In fact, he was not to return to Ireland until 30 April 1923, but in the interim, as we shall see, he was to throw himself into the revolutionary movement in the United States.[28]

Connolly in Charge

How did Connolly respond to the setbacks of 1914? The lockout had ended in a victory for the employers, the Home Rulers had accepted partition, the international working class had proved incapable of stopping the war, and the Irish people, including the great majority of the Volunteers, had rallied to the British Empire. The accumulation of defeats seems to have cut him loose from the politics he had championed since the late 1890s. The amalgam of De Leonism and Syndicalism that he had developed proved unable to cope with the crisis. Confronted with the absence of mass resistance to the war either internationally or in Ireland, Connolly was to become the impassioned advocate of revolutionary action even by a tiny minority, even by the few hundred men and women of the Citizen Army. Moreover this insurrectionism was posed in nationalist terms with only the occasional gesture towards socialist politics. This is not to say that he abandoned socialism. Indeed, he remained a socialist, but a socialist who had concluded that in the circumstances of the time, a republican insurrection had become the political priority. Preparations for this insurrection came completely adrift from both his socialism and from his trade union activities, from the rebuilding of the ITGWU. To all intents and purposes the Citizen Army and the ITGWU became separate, distinct spheres of activity. They shared the same building, Liberty Hall, but went about completely different business, the one Ireland's business, the other the business of the working class. And at the same time, Connolly became a staunch defender of Imperial Germany as the victim of British Imperialist aggression, as the most progressive of the great powers involved in the conflict, as the country closest to socialism. We shall return to this last point.

Once Connolly had famously insisted (in January 1897) that even if ' you remove the English army tomorrow and hoist the green flag over Dublin Castle, unless you set about the organisation of the Socialist Republic your efforts will be in vain. England would still rule you'.[29] Whereas the emancipation of the working class and the winning of freedom for Ireland had once been inseparably linked in his thinking, now they had come apart, with the emancipation of the working class postponed, while a blow was struck for Ireland. The transformation in his thinking was made explicit in an article that appeared in his *Workers' Republic* newspaper in late January 1916. Here he made a crucial distinction between the struggle for socialism in a time of peace and for national liberation in a time of war. 'Our programme', he wrote, 'in time of peace was to gather into Irish hands in Irish trade unions the control of all the forces of production and distribution in Ireland', but 'in times of war we should act as in war'. He went on: 'While the war lasts and Ireland still is a subject nation we shall continue to urge her to fight for her freedom ... the time for Ireland's battle is NOW'.[30] The notions of socialism and national liberation continued to co-exist in his mind, but whereas his socialist pronouncements remained propagandist exercises, his republican commitment was to be realised in practice on the streets of Dublin.

His development was closely observed by Sean O'Casey. Although he was no longer a member of the Citizen Army, he remained on friendly terms with some of those who were and was a keen observer of developments. He had, of course, been strongly opposed to any close relationship between the Citizen Army and the Volunteers, and now that Connolly was in charge his worst fears were realised. O'Casey considered that by the time of the 25 October Volunteer convention in 1914 it was already clear to all 'that carefully reflected upon passing events ... that the Citizen Army was really becoming the militant Left Wing of the Irish Volunteers'. He wrote of how relations between Connolly

and the militant members of the Volunteer Council soon became cordial. It is difficult to understand the almost revolutionary change that was manifesting itself in Connolly's nature. The labour movement seemed to be regarded by him as a decrescent force, while the essence of nationalism began to assume the finer elements of his nature. His articles that now appeared in the *Workers' Republic* with consistent regularity, the speeches that he delivered at various demonstrations and assemblies, all proclaimed that Jim Connolly had stepped from the narrow byway of Irish Socialism onto the broad and crowded highway of Irish nationalism .... The high creed of Irish Nationalism became his daily rosary, while the higher creed of international humanity that had so long bubbled from his eloquent lips was silent forever and Irish labour lost a leader.[31]

This was written in 1919 and while O'Casey's language is overly dramatic, he nevertheless correctly delineated the nature of the transformation that had overcome Connolly.

One question worth considering here is Connolly's understanding of Irish nationalism at this time. It is clear from his writings that the Marxist analysis of Irish nationalism and the Irish national struggle that he had begun to develop in the 1890s and that resulted in his *Labour in Irish History* was abandoned for a romantic Fenian nationalism that had little if anything to do with Marxism. As far as Connolly was concerned Redmond's crime was that he had betrayed 'the soul of Ireland'. In 1914 Connolly had believed that the Irish people, because of partition and the war, could be won over from their allegiance to the Home Rulers, but this was shown to be a pipe-dream. Instead, he came to the conclusion that a small, determined minority must be prepared, if necessary, to sacrifice themselves in order to save the soul of the nation. More and more this involved himself identifying with a particular strand of the Irish republican tradition, that identified with Padraic Pearse.

On 1 August 1915 the Volunteers and the Citizen Army jointly commemorated the funeral of Jeremiah O'Donovan Rossa, a Fenian veteran of the 1860s who had remained true to the cause, and whose body had been returned from America for burial. In a memorial that he wrote for the occasion, Connolly discoursed at length on 'the soul of the nation'. 'Slavery', he argued, 'was a thing of the soul .... Before a nation can be reduced to slavery its soul must have been cowed, intimidated or corrupted by the oppressor'. While the body seeks to preserve itself by compromise 'with the foes of its national existence', the unconquered soul 'declares its sanctity to be more important than the interests of the body'. For generations there had been a conflict in Ireland between the sanctity of the soul and the interests of the body. The soul 'preached revolution, declared that no bloodletting could be as disastrous as a cowardly acceptance of the rule of the conqueror' and in 'fitful moments of spiritual exaltation Ireland accepted that idea'. These moments passed, however, and Ireland 'sank again into its slavery'. O'Donovan Rossa's funeral raised 'in the mind of every worker the question of his or her own mental attitude to the powers against which the departed hero was in revolt'. And Connolly answered for the Citizen Army:

> The Irish Citizen Army in its constitution pledges its members to fight for a Republican Freedom for Ireland. Its members are, therefore, of the number who believe that at the call of duty they may have to lay down their lives for Ireland, and have so trained themselves that at the worst the laying down of their lives shall constitute the starting point of another glorious tradition – the tradition that will keep alive the soul of the nation.[32]

In this way he pledged the working class, or rather those few of its number enrolled in the Citizen Army, to sacrifice themselves for the very republican tradition that he had himself earlier subjected to such searching criticism from a socialist standpoint.

A week after the funeral, he wrote in the *Workers' Republic* that

> For twelve months, twelve very long dreary agonising months we have seen war in Ireland, war upon the soul of the Irish people .... Never has a nation suffered such an onslaught. Belgium in its agonies under the heel of the invaders, nor Poland in its awful travail, cannot claim to have suffered as Ireland has suffered since war was declared .... The fighting in Belgium and Poland was for the material possession of towns and cities, the fight in Ireland has been for the soul of the race.[33]

This was a really quite incredible piece. For all practical purposes Connolly had abandoned the terrain of socialist politics for the imaginary landscape of Pearse's messianic nationalism, substituting rhetorical excess for analysis. But this is not to say he was no longer a socialist. He continued to advocate socialism, indeed he published a substantial exposition of syndicalist politics, *The Reconquest of Ireland*, in 1915, but for the time being the struggle over the soul of Ireland and preparations for a rising altogether dominated his immediate political concerns.

The wheel came full circle in a crucial article, 'The Ties that Bind', that appeared in the *Workers' Republic* on 5 February 1916, less than three months before the Easter Rising. This is worth quoting at some length because here he revealed that as far as he was concerned the Irish working class was itself a party to the betrayal of Ireland, had sold its soul for a mess of pottage, and could only be redeemed by a blood sacrifice:

> Recently we have been pondering deeply over the ties that bind this country to England. It is not a new theme for our thoughts: for long years we have carried on propaganda in Ireland pointing out how the strings of self-interest bound the capitalist and landlord classes to the Empire, and how it thus became a waste of time to appeal to those classes in the name of Irish Patriotism. We have said that the Working Class was the only class to whom the word "Empire" and the things of which it was the symbol did not appeal. That to the propertied classes "Empire" meant high dividends and financial security, whereas to the Working Class that meant only the things it was in rebellion against. Therefore, from the intelligent working class could alone come the revolutionary impulse. Recently we have seen the spread of those ties of self-interest binding certain classes and individuals to the Empire – we have seen it spread to a most astonishing degree until its ramifications cover the island like a foul disease. It would be almost impossible to name a single class or section of the population not evilly affected by this social, political and moral leprosy .... In all the grades of Irish Society the only section that has not furnished even one apostate to the cause it worked for in times of peace is that of the much hated and traduced Militant Labour Leaders. But if the Militant Labour Leaders of Ireland have not apostatised the same cannot be said of the working

class as a whole. It is with shame and sorrow we say it, but the evil influence upon large sections of the Irish Working Class of the bribes and promises of the enemy cannot be denied .... For the sake of a few paltry shillings per week thousands of Irish workers have sold their country in the hour of their country's greatest need and hope. For the sake of a few paltry shillings Separation Allowance thousands of Irish women have made life miserable for their husbands with entreaties to join the British Army .... Deep in the heart of Ireland has sank the sense of the degradation wrought upon its people – our lost brothers and sisters – so deep and humiliating that no agency less potent than the red tide of war on Irish soil will ever be able to enable the Irish race to recover its self-respect, or re-establish its national dignity in the face of a world horrified and scandalised by what must seem to them our national apostasy. Without the slightest trace of irreverence but in all due humility and awe we recognise that of us, as of mankind before Calvary, it may truly be said: "Without the shedding of Blood, there is no Redemption".[34]

Connolly's state of mind at this time is perhaps best captured by an article he wrote commemorating the execution of the Manchester Martyrs in November 1867. Here he detailed the considerations that had argued against their actions: they were surrounded by a hostile population, they were playing into the British government's hands by exposing their organisation to repression, they were discouraging the Irish people through another failure. Such considerations he contemptuously dismissed as 'the sound sensible arguments of the prudent, practical politicians and theoretical revolutionists. But "how beggarly appear the words before a defiant deed!" The Manchester Martyrs - ALLEN, LARKIN and O'BRIEN died that the right of their small nationality to independence might be attested by their blood – died that someday an Irish Republic might live'.[35] This was written as a challenge to MacNeill and the moderate leaders of the Volunteers, as part of an attempt to push them into an insurrection. Soon after, in January 1916, the military council of the IRB were to bring him into their plans for a rising, which will be examined in the next chapter. Connolly was to be initiated into the Brotherhood and was co-opted onto the military council as its sixth member. His embrace of republicanism was now official.

The German Empire

What of Connolly's attitude towards Imperial Germany and the Great War? For many years, it was accepted with only minor qualification that Connolly's attitude was the same as that of Lenin and the Bolsheviks, that he had adopted a position of revolutionary defeatism. C. Desmond Greaves, for example, in his biography of Connolly, argued that 'Connolly's thought ran parallel with Lenin's ... almost phrase by phrase'.[36] Another study of Connolly's political ideas by Bernard Ransom, argued along similar lines that 'Connolly's internationalist stand on the war issue was substantially similar to that of Lenin'.[37] The problem is that the evidence of what Connolly actually wrote starkly contradicts this proposition and reveals that the position he adopted was very much a pro-German one. As early as 29 August 1914 he wrote in the *Irish Worker* that having failed to beat Germany economically, the British had determined to beat her 'unfairly by organising a military and naval conspiracy against her'. This was 'a conception worthy of fiends'. 'The British capitalist class', he wrote:

> have planned this colossal crime in order to ensure its uninterrupted domination of the commerce of the world. To achieve that end it is prepared to bathe a continent in blood, to kill off the flower of the manhood of the three most civilised great nations of Europe, to place the iron heel of the Russian tyrant upon the throat of all liberty-loving races and peoples from the Baltic to the Black Sea, and to invite the blessing of God upon the spectacle of the savage Cossack ravishing the daughters of a race at the head of the christian civilisation. Yes, this war is the war of a pirate upon the German nation.[38]

He welcomed British defeats because the weaker Britain became, 'the stronger becomes every revolutionary force … as conversely the stronger he becomes the more defiant and unyielding he will be to every influence for in good in Ireland'. This was an attitude with which Lenin would have had some sympathy, but Connolly went on to celebrate German victories as the victories 'of the most enlightened nation in Europe – the nation whose democracy is most feared by the cunning capitalist rulers of the world'. Whereas Lenin considered the war to be an imperialist war on both sides, Connolly held that it was imperialist only on the British side and that Germany was a peaceful, progressive nation, subjected to unprovoked aggression. He seems to have considered Germany the country in Europe that was closest to socialism, the county 'whose working class had advanced nearest to the capture of the citadels of capitalism'. A German victory would be a victory for international progress and would clear a path for Germany's transition to socialism.[39]

In the early months of the war, Connolly expended much effort explaining away the German invasion of Belgium and the reprisals German troops had taken against resistance fighters and civilian hostages. If only the Belgians had contented themselves with peaceful protests against the passage of German troops through their territory, then 'her soldiers would all be alive … none of her civilian population would have lost their lives, homes or domestic treasures, or be scattered as exiles on the charity of strangers'. It was all the fault of 'her stupid governing class, and the wily heartless English diplomacy that sacrificed Belgium in a quarrel not her own'.[40] He elaborated upon 'the perfectly conscienceless character of the governing class of Belgium' and 'the thoroughly fiendish nature of many of its military tools' the following month. Belgium, he was reliably informed, had agreed 'to become part of the scheme against Germany, to abandon her neutrality and be an accomplice of the English and French cabinets' in return for 'the withdrawal of the journalistic and government-inspired exposure of Belgian atrocities in the Congo'. If this had not been agreed, Britain and France would have annexed the Congo ' in the interests of humanity'. The Belgian people were having to pay the price for the greed and blood-guiltiness of their rulers'.[41] Connolly condemned the 'newspaper wail over the suffering of "poor catholic Belgium"' as hypocrisy. The French had planted machine guns in the churches at Louvain and field artillery before the cathedral at Rheims thereby compelling the Germans to fire upon these buildings 'in self-defence'. The damage caused was then 'made the basis of an allegation that the Germans were making war upon religion'. To reinforce this blackening of the German army, 'hundreds of little Belgian children have been deported to Great Britain and Ireland, and are now being scattered up and down the land so that catholics may be moved to sympathy with their suffering to go out and fight'.[42] Connolly's belief that Germany was the victim of aggression inevitably led him into the role of apologist.

This pro-German propaganda led to the suppression of the *Irish Worker* in December 1914 and its replacement by the *Workers' Republic*. The new paper gave less space to pro-German material and focused more on fostering the spirit of Fenianism. Even so it still carried some remarkable features identifying the German cause as the cause of progress. On 4 December 1915 the *Workers' Republic* carried an interview with Kaiser Wilhelm conducted by a German Social Democrat, Anton Ferdrich. This made clear 'the Kaiser's love for peace' and argued that while he might not be a socialist 'there is no doubt that he understands the aims of the radical left in parliament far better and has more sympathies for them than the world knows'.[43] And an even more remarkable article was published in February the following year, once again only months before the Easter rising, extolling the virtues of German state socialism. This was an extract from a book, *Socialized Germany*, written by an American, Frederick C. Howe. Connolly gave over nearly two pages to this eulogy. According to Howe, Imperial Germany 'presents a new conception of the state' and one of the most remarkable features of this conception is its 'emphasis on human welfare'. The German nation 'thinks and act as a great human mechanism, adjusted in all its parts to efficiency and the advancement of the fatherland'. No one social class has been permitted 'exclusive control of the state', but rather each class 'has accepted sacrifices and limitations on its privileges when the national welfare was at stake'. No other country has 'so greatly improved the well-being of so large a portion of her people', and it is this that 'lies back of her military achievements'.[44]

The following month Connolly himself returned to the defence of the German Empire. The British Empire, he wrote, was 'a heterogeneous collection in which a very small number of self-governing communities connive at the subjugation, by force, of a vast number of despotically ruled subject populations'. The German Empire, however, was 'a homogeneous empire of self-governing peoples'. While he did not wish to be subject to either, nevertheless he believed that the German Empire 'contains in germ more of the possibilities of freedom and civilization' than the British. Moreover, British control of the high seas was an obstacle to the 'free industrial development' of the rest of the world upon which socialism waited. Only the full development of the capitalist system would, Connolly argues, 'make socialism possible', and the British Empire stood in the way.[45] A German victory would therefore bring socialism nearer. What all this nonsense was intended to do was to prepare his readership for the coming rising, a rising that was to ally itself quite openly with the German Empire. From this we can see quite clearly that Connolly's position was very different from Lenin's, but while his pro-German stance can be seen as seriously mistaken, it was nevertheless preferable to a pro-British stance. Connolly still recognised that the main enemy was at home.[46]

Connolly's Reputation

Before going on to look at the Easter Rising itself in the next chapter, it is worth considering the development of the historical and critical writing on Connolly and his embrace of Fenianism. Essentially the question at issue is whether or not Connolly's participation in the Rising involved a rupture in his politics or was the logical conclusion of his politics. O'Casey's 1919 critique of his political trajectory, *The Story of the Irish Citizen Army*, which argued for a dramatic break, almost an apostasy, had very little impact. It appeared at a time when Connolly and the other leaders of the Rising were still undergoing canonisation and were consequently beyond criticism. Much more important were the books written by W.P. Ryan of the *Daily Herald* and by his son Desmond Ryan, who actually fought in the Rising. In his *The Irish Labour Movement*, published in 1919, W.P. Ryan argued that the politics that Connolly had developed in the 1890s were those that he acted out in 1916. There was 'no evolution in Connolly's teaching' and everything he wrote after the 1890s was merely 'illustration, elucidation, not further discoveries'.[47] His son, Desmond, in his 1924 biography, *James Connolly*, went along with this, arguing that in 'the final phase one finds his early ideas in action' and that he was 'unchanging but developing until life gave out'. Nevertheless in the final chapter of the book, 'Connolly's Last Fight', where he actually presented a detailed discussion of Connolly's participation in the Rising, he proceeded to throw this thesis out the window. 'Why', Desmond Ryan asked, 'did James Connolly take part in the insurrection, he whose *Labour in Irish History* is one of the most damaging criticisms of mere insurrectionism imaginable'. He concluded that Connolly had been 'embittered, horrified, depressed and stung to militant action by the war's reactions on Ireland, by the works of a lifetime apparently perishing in an imperialist holiday, by national apostasy, by a mood in which love for the Irish people … mingled with a profound and proud despair'. This despair drove him into the arms of Padraic Pearse, the 'apostle of blood sacrifice to rouse a people', into 'a comradeship of despair as much as a comradeship of aspiration'.[48] Interestingly it was to be the thesis of continuity rather than the evidence of rupture that prevailed.

Certainly the most important contribution to the continuity thesis was C. Desmond Greaves' biography, *The Life and Times of James Connolly*, published in 1961. A staunch communist, Greaves argued that over the years Connolly had developed a political programme that prefigured that of the Communist International; that he was, in effect, the Irish Lenin. The two key elements that Greaves identified were Connolly's development of a 'stages theory' regarding the Irish revolution and his support for cross-class alliances. What this involved was an understanding on Connolly's part that Ireland was not ready for a socialist revolution in 1916, but was only at the 'democratic' stage and that this would have to be accomplished through an alliance with other social groups, for example, the middle-class Volunteers. Of course, this particular theory of revolution owes considerably more to Stalin than it does to Lenin. What it did, however, was enable Greaves to present Connolly's embrace of Fenianism not as a surrender produced by despair and desperation, but a deliberate step in a worked-out Marxist theory of revolution. Consequently, the Easter Rising was not a republican insurrection but a blow for socialism. He made much in this regard of Connolly referring to 'the first stage of freedom' as evidence of the stages theory. This might seem pretty conclusive, but unfortunately, it is a misquotation. What Connolly actually wrote was about 'the first days of freedom' so that the evidence produced to support the contention that Connolly had developed a stages theory actually supports the argument that he didn't. While on this occasion it seems likely that Greaves was merely guilty of over-enthusiasm, there can be little doubt that to establish that Connolly was the Irish Lenin he deliberately suppressed the evidence of his pro-German stance during the war.[49] In effect Greaves bent and twisted Connolly out of shape to make his ideas fit his Stalinist stages theory. The motive behind this exercise was a contemporary concern that the Irish left should see allying itself with and influencing the republican movement as the way forward. The book was first published, it should be remembered, in 1961.

One other point worth taking up concerns another crucial quotation that appears in Greaves' account and that has since been accepted as one of the keys to understanding Connolly's attitude in 1916. According to Greaves, shortly before the Rising, Connolly addressed the Citizen Army and told them 'to hold on to your rifles, as those with whom we are fighting may stop before our goal is reached. We are out for economic as well as political liberty'.[50] The trouble with this quotation, which is routinely reproduced in numerous books and articles, is that it has no reliable provenance, that there is no contemporary evidence that he actually said it. Moreover, it is starkly contradicted by just about everything we know for certain he did say and write. His criticisms of the republicans at the time were not that they weren't socialist, but that they weren't republican enough. And, of course, when they convinced him they were, he actually joined the IRB and was, as we shall see, to command the republican forces, both the

Volunteers and the Citizen Army, in Dublin during Easter Week. The fact is that Connolly did not argue that the Easter Rising was a blow in the struggle for socialism, but rather that it was an attempt to save the soul of the nation. The weight of evidence is overwhelming. W.K. Anderson's reassertion of the Greaves' position in his *James Connolly and the Irish Left*, published in 1994, demonstrates the problems this can cause. He insists that it is 'abundantly clear' that Connolly was fighting for socialism in 1916, but then goes on to say that some 'statement, perhaps even a proclamation of some kind stating clearly the goal of a Workers' Republic, would have been of immense assistance'.[51] This is really a remarkable way of proceeding. Apparently, Connolly forgot to make clear that the Rising had a socialist agenda. The evidence of what Connolly did say is ignored in favour of the evidence of what he did not say!

A number of historians coming from a variety of different political perspectives have challenged the Greaves thesis since the mid-1980s, myself, David Howell and Austen Morgan,[52] but certainly the most important contribution to the discussion has been Kieran Allen's *The Politics of James Connolly*, published in 1990. Allen presents a rigorously honest account of Connolly's political development, making clear where he thinks he was mistaken rather than trying to rewrite the man's life as if he shared his, that is Allen's, politics. This is certainly the right way to proceed. Indeed, a good case can be made that on occasions he is too critical of Connolly, judging him by a Bolshevik standard that had not yet emerged. Nevertheless, Allen confronts the problems in Connolly's politics in a way that puts Greaves to shame. Connolly's embrace of Fenianism is discussed as a product of his 'extreme pessimism' which led to a 'crisis in Connolly's political perspective'. Allen writes of him 'pandering to republican ideas', of his openly embracing 'the Fenian conception of insurrection' and of his justifying the Rising not in socialist, but in true Fenian terms'.[54] There is no doubt that Allen's account is borne out by the evidence. Where the current writer would disagree with him is with regard to his characterisation of the Easter Rising itself. We will turn to this now.

Notes

1   *Irish Worker*, 24 January 1914.
2   *Irish Worker*, 7 February 1914.
3   *Irish Worker*, 21 February 1914.
4   P.O. Cathasaigh, *The Story of the Irish Citizen Army*, (Dublin 1919) p. 13, 14.
5   *Irish Worker*, 9 May 1914.
6   *Irish Worker*, 23 May 1914.
7   *Irish Worker*, 30 May 1914. The *Irish Worker* was not alone in seeing the Irish Volunteers as potential strike-breakers. Patrick McIntyre in *The Toiler* was positively enthusiastic about the prospect.
8   *Irish Worker*, 6 June 1914.
9   *Irish Worker*, 27 June 1914.
10   *Irish Worker*, 27 June 1914.

11 O Cathasaigh, op cit. p. 45. This version of events has been challenged by C. Des-mond Greaves in his study of O'Casey's politics, *Sean O'Casey – Politics and Art* (London 1979) where he reduces the episode to an argument over a piano (p. 7). For a fuller discussion of this and other issues see my '"In the Hunger-Cry of the Nation's Poor is Heard the Voice of Ireland": Sean O'Casey and Politics 1908-1916', *Journal of Contemporary History*, 20, 1985.

12 See F.X Martin, *The Howth Gun-Running*, Dublin 1964.

13 *Forward*, 30 May 1914.

13 *Irish Worker*, 1 August 1914.

15 *Irish Worker*, 14 March 1914.

16 *Forward*, 21 March 1914.

17 *Irish Worker*, 21 March 1914.

18 *Irish Worker*, 30 May 1914.

19 *Irish Worker*, 8 August 1914. The same issue also lamented the fact that even staunch ICA members were enlisting in the British Army. For the attitude towards the war taken by Lenin and the Bolsheviks see in particular Tony Cliffe, *Lenin* 2 London 1976 Marcel Liebman, *Leninism Under Lenin*, London 1975, and O.H. Gankin and H.H. Fisher, *The Bolsheviks and the World War: The Origins of the Third International*, Stanford 1940. For Rosa Luxemburg's position on the war see J.P. Nettl, *Rosa Luxemburg* 2, London 1966.

20 *Irish Worker*, 15 August 1914.

21 *Irish Worker*, 26 September 1914.

22 *Irish Worker*, 10 October 1914.

23 *Irish Worker*, 17 October 1914.

24 *Irish Worker*, 3 October 1914.

25 *Irish Worker*, 10 October 1914.

26 Samuel Levenson, *James Connolly*, London 1973, p. 268.

27 Kieran Allen, *The Politics of James Connolly*, London 1990, p. 135.

28 See in particular Emmet Larkin, *James Larkin*, London 1965, p. 166.

29 *Shan Van Vocht*, January 1897.

30 *Irish Worker*, 23 January 1916.

31 O Cathasaigh, op cit, pp. 51-52.

32 *Rossa Souvenir*, July 1915.

33 *Workers' Republic*, 7 August 1915.

34 *Workers' Republic*, 5 February 1916.

35 *Workers' Republic*, 20 November 1915.

36 C. Desmond Greaves, *The Life and Times of James Connolly*, London 1972, p. 353.

37 Bernard Ransom, *Connolly's Marxism*, London 1980, p. 79.

38 *Irish Worker*, 29 August 1914.

39 *Irish Worker*, 5 September 1914.

40 *Irish Worker*, 17 October 1914.

41 *Irish Worker*, 14 November 1914.

42 *Irish Worker*, 26 September 1914.

43 *Workers' Republic*, 4 December 1915.

44 *Workers' Republic*, 9 February 1916.

45 *Workers' Republic*, 18 March 1916.

46   Larkin adopted a similar pro-German stance in America. On one occasion he celebrated Imperial Germany as 'The Friend of Small Nationalities', see David Emmons, *The Butte Irish: Class and Ethnicity in an American Mining Town 1875-1925*, Urbana 1989, p. 353.

47   W.P Ryan, *The Irish Labour Movement*, Dublin 1919, p. 237.

48   Desmond Ryan, *James Connolly*, Dublin 1924, pp. 97-100. Ryan went on to edit the first collections of Connolly's writings: *James Connolly: Socialism and Nationalism*, Dublin 1948; *James Connolly: Labour and Easter Week*, Dublin 1949; and *James Connolly: The Workers' Republic*, Dublin 1951.

49   Greaves, *Connolly*, op cit, pp. 384, 425. For his misquotation of Connolly see John Hoffman, 'The dialectic between democracy and socialism in the Irish national quarter', in Austen Morgan and Bob Purdie, eds, *Ireland: Divided Nation, Divided Class*, London 1980, p. 180.

50   Greaves, *Connolly*, op cit, p. 403.

51   W.K. Anderson, *James Connolly and the Irish Left*, Blackrock 1994, pp. 64, 75.

52   See my 'James Connolly and the Easter Rising', *Science and Society* 47, 1983; David Howell, *A Lost Left*, Manchester 1986; and Austen Morgan, *James Connolly: A Political Biography*, Manchester 1988.

53   Allen, op cit, pp. 132, 143, 147.

Chapter VII
The Rising

Was the Easter Rising carried out with a view to military success, to inflicting a serious defeat on the British, or was it merely intended as an armed demonstration, as a 'blood sacrifice' to keep alive 'the soul of the nation'? Historians of all political persuasions are divided over this. For Kieran Allen, Connolly was much too hard-headed to fall for any 'blood sacrifice' nonsense and the strategy behind the Rising was definitely 'premised on the chance of success'.[1] From a very different political perspective, Joe Lee insisted that the rebels struck when they 'felt they had the maximum chance of success'. Their judgement might have been faulty, but it was only once they were defeated that they couched 'their last testaments in terms of blood sacrifice'.[2] Moreover, one of the most recent accounts of the Rising itself, by Michael Foy and Brian Barton, argues that while the likes of Pearse and Plunkett ('literary men') might have been sympathetic to the concept of a 'blood sacrifice', the revolutionary enterprise was driven 'most of all by Clarke and MacDermott ... very practical and down-to-earth men' who felt they had a fighting chance.[3] According to Michael Laffan, however, while the rebels 'hoped and planned for a successful revolt ... their main concern was to make a heroic and principled gesture, to salvage what they viewed as the remnants of Ireland's tarnished honour'. For at least some of the leaders, while victory would have been 'a bonus', it was in reality a 'secondary consideration' because their real objective was to 'renew the tradition of insurrection'.[4] Most eccentrically, W.K. Anderson wrote enthusiastically of the Rising as 'a ridiculous, arguably insane enterprise' that was nevertheless 'a work of art ... the ultimate street theatre ... a brilliant theatrical success'.[5] And for Charles Townshend, while '(t)he evidence remains ambiguous' and the Military Council's plans 'can be read both ways', at the end the rebels went into the fight knowing they had no chance of success.[6]

What we shall attempt in this chapter is first of all a consideration of the evidence regarding the blood sacrifice or military success debate, secondly an assessment of how serious the prospects for military success actually were at the time, and thirdly attempt to place James Connolly in the context of these discussions. The chapter will also examine the religiosity of the rebels and the response of the left to the Rising.

Planning The Rising

The Easter Rising was the work of the Irish Republican Brotherhood, or more particularly of a faction within its leadership. Even though Redmond had secured the allegiance of the great majority of Volunteers in 1914, the IRB leadership nevertheless resolved to seize the opportunity provided by the war to prepare for an insurrection against British rule. There was, however, no agreement within the IRB as to what would be the appropriate circumstances for the staging of an insurrection. The IRB Constitution of 1873 specifically prohibited military action without popular support: 'The IRB shall await the decision of the Irish nation, as to the fit hour of inaugurating a war against England'.[7] This was a response to the failed 1867 Rising. There were many within the organisation who still felt that this was the correct approach, but others took the decision to subvert this prohibition. The key individuals involved in this enterprise were Tom Clarke and Sean MacDermott. To this end, they had established a military committee to plan the rising, but this body in effect constituted itself as an alternative leadership, as a Military Council superseding the Supreme Council. Bulmer Hobson was later to describe the Military Council as 'a secret society organised within a secret society'.[8] Together with their supporters in the American Clan-na-Gael, the Military Council prepared for an insurrection, regardless of popular support, in alliance with the German Empire. These proceedings were kept secret, not just from a majority of IRB members but also from those in the leadership known to be opposed to a premature rising. This was a quite remarkable way of proceeding and many of the difficulties that were to be encountered over the Easter weekend in 1916 derived from the extent to which MacDermott and company were deceiving their own comrades as to their intentions.

What evidence is there regarding the state of popular opinion at the time? One simple exercise is to compare the numbers of those in the Irish Volunteers with the number of those who volunteered to fight for the British Empire. At the time of the breakaway from Redmond's Volunteers in 1914, the reconstituted Irish Volunteers probably had a membership of some 5,000. By Easter 1916 this had increased to around 15,000. When war broke out in 1914 there were already 58,000 Irishmen in the British Army and subsequently another 140,000 were to volunteer. These 200,000 men together with their families and friends constituted a significant body of opinion supporting the British war effort. Moreover, there is no reason to doubt that Irish public opinion generally was behind them. During Easter Week, while sixty-four rebels were to be killed fighting in Dublin, 570 men of the 16th (Irish) division were to be killed fighting at Hulluch on the

Western Front.[9] This is not to say that support for the war was not weakening by 1916 and that as the slaughter continued war weariness and disillusion would certainly increase. It did in every combatant country, and Ireland would certainly not have been exempt. But at the time of the Easter Rising Irish popular opinion certainly did not support rebellion against the British in alliance with the German Empire.

It seems clear that the Military Council intended to compensate for lack of popular support by means of German assistance, indeed it was hoped that the landing of German troops in Ireland would actually begin the process of rallying popular support. To secure this German involvement, Sir Roger Casement and Joseph Plunkett, representing both Clan-na-Gael and the IRB, were sent to Germany. Here Casement tried unsuccessfully to recruit Irish prisoners-of-war to the rebel cause and together they presented the German High Command with their plans for a rising. What they envisaged was the landing of 12,000 German troops in the west. This force was to seize Limerick and rally popular support, equipping the thousands expected to flock to the cause with the 40,000 rifles they were to bring with them. The arrival of German troops would provide the signal for the rebels to seize control of Dublin which would be held until the German-Irish forces could march to the relief. The plan was explicitly modelled on the French landings at Killala in County Mayo during the 1798 rebellion. Once success was achieved there would be 'a victory parade down O'Connell Street by Irish Volunteers and Prussian grenadiers with crowds cheering and throwing flowers as bands played "A Nation Once Again" and "Deutschland Uber Alles"'. The newly independent Irish state would ally itself with Germany, Austria-Hungary, Bulgaria and Turkey and provide the German Navy with bases.[10] Would this new state be a republic? According to two leading members of the IRB, Desmond Fitzgerald and Ernest Blythe, both supporters of the Rising, there were those among the IRB leadership, including Pearse, Plunkett and Mac-Donagh, who were contemplating the establishment of an independent Ireland with a German prince on the throne, obviously not a Protestant Hohenzollern, but a Catholic Bavarian, Prince Joachim.[11] What Connolly would have made of this we have no way of knowing, but it is hard to imagine him enthralled at the prospect.

Regardless of the rights and wrongs of the German alliance, Foy and Barton in their account of the Rising make the point that the Casement-Plunkett plan was clear evidence of the seriousness of the Military Council's military intention: they had a plan for military victory, not a plan for a blood sacrifice, and every intention of driving the British out of Ireland. So much seems incontrovertible. Nevertheless, they do go on to acknowledge that there were people on the Military Council who did think in terms of a 'blood sacrifice'.[12] It will be the contention here that once it became clear that a German landing was not a serious proposition, it was the 'blood sacrifice' concept that came to the fore, not least as far as Joseph Plunkett himself was concerned. Moreover, the blood sacrifice was embraced, not just by the likes of Pearse, but also by the hard-nosed realists, in particular, Jim Connolly and Sean MacDermott.

How realistic was the Casement-Plunkett plan on its own terms? There was the assumption that a German landing would be greeted as a liberation by the majority of the Irish people. There was, however, no evidence to support this belief, indeed all the evidence pointed the other way. Plunkett and his comrades were engaged in the most monumental self-delusion in this regard. Moreover, this delusion was not shared by the German High Command that had no intention of sacrificing 12,000 troops to such a scheme. Without the support of a popular uprising and with British control of the seas such an expeditionary force clearly would have been doomed. Without the prospect of German intervention, even on the Military Council's own terms, any prospect of success was gone.

Pearse

Padraic Pearse was to emerge as the chief exponent of the doctrine of the 'blood sacrifice' in both his literary and his political writings. The head of a Catholic private school, St. Enda's and a leading member of the Gaelic League, Pearse had supported Home Rule up until the Unionists had armed to prevent it. This had converted him to physical force and in December 1913 Bulmer Hobson had sworn him into the IRB. By May 1915 he was a member of the Military Council. While Clarke and MacDermott were certainly the driving force behind preparations for a rising, Pearse was to become its chief ideologist, its public spokesperson and, indeed, a strong case can be made that it was his imaginative conception of revolution as redemption that was to be realised on the streets of Dublin. His role was not just symbolic, however. Pearse's success in establishing a rapport with Connolly was a crucial element in the Military Council's preparations. Moreover, as Director of Organisation of the Volunteers he had a vital practical role to play in the actual launching of the Rising. Pearse was in the key position where he could mobilise the Volunteers for rebellion without the knowledge of either the official leadership or the rank and file. His role in 1916 was pivotal.[13]

Pearse was first and foremost a devout Catholic. No understanding of his politics is possible without grasping this. He firmly believed in the immanence of God. In his play, *Iosagan*, for instance, the child Jesus is shown playing with contemporary Irish children and bringing a priest to hear the last confession of a repentant anti-cleric. Pearse argued that there was 'nothing improbable' in this, that it was not 'outside the bounds of everyday experience'. He insisted

> I know a priest who believes that he was summoned to the death-bed of a parishioner by Our Lord in person; and there are many hundreds of people in the countryside I write of who know that on certain nights Mary and her child walk through the villages and if the cottage doors be left open, enter, and sit awhile at the firesides of the poor.[14]

In another play, *The Master*, the Archangel Michael appears as a sign to the king who is demanding proof of Christianity.

It is important to recognise that for Pearse and for many other republicans their nationalism was a Catholic nationalism. Steadfast adherence to the Catholic faith through the long years of persecution at the hands of the Protestant Ascendancy was one of the hallmarks of Irish nationalism. This is not to say that theirs was an exclusive or sectarian nationalism, indeed Protestants were positively welcomed to enlist in the national cause, a sharp contrast with Orangeism. Nevertheless they saw Irish nationalism and Catholicity as inseparably entwined. Pearse gave powerful voice to this belief. One of his sharpest objections to the Home Rule leaders was that they 'have not recognized in their people the image and the likeness of God. Hence, the nation to them is not all holy, a thing inviolate and inviolable, a thing that a man dare not sell or dishonour on pain of eternal perdition', whereas for him national freedom was like 'a divine religion' bearing 'the marks of unity, of sanctity, of catholicity, of apostolic succession'. He was prepared to 'stake my mortal and all my immortal hopes' on the conviction that republicanism was divinely inspired, and 'I ask the men and women of my generation to stake their mortal and immortal hopes with me'. Of considerable importance in his political writings was his seldom noticed celebration of 'the Fenian priest'. Of him 'it was said that he had a Sodality of the Sacred Heart composed to a man of sworn Fenians' and that the Fenians came from miles around for confession with him in preference to their own parish priests. He warned Pearse of the danger of missed opportunities when Britain was at war with the Boers: 'GOD ALMIGHTY WON'T GO ON GIVING US CHANCES if we let every chance slip. You can't expect He'll give more chances than He gave the Jews. He'll turn his back on us'. In his writings Pearse assimilated Wolfe Tone, Robert Emmet, Thomas Davis and John Mitchel, all Protestants, into the pantheon of Catholic nationalism: 'God spoke to Ireland through Tone'; Emmet died 'that his people might live, even as Christ died. Be assured that such a death always means a redemption'; Mitchel, he fervently believed, 'did really hold converse with God; he did really deliver God's word to man, delivered it fiery tongued'. These were not empty rhetorical flourishes, but statements of deeply felt literal belief. The role of God's instrument was the role in which Pearse cast himself and his comrades: 'Who like us', he asked a republican audience in New York, 'has carried Christ's word of charity about the earth? But the Christ that said, "My peace I leave you, My peace I give you", is the same Christ that said, "I bring not peace but a sword". There can be no peace between right and wrong, between truth and falsehood'. 'Ireland', he wrote elsewhere, 'will not find Christ's peace until she has taken Christ's sword'.[15]

In his own mind Pearse managed to merge pre-Christian Gaelic mythology with contemporary Irish Catholicism. He was a particular admirer of 'the heroic figure of Cuchulainn' and attempted to inculcate his warrior virtues to such effect at St. Enda's that Desmond Ryan, a student at the school, described Cuchulainn as 'an invisible member of the school staff'.[16] As Aodh de Blacam recalled, at St. Enda's 'the sagas were a vital part of his education scheme. He loved to dwell on the tale of Cuchulain, boy hero of Ulster…'.[17] For Martin Daly, Pearse 'hoped no less than to see Ireland teeming with Cuchulains; he conceived education, apart from its essential Reading, Writing and Arithmetic, as the art of giving Cuchulains to the country' Pearse's 'ideal Irishman … was a Cuchulain baptised'.[18] And indeed, it seems that his original conception of his life's work was that it would be his students, some of the boys trained by him, who would take up arms to free Ireland rather than himself. In May 1913 he wrote that

> I dreamt that I saw a pupil of mine, one of our boys at St. Enda's, standing alone upon a platform above a mighty sea of people; and I understood that he was about to die there for some august cause, Ireland's or another. He looked extraordinarily proud and joyous, lifting his head with a smile of amusement … I felt an inexplicable exhilaration as I looked on him and this exhilaration heightened rather than diminished by my consciousness that the great silent crowd regarded the boy with pity and wonder rather than with approval – as a fool who was throwing away his life rather than a martyr that was doing his duty. It would have been so easy to die before an applauding crowd or before a hostile crowd: but to die before that silent unsympathetic crowd.[19]

In fact, he was to cast himself in the role of the fool, of the man, whose sacrifice would be vindicated.

Pearse advocated insurrection as a means of redeeming the Irish nation from its apostasy, from its support for the British Empire and its abandonment of separatism. He envisaged the Rising not as a military operation, but as a deliberate blood sacrifice. The handful of rebels in their hopeless adventure would save the Irish people. In his last and most self-consciously autobiographical play, *The Singer*, he wrote: 'One man can free a people as one Man redeemed the world. I will take no pike, I will go into battle with bare hands. I will stand up before the Gall as Christ hung naked before man on the tree'.[20] Once it became clear that German intervention, the military justification for the rising, was not forthcoming, it was the conception of revolution as blood sacrifice that gripped the rebel leadership, Connolly included. During the actual fighting, Ryan was with Pearse in the GPO:

> I stood beside him as he sat upon a barrel, looking intently at the flames, very silent, his slightly-flushed face crowned by his turned-up hat. Suddenly he turned to me with the very last question that I ever expected to hear from him: 'It was the right thing to do, was it not?' he asked curiously. 'Yes', I replied in astonishment …
> . He spoke again. 'When we are all wiped out, people will blame us for everything, condemn us. But for this protest, the war would have ended and nothing would

have been done. After a few years they will see the meaning of what we tried to do .... Dublin's name will be glorious for ever.[21]

Pearse was not the only advocate of the blood sacrifice. We have already noticed Connolly's proclamations that 'the fight in Ireland has been for the soul of the nation' and that 'no agency less potent than the red tide of war on Irish soil will ever be able to enable the Irish race to recover its self-respect'.[22] They were joined in their advocacy by Sean MacDermott. The man who is most often singled out as the best guarantee that the Rising was not a blood sacrifice actually toured the country preparing the IRB membership for that very thing. MacDermott told a meeting in Kerry that

Nationalism as known to Tone and Emmet is almost dead in the country and a spurious substitute, as taught by the Irish Parliamentary Party, exists. The generation now growing old is the most decadent generation nationally since the Norman invasion, and the Irish patriotic spirit will die forever unless a blood sacrifice is made in the next few years. The spark of nationality left is the result of the sacrifice of the Manchester Martyrs nearly half a century ago, and it will be necessary for some of us to offer ourselves as martyrs if nothing better can be done to preserve the Irish national spirit and hand it down unsullied to future generations.[23]

Into Battle

While the IRB Military Council was secretly planning and preparing for a rising, as far as Connolly was concerned the Volunteers under MacNeill's leadership had adopted a passive stance. He was completely unaware of the Military Council's activities. Indeed, he despaired of the Volunteers ever taking up arms and in his desperation made clear on a number of occasions that if necessary he would lead his few hundred, poorly armed Citizen Army members into battle alone. This in itself is enough to call into question the basis upon which he was making his political judgements at the time. In October 1915 the Citizen Army carried out a mock attack on Dublin Castle, positively inviting suppression. To prevent him from acting prematurely and calling down repression on the whole movement, in January 1916 Connolly was kidnapped on the orders of the IRB Military Council, informed of the secret preparations that were underway, and of the proposed date for the rising – 23 April, Easter Sunday. He was, as we have already seen, initiated into the Brotherhood and co-opted onto the Military Council as its sixth member. Connolly had embraced Fenianism.

The Military Council's intention was to turn the country-wide Volunteer manoeuvres planned for Easter Sunday into an insurrection on the pretext of a British attempt to suppress the organisation. With the official leadership of the Volunteers opposed to a rising except in self-defence, the Military Council planned to stampede the by now 15,000 strong force into an armed confrontation with the British. To this end, Joseph Plunkett, returned from Germany, produced forged British documents ordering the suppression of the Volunteers and the arrest of not just republicans, but Home Rulers, and the Archbishop of Dublin. The plan was that once the Volunteers had assembled on Easter Sunday, MacNeill would order them into action to forestall the British. This tricking of their unwitting comrades into insurrection is quite unprecedented. Not only did the insurrection not have any popular support, but as Michael Collins later confessed, most of the Volunteer rank and file shared MacNeill's views: 'it was we who were in a minority'.[24] The rising was intended to coincide with the landing of arms and ammunition from a German ship, the *Aud*, in Tralee Bay. There were to be no German troops, but by now even the arrival of German arms was irrelevant and no steps were taken to organise their safe unloading and distribution.[25] These plans were a closely guarded secret, so secret that even the IRB President, Denis McCullough, was not informed until he insisted on being told what was going on a week before Easter weekend. Other members of the Supreme Council were not told until Good Friday or Easter Saturday. This was patently not the way to organise a successful insurrection. Inevitably the plans miscarried.

Meanwhile, Casement was on his way back to Ireland by German submarine, ostensibly to join the rising as one of its leaders, but in reality to urge the Military Council to call it off. Without German intervention or popular support, he regarded the enterprise as doomed. With him was Robert Monteith. They landed at Banna Strand on 20 April and Casement was promptly arrested. Only at this point did MacNeill finally realise that he was being deliberately and systematically misled and made clear his intention of cancelling the Sunday manoeuvres. He was, however, persuaded to accept the inevitability of insurrection by Pearse who informed him that the *Aud* was on the seas with a consignment of arms. At this point, Hobson, still a leading IRB member in Dublin, was kidnapped at gunpoint by men loyal to the Military Council to prevent him interfering with their plans. When news reached MacNeill that the *Aud* had been intercepted by the British and scuttled by her captain, he went ahead and issued an order of cancellation. It is worth remembering that for the great majority of Volunteers what was being cancelled was not an armed insurrection, but Sunday manoeuvres. Pearse pretended to accept his decision. The Military Council's plans were thrown into chaos. After much discussion they decided to stage the rising on Easter Monday with such forces as they could rally. Pearse replaced MacNeill as commander-in-chief of a rump of the Volunteers and at the head of a joint force of some 700 Volunteers and 120 members of the Citizen Army, he seized control of the centre of Dublin.[26]

The Easter Rising took place without any popular support whatsoever. Patrick O'Hegarty, himself a leading IRB member subsequently wrote:

The insurrection came upon a people like a thunderbolt. They had not been expecting it, and they did not want it …. The insurrection was therefore universally and explosively unpopular. The populace fraternised with the British soldiery during the fighting, gave them food and smiles … the resolutions of the various public bodies in the country condemning the rising may still be read. If Ireland as a whole could have got hold of Tom Clarke and his Comrades during that week it would have torn them to pieces …. The insurrection of 1916 was a forlorn hope and a deliberate blood sacrifice. The men who planned it and led it did not expect to win. They knew they could not win. They knew that the people were against them and that the people would hate them for it. But they counted upon being executed afterwards and they knew that that would save Ireland's soul.[27]

Connolly certainly knew that he was leading the men and women of the Citizen Army out to certain defeat. Early on the morning of Easter Monday, he met William O'Brien at Liberty Hall, and told him 'We are going out to be slaughtered'. O'Brien asked 'Is there no chance of success' and Connolly replied 'None whatsoever'.[28]

The Rising as a Military Affair

Looking back on the rising, Robert Monteith wrote:

It is hard to see what the Council hoped to accomplish by marching and taking up positions in the General Post Office, the Four Courts, Boland's Mills and Stephen's Green, or any of the positions occupied … without artillery or machine-guns their position was hopeless from the very beginning; their zone of fire bounded by the length or width of a street. They were there to await the closing of the ring of death around them.[29]

Under Connolly's command the rebel forces occupied the centre of Dublin and prepared entrenched positions to await British attack. Few in number and equipped with only light weapons, their fate as Monteith observed, was certain. There was to be no spontaneous rallying of popular support and no German landing. Indeed, their survival was really only a matter of how long it took the British to assemble a large enough force to encompass their destruction. They could do nothing to hinder that process. All their courage and determination would simply be overwhelmed by the numbers and firepower the British were able to concentrate against them. By the end of the fighting the British outnumbered the rebels twenty to one.[30]

To what extent was Connolly responsible for this strategy? He was in command of the rebels' Dublin forces, of both the Volunteers and the Citizen Army, reconstituted as the Irish Republican Army. More to the point this was precisely the strategy that he had advocated in the articles on revolutionary warfare that he had written for the *Workers Republic*. Here Connolly argued that in the sort of urban fighting the Citizen Army was going to be engaged in 'the defence is of almost overwhelming importance'. What was secondary was to seize and fortify positions that threatened 'the supremacy and existence of the enemy' so that they could be compelled to attack them. If the defence was conducted with the necessary 'combination of genius, skill and courage' out of it would 'grow the flower of military success'. As far as the deployment of artillery against the rebel positions was concerned, he drew on what he believed to be the experience of the 1905 insurrection in Moscow. He argued quite erroneously that the use of artillery in 'the close quarters of street fighting was against all the teaching of military science'. Had it not been for a lack of rifles (he thought 800 rifles would have been enough), the Moscow revolution 'would have ended in the annihilation of the artillery' and the Tsarist forces could 'only have taken Moscow from the insurgents at the cost of an appalling loss of life'. He actually used the Alamo as an example to be emulated: it was 'one of those defeats which are often more valuable to a cause than many loudly trumpeted victories'.[31] On other occasions, Connolly argued that the British would never use artillery in Dublin because of the damage to capitalist property that would result. Darrell Figgis, a republican activist, wrote that 'he, the mocker of national illusions, nursed illusions that none of the others did' and held him 'mainly responsible for the mistaken strategy of occupying public buildings'.[32]

What happened in Dublin during Easter Week was that the British did indeed attempt to storm the rebel positions and suffered heavy casualties. The experience that the British had at Mount Street Bridge, where a handful of volunteers under Lieutenant Michael Malone, held up their advance, was testimony to the defensive potential of even poorly armed and trained troops when capably led and fiercely determined. For the loss of only five men killed, the volunteers inflicted 242 casualties, killed and wounded, on the British, before being forced to withdraw. A large proportion of total British losses was suffered here.[33] Once the British had learned a proper respect for their opponents, however, frontal assaults were abandoned and artillery was deployed. The fate of the Rising was sealed. The rebel headquarters in the GPO was subjected to a relentless bombardment to which they had no answer and the rebels were inevitably forced to surrender.

In retrospect, it seems clear that Connolly's military writings were fundamentally mistaken and that the rebel dispositions for which he was in good part responsible ensured their complete and total defeat. Nevertheless this has not stopped some of his admirers praising his military expertise. For Michael O'Riordan he was 'a proficient military scientist' and even more extravagantly Peter Beresford Ellis considers him 'a revolutionary soldier whose concepts and methods have been proved on countless anti-imperialist battlefields in all parts of the world'.[34] Connolly's tragedy, of course, was that he did not live to learn from his mistakes. Too many of his admirers either do not acknowledge or even positively celebrate those mistakes.

It is worth briefly comparing Connolly's understanding of the lessons of Moscow in 1905 with Leon Trotsky's. In *1905* Trotsky wrote quite categorically

Also comrades, do not occupy fortified buildings. The troops will always recapture them or simply destroy them by artillery fire. Let our fortresses be courtyards with entrances front and back, and all places from which it is easy to fire and withdraw. Even if they capture such a place, they will find no one yet it will cost them dear.

Of course, this sort of mobile guerrilla fighting was predicated on popular support. As Trotsky once again put it, the city's working class 'formed a living wall between the guerrillas and the government troops' and 'surrounded the armed revolutionaries with an atmosphere of active sympathy'. Indeed, for Trotsky preparing for an insurrection specifically did not mean that the revolutionaries proceed 'to lay in stocks of arms, prepare a plan of military operations, consign the participants of the rising to particular places'. This was to mirror how the military authorities would proceed. What preparing an insurrection meant for Trotsky was 'first and foremost, enlightening the people, explaining to them that open conflict was inevitable, that only might can defend right, that the struggle had to be continued to the end, that there was no other way'.[35] But, of course, what Trotsky was advocating was the way that a working-class revolutionary struggle should be conducted, whereas what Pearse, MacDermott *and* Connolly were engaged in was something completely different.

Even before the Rising there were those arguing that guerrilla warfare was the only way for Irish revolutionaries to effectively confront the British Empire. Sean O'Casey, Robert Monteith, Bulmer Hobson and others had all urged a guerrilla strategy, but had been ignored. Others were to survive to learn from the Easter experience. Michael Collins, for example, remarked that 'we were literally a corporal's guard planning to attack the armed forces of an Empire'.[36] The Rising, he believed, 'had the air of a Greek tragedy about it .... On the whole I think the Rising was bungled terribly, costing many a good life'. He still thought highly of Connolly: he was 'a realist .... There was an air of earthy directness about Connolly .... I would have followed him through hell had such action been necessary'.[37] There was to be no repeat of Easter Week during the War of Independence though.

The Working Class and Easter Week

In his memoir of the Rising, *Enchanted By Dreams*, Joe Good, a young London Irishman recalled a middle-aged man, 'an American and a revolutionary', approaching the assembling volunteers and asking to be allowed to join the fight. He called people 'comrade'. Good recognised the man from Hyde Park corner in 1913, where he had been 'speaking on a platform ... on behalf of the IWW'. He was in Dublin to see Connolly who he knew from America and was determined to strike a blow against the British Empire. As Good observes, he 'was to die fighting with us and for us, but we do not know where he was buried and I have never found out his name'.[38] The heroic stand of this unknown American exemplifies the courage of the men and women who went out to confront overwhelming odds on Easter Monday. No amount of criticism of the politics of the enterprise should detract from their bravery and dedication.

Connolly himself fought bravely throughout Easter Week until he was seriously wounded on the Thursday. He impressed all those who came into contact with him with his leadership and his courage. According to Joe Good, despite his distinctly unmilitary appearance ('rather pot-bellied with bandy legs and a disorderly moustache'), 'it was the courage of Connolly, more than any other leader, which held the men together'. As for the Citizen Army men, they 'were hard-bitten men: far better to have with you than against you, veterans of South Africa and economic wars'.[39] The Citizen Army, of course, practised equality between the sexes and there were also a number of remarkable women taking part in the fighting: Constance Markiewicz is the best known, but there was also Helena Maloney, actress and trade union activist, Kathleen Lynn, doctor and socialist, who later founded St. Ultan's Hospital for infants, Winifred Carney, Connolly's secretary and trade union activist, and others.[40] They were without any doubt a heroic band of men and women. But recognition of this should not be allowed to conceal the extent to which they were acting in isolation from the Dublin working class.

While Connolly claimed to speak for the working class, the Citizen Army had only mobilised around 150 members for the fight. Connolly was the only member of the ITGWU's fourteen man executive to take part in the Rising and in fact had made no serious attempt to rally the union's rank and file. In 1916 the ITGWU only had some 5,000 members and was still recovering from the Great Lockout. He made no attempt to call a general strike either against the war or in support of the Rising, instead the union's members remained by and large passive observers. One simple reason for his failure to issue a strike call was the knowledge that there was no popular support for their cause and that anyway the labour movement was too weak. Indeed, in 1916 there were considerably more ITGWU members fighting with the British Army in France than took part in the Easter Rising.[41] A good case can be made that working-class participation in the events of Easter Week was largely confined to taking advantage of the disappearance of the police to engage in widespread looting. As the *Irish Times* 'Rebellion Supplement' complained:

> The 'underworld' of the city quickly realised their opportunity, and first tackled the shops in Lower Sackville Street. The windows were smashed, and hordes of people crowded into the shops, returning with bundles of wearing apparel of all descriptions .... More looting took place in the streets in the vicinity of Nelson's Pillar. Messrs. Lawrence's large photographic and toy emporium in Upper Sackville Street was one of the principal places cleared. The crowd of looters had

matters all their own way for hours, and revelled in the destruction of the property. Some exciting scenes were witnessed when the fireworks were brought out and exploded. Rockets rushed up in the air and burst with a sound like a cannon, and all the smaller sorts of fireworks were thrown whizzing about amongst the crowd. Finally the premises were set on fire and burned to the ground.[42]

According to one contemporary account, 'for days to come all kinds of luxuries could be bought in Dublin slums for a trifle. You could have a silver fox for a shilling or two; a pair of hand-made boots for what you cared to give; and a gold watch for half-a-crown'. The post-Rising police raids in working-class districts were not in search of fleeing rebels, but searches for stolen property'.[43]

Keeping Faith

One aspect of the Rising that is still generally neglected is the extent to which Catholicism informed the rebels' beliefs and helped sustain them through the fight. Pearse was not alone in his devotions. In his account of the Rising, Brian O'Higgins, a rank-and-file participant, recalled how there

> was hardly a man in the Volunteer ranks who did not prepare for death on Easter Saturday, and there were many who felt as they knelt at the altar rails on Easter Sunday morning that they were doing no more than fulfilling their Easter duty – that they were renouncing the world and all the world held for them and making themselves worthy to appear before the Judgment Seat of God.

O'Higgins was stationed on the roof of the GPO building throughout the fighting, and he recounts how, together with his comrades-in-arms, he took turns reciting the rosary, every half hour, day and night.[44] Margaret Skinnider, a Citizen Army member, who was wounded three times while trying to bomb a British machine gun post in the Shelbourne Hotel, wrote later of how

> Whenever there came a lull in business or fighting, the men would begin to sing either rebel songs or those old lays dear to Irishmen the world over. And sometimes they knelt in prayer. Protestants and Catholics side by side. From the very beginning there was a sense of the religious character in what we were doing. This song and prayer at the post office were all natural, devoid of self-consciousness. A gay song would follow a solemn prayer, and somehow was not out of harmony with it.[45]

The rebels were convinced in their own minds that they were fighting for both Faith and Fatherland. Only by recognising the religious fervour (not too strong a word) that gripped them does the Military Council's despatch early in April 1916 of Joseph Plunkett's father, George, a papal count, to Rome to seek Pope Benedict XV's blessing for the imminent insurrection become in any way explicable.[46] On the actual morning of the Rising, as an act of courtesy, he was sent to inform the Archbishop of Dublin of the rebels' intentions.[47]

At first sight it might seem that the Citizen Army's participation in the Rising might involve some qualification of its 'Catholic' character. This is not the case. Indeed, the religiosity of the Citizen Army men and women really proves the case. According to Desmond Ryan, it was Padraic Pearse who persuaded Connolly to receive the last rites before facing the firing squad. When told that Connolly had agreed to this, Pearse remarked 'Thank God. It was one thing I was anxious about'.[48] The sincerity of his reconciliation with the Church is positively demonstrated by his last request to his wife, Lily, a Protestant, that she should 'go under instruction in the Catholic Faith and then, if you feel you can do so, be received into the Catholic Church'. Connolly acknowledged that 'he had not always been an exemplary Catholic, but he wanted very much now, that she would do this for him'.[49] The Citizen Army's second-in-command, Michael Mallin, secretary of the Silk Weavers' Union who had spent twelve years in the British Army, also made his peace with the Church. While awaiting execution, he wrote to his pregnant wife urging that his daughter, Una, should be directed towards becoming a nun, and his son, Joseph, towards becoming a priest, 'as penance for our sins'. He consoled her that 'I do not believe our Blood has been shed in vain. I believe Ireland will come out greater and grander but she must not forget she is Catholic she must keep faith'.[50] Neither Connolly nor Mallin made any declaration of their socialist beliefs on their way to the firing squad, something that seems to show pretty conclusively that the Rising had no connection with those beliefs as far as they were concerned. This is not to say that they had abandoned socialism, but rather that they did not consider it relevant in 1916.

Of equal moment with Connolly's reconciliation with the Church was the part the experience of the rising played in bringing about the conversion of its two most prominent Protestant participants: Sir Roger Casement and Countess Markiewicz. Casement asked to be received into the Church while awaiting execution although this appears to have been the culmination of a protracted search for a faith.[51] After he had been hanged, a manuscript was found among his papers in which he had written:

> If I die tomorrow, bury me in Ireland, and I shall die in the Catholic Faith, for I accept it fully now. It tells me what my heart sought long – but I saw it in the faces of the Irish. Now I know what it was I loved in them – the chivalry of Christ speaking through human eyes.[52]

As for Markiewicz, she had her outlook transformed by the religious devotion she had observed among the Citizen Army rank and file during Easter Week. Her friend, Esther Roper wrote that

> Many years afterwards she described to me the last night at the College of Surgeons. There were wounded to be nursed, as well as military duties done. In all this she

took part. Through the night those assembled there prayed for the dead and the living. A great peace was over them waiting for the end. Constance wanted to join in the prayers, ... face to face with death she was deeply impressed by the reality of spiritual things to these men and women among whom she had lived. As she shared their prayers there came to her a vision of the Unseen, which wrought such a change in her that from that moment to her, too, the things that are seen became temporal and things that are unseen, eternal.

According to Hanna Sheehy Skeffington, it was 'the heroic ease by which the simple unlettered men of the Irish Citizen Army went to meet their deaths' that determined the Countess to become a Catholic.[53] Markiewicz subsequently commemorated her experience in the College of Surgeons in a poem originally entitled 'To A Comrade' but later retitled 'The Rosary'. It was dedicated to William Partridge, who had fought in the Rising and died soon after his release from prison in July 1917:

On our rough altar white flowers shine and bloom
Intensifying dusky waves that move
Around the tall black Cross. One hope, one prayer
Filled all our hearts, one perfect holy Faith
Lifted our souls. As we knelt humbly there,
Your silvery voice, soft as a dying breath
Was answered by a hundred strong and clear,
Craving a grace from her whom all hold dear –
"Mary! Be with us at the hour of death".[54]

She was received into the Catholic Church in June 1917.

The Surrender

The rebels surrendered unconditionally on Saturday 29 April, although it took another two days for the process to actually be completed. Casualties on both sides were surprisingly light in the circumstances. The British had 132 soldiers and police killed, while the rebels had 64 killed, including eleven Citizen Army members. Around 250 civilians were killed, at least some of them shot out of hand by British troops, sometimes acting under orders, sometimes not. The British commander in Ireland, General Sir John Maxwell, confessed to his wife that there may have been cases where troops 'murdered innocent civilians in cold blood' but to Field Marshal Lord Kitchener he wrote: 'I wonder there was not more'.[55] Among the innocent civilians murdered by the British was the Dublin socialist and Herald Leaguer, Francis Sheehy Skeffington. He regarded the Rising as a mistake and rather than take part tried to organise socialists and suffragettes to put a stop to the looting. He was arrested by British troops and summarily executed on the orders of Captain Bowen Colthurst.[56] Of the actual rebel prisoners who surrendered, 183 were court-martialled and fifteen of these were subsequently executed by firing squad: Thomas MacDonagh, Tom Clarke, Padraic Pearse, Michael O'Hanrahan, William Pearse, Eamon Ceannt, Joseph Plunkett, Sean Heuston, Con Colbert, John McBride, Thomas Kent, Michael Mallin, Sean MacDermott and James Connolly. Connolly was the last to be shot, tied to chair because of his leg wound. According to Maxwell, Connolly and MacDermott were 'the worst of the lot'.[57]

When the rebels surrendered they were left in little doubt as to the hostility of most Dubliners. Frank Robbins, in his memoir, remembered how on a number of occasions during the fighting they had been attacked by outraged civilians, but now as they were marched through the streets under British guard, 'we were left in no doubt as to the opinion of the vast majority of the citizens of Dublin'. The British troops were cheered: 'The shouts of "good old Staffords", "Shoot the traitors" and "Bayonet the bastards" seem now almost incredible'.[58] Joe Good remembered how 'Women ran out of the side streets, screaming at us, and would have attacked us, no doubt, but for our British escorts … they shouted "Bayonet them! Bayonet them!"'. Some of these women were well-to-do, but most were 'poor "shawlies" from the back streets'.[59] Batt O'Connor recalled one particular woman, 'who called out to my guard not to take the trouble to take me prisoner but to shoot me'.[60] As Robert Brennan recalled: 'The crowd left no doubt in our minds as to what they wanted done to us'. He was still surprised to see some of Redmond's Volunteers 'jeering at us'. If the British had only had the sense not to execute the rebel leaders, 'our political opponents would have ridiculed us to death'.[61] Even at this moment, however, there is evidence that at least some Dubliners were already beginning to show sympathy. F.A Mackenzie saw the prisoners cheered where he was observing the scene and believed that there was already considerable sympathy for them 'in poorer districts'.[62]

What transformed the situation though was the executions. John Dillon, one of the Home Rule leaders told the House of Commons on 11 May that the Rising was 'the first rebellion that ever took place in Ireland where you had the majority on your side'. This was the life's work of people like him 'and now you are washing out our whole life work in a sea of blood'.[63] The executions led to a posthumous rallying behind the rebel cause that was to eventually sweep away the Home Rulers, elevate Sinn Féin to a position of political dominance and provide the popular support necessary for the successful waging of a guerrilla war against the British. The politics that triumphed, however, were those of Padraic Pearse.

The Rising and the Left

Shortly before his execution, Connolly told his daughter, Nora, that the socialists 'will never understand why I am here. They all forget I am an Irishman'.[64] In effect this was an acknowledgement that the Rising had no socialist credentials and that consequently his involvement would be incomprehensible to many of his former comrades in Britain and elsewhere. Thomas Johnston, the editor of the Glasgow socialist newspaper, *Forward* that had carried many of Connolly's articles and was banned in January 1916, later remembered how puzzled he had been that Connolly, 'a cool level-headed analyst, precise, careful and accustomed to weighing evidence and words … had ever come to be a leader in an armed rebellion against the British Government, when his Citizen Army insurgents could only muster 118 rifles'. None of Connolly's articles for *Forward* had 'ever give a hint that he was developing into a military insurrectionist Sinn Féiner'.[65] Most sympathetic at the time was Sylvia Pankhurst's socialist-feminist newspaper, *The Woman's Dreadnought* which described the Rising as 'mistaken' but nevertheless praised the courage of the rebels and insisted that 'their desperate venture was undoubtedly animated by high ideals'. It went on: 'To many of us who believe that neither race nor creed should separate the workers of the world, it is a matter of regret that the old position of Larkin and Connolly should now seem to be somewhat obscured'. The paper made clear its opposition to repression in Ireland and declared on it front page that 'Justice can make but one reply to the Irish rebellion and that is to demand that Ireland shall be allowed to govern herself'.[66] Even this, in the circumstances of the time, brave defence of the Easter rebels was confused with regard to their politics, but Pankhurst and her comrades did defend the right of the Irish to self-determination, a crucial test.

The decisive intervention, however, was that of the Russian revolutionary, Lenin, writing some six months after the event. He forcefully defended Connolly and his comrades against accusations of putschism:

> The term "putsch," in its scientific sense, may be employed only when the attempt at insurrection has revealed nothing but a circle of conspirators or stupid maniacs, and has caused no sympathy among the masses. The centuries-old Irish national movement, having passed through various stages and combinations of class interest … manifested itself in street fighting, conducted by a section of the urban petty bourgeoisie and a section of the workers after a long period of agitation, demonstrations, suppressions of newspapers, etc. Whoever calls such a rebellion a "putsch" is either a hardened reactionary or a doctrinaire hopelessly incapable of envisaging a social revolution as a living phenomenon.[67]

This powerful endorsement is quoted time and again. The problem is, however, that when Lenin wrote these words he had no reliable information regarding what had actually taken place in Dublin and was mainly concerned with using the episode to demonstrate the importance for socialists of the right of nations to self-determination. In retrospect, it is absolutely clear that 'the attempt at insurrection' was the work of 'a circle of conspirators' who had 'no sympathy among the masses'. In fact the Easter Rising was a classic instance of a putsch, according to Lenin's own Marxist definition.

In his 'Letter To Comrades' Lenin wrote that

> Military conspiracy is Blanquism if it is not organised by a party of a definite

class. If its organisers have not analysed the political moment in general and the international situation in particular. If the party has not on its side the sympathy of the majority of the people as proved by objective facts. If the development of revolutionary events has not brought about a practical refutation of the conciliatory illusions of the petty bourgeoisie. If the majority of the Soviet-type organs of revolutionary struggle that have been recognised as authoritative or have shown themselves to be such in practice have not been won over ....[68]

Of course, Lenin was writing about the Russian situation here, but nevertheless he does provide a useful set of criteria with which to consider the Irish situation. In Ireland in April 1916 there was no proletarian party, only a republican secret society, the IRB with some 2,000 members, and a working-class militia, the Citizen Army with some 200 members; the people were known to be opposed to a rising and to still support the Home Rulers; the Rising had no significant support among the Irish working class and it was not accompanied by any strikes or factory occupations; there were no 'Soviet-type organs of revolutionary struggle', indeed the labour movement had still not recovered from the 1913-14 Lockout; and as for the revolutionary leadership having 'analysed the political moment', they were, in fact, gripped by Pearse's conception of the revolution as blood sacrifice, having given up all hope of a successful outcome. For Lenin, 'if the revolutionary party has no majority in the advanced contingents of the revolutionary classes and in the country, insurrection is out of the question'.[69] Once Connolly would have agreed wholeheartedly with this, indeed he had criticised the politics of republicanism from this very standpoint, but in April 1916 he was engaged in a very different undertaking.

In his October 1916 defence of the Rising, Lenin did acknowledge that the misfortune 'of the Irish was that they rose prematurely, when the European revolt of the proletariat had not yet matured'.[70] This surely has to be the starting point for any Marxist consideration of the Rising. If Connolly had survived even a year the international situation would have been transformed by the February Revolution in Russia and the overthrow of Tsarism. By the end of 1917 war weariness and popular unrest was growing in both Britain and Germany, the ITGWU was increasing in strength throughout the whole of Ireland, and the October Revolution had seen the establishment of the first workers' state. Early in 1918 the Conscription crisis provided the basis for mass opposition to both the war and British rule and, by the end of the year, the Kaiser had been overthrown and Germany was in the grip of revolution. There can be no doubt whatsoever that the despair that led him into his fatal alliance with the republicans would have been replaced by hopes of international working-class revolution. What conclusions can we draw from this? It seems quite clear, in retrospect, that far from urging the IRB into precipitate action, Connolly should have urged patience, should have argued for keeping the movement intact until the situation had turned to their advantage, until the conditions were right for a successful mass challenge to the British Empire. In the circumstances of April 1916 he should have opposed a rising. His failure to do this cost him his life. This was Connolly's tragedy, a tragedy for both the Irish and the British labour movements, who could ill afford to lose such a revolutionary.[71]

Notes

1   Kieran Allen, *The Politics of James Connolly*, London 1990, p. 151.

2   J.J. Lee, *Ireland 1912-1985: Politics and Society*, Cambridge 1989, p. 25.

3   Michael Foy and Brian Barton, *The Easter Rising*, Stroud 2000, p. 18.

4   Michael Laffan, *The Resurrection of Ireland: The Sinn Féin Party 1916-1923*, Cambridge 1999, p. 35.

5   W.K. Anderson, *James Connolly and the Irish Left*, Dublin 1994, p. 72.

6   Charles Townshend, *Ireland: The Twentieth Century*, London 1999, pp.74, 75.

7   T.W. Moody and Leon O'Broin, 'Select Documents: The IRB Supreme Council 1868-1878, *Irish Historical Studies* 75, 1975, p. 314.

8   Bulmer Hobson, *Ireland Yesterday and Tomorrow*, Tralee 1968, p. 72.

9   Keith, Jeffrey, *Ireland and the Great War*, Cambridge 2000, p. 51. Those historians and others who criticise the violence of the Easter Rising often overlook the far greater violence on the Western Front. While Pearse, Connolly, MacDermott and their comrades bear responsibility for the 450 people who died during Easter Week, what of Redmond's responsibility for the 30,000 Irishmen (a conservative estimate) who died fighting for the British.

10   Moy and Barton, op cit, pp. 12-19.

11   Desmond Fitzgerald, *Memoirs 1913-1916*, London 1969 pp. 140-141 and F.X. Martin, '1916 – Myth, Fact and Mystery', *Studia Hibernica* 7, 1967, pp. 69-70.

12   Moy and Barton, op cit, p. 18.

13   There is a large literature on Pearse but see Ruth Dudley Edwards, *Patrick Pearse: The Triumph of Failure*, London 1977 and Sean Farrell Moran, *Patrick Pearse and the Politics of Redemption*, Washington DC 1994.

14   Padraic Pearse and Desmond Ryan, *The Story of a Success*, Dublin 1917, p. 44.

15   Padraic Pearse, *Collected Works: Political Writings and Speeches*, Dublin 1922, pp. 71, 77, 193-194, 215, 225-226, 293, 365.

16   Desmond Ryan, *The Man Called Pearse*, London 1919, p. 83.

17   Aodh de Blacam, *What Sinn Féin Stands For*, Dublin 1921, p. 59.

18   Martin Daly, *Memories of the Dead*, Dublin 1916, p. 17.

19   Pearse and Ryan, op cit, pp. 76-77.

20   Padraic Pearse, *Collected Works: Plays, Stories and Poems*, Dublin 1917, pp. 43-44.

21   Ryan, op cit, pp. 57-58.

22   *Workers' Republic* 7 August 1915 and 5 February 1916.

23   D.G. Boyce, *Nationalism in Ireland*, London 1982, p. 308.

24   Hayden Talbot, *Michael Collins' Own Story*, London 1923, p. 42.

25   For the Kerry fiasco see T. Ryle Dwyer, *Tans, Terror and Troubles: Kerry's Real Fighting Story 1913-23*, Cork 2001, pp. 57-90.

26   There are numerous accounts of the events leading up to the Rising but see Foy and Barton, op cit for the most recent.

27   P.S. O'Hegarty, *The Victory of Sinn Féin*, Dublin 1924, pp. 3-4.

28   William O'Brien 'Introduction' in *James Connolly: Labour and Easter Week*, Dublin 1949, p. 21.

29   Robert Monteith, *Casement's Last Adventure*, Dublin 1953, pp. 220-221. It is interesting to note that Monteith, an IRB member himself, blamed the Easter weekend confusion on the Military Council. He wrote that 'the responsibility for the confusion existing in Dublin and the country … must be borne by the Military Council …. It would appear that no one outside the Council was to be fully trusted and that those within the Council did not trust one another.' He was also censorious of the failure to prepare for the arrival of the *Aud*, arguing that because of this the ship 'was lost' before it even reached Tralee Bay (pp. 220, 227).

30   John P. Duggan, *A History of the Irish Army*, Dublin 1991, p. 12.

31   James Connolly, *Revolutionary Warfare*, Dublin 1968, pp. 6, 19, 32, 34.

32   Darrell Figgis, *Recollections of the Irish War*, London 1927, pp. 87-88.

33   Foy and Barton, op cit, pp. 77-83.

34   Connolly, *Revolutionary Warfare*, op cit, p. IV and Peter Beresford Ellis, *A History of the Irish Working Class*, London 1972, p. 220.

35   Leon Trotsky, *1905*, London 1972, pp. 240, 246, 396.

36   Talbot, op cit, p. 41.

37   Rex Taylor, *Michael Collins*, London 1958, pp. 57-58.

38   Joe Good, *Enchanted By Dreams*, Dublin 1996, p. 41.

39   Ibid, pp. 30, 44.

40   For recent biographical studies see Helga Woggon, *Silent Radical – Winifred Carney 1887-1943: A Reconstruction of Her Biography*, Dublin 2000 and Medb Ruane, 'Kathleen Lynn' and Nell Regan, 'Helena Maloney' both in Mary Cullen and Maria Luddy, eds, *Female Activitists: Irish Women and Change 1900-1960*, Dublin 2001.

41   On 25 April, the 2 Dublin Fusiliers lost 510 men killed and wounded in an attack on the Western Front. During the advance, the cry was raised 'three cheers for Jim Larkin': Tom Johnstone, *Orange, Green and Khaki*, Dublin 1992, p. 75.

42   *Sinn Féin Rebellion Handbook*, Dublin 1917, pp. 9-10.

43   F.A. Mackenzie, *The Irish Rebellion – What Happened and Why*, Dublin 1917, pp. 60-61, 77.

44   Brian O'Higgins, *The Soldier's Story of Easter Week*, Dublin 1925, pp. 19, 34. Another rank-and-file fighter, Frank Robbins of the Citizen Army later remembered that 'I attended to my spiritual duty by going to Mass in St. Agatha's Church.' Even in old age, Robbins still followed the advice a nun had given him in his youth, 'sleeping at night with arms crossed, so as to be "near to God"': Frank Robbins, *Under The Starry Plough*, Dublin 1977, pp. 14, 78.

45   Margaret Skinnider, *Doing My Bit For Ireland*, New York 1917, p. 128.

46   Geraldine Plunkett Dillon, 'The North Roscommon Election', *Capuchin Annual* 1967, p. 338; David W. Miller, *Church, State and Nation in Ireland 1898-1921*, Dublin 1973, p. 341.

47   Thomas J. Morrissey, *William J. Walsh, Archbishop of Dublin 1841-1921*, Dublin 2000, p. 282-283.

48   Ryan, *Connolly*, op cit, p. 96; Dudley Edwards, op cit, p. 320.

49   Annie Smithson, *Myself – And Others*, Dublin 1944, pp. 272-273. Smithson was a

lifelong republican, a successful popular novelist and for many years secretary of the Irish Nurses Union. She too converted to Catholicism.

50   Piaras F. Mac Lochlainn, *Last Words*, Dublin 1917, p. 122.
51   Brian Inglis, *Roger Casement*, London 1974, pp. 383-384, 386.
52   Mac Lochlainn, op cit, p. 206.
53   Esther Roper, *Prison Letters of Countess Markiewicz*, London 1934, pp. 21, 73.
54   Jacqueline Van Voris, *Constance De Markiewicz: In The Cause of Ireland*, Massachusetts 1967, p. 203.
55   Brian Barton, *From Behind A Closed Door: Secret Court Martial Records of the 1916 Rising*, Belfast 2002, p. 15.
56   For the execution of Francis Sheehy Skeffington see Leah Levenson, *With Wooden Sword*, Boston 1983, pp. 217-233. His wife and partner, Hanna, was much more sympathetic to the rebels and helped supply them with food and carried messages, see Margaret Ward, *Hanna Sheehy Skeffington: A Life*, Cork 1997, pp. 184-161.
57   Barton, Ibid, p. 73.
58   Robbins, op cit, p. 128.
59   Good, op cit, pp. 76-77.
60   Batt O'Connor, *With Michael Collins In The Fight For Irish Independence*, London 1925, p. 54. O'Connor, who was to serve alongside Collins throughout the War of Independence, provides more evidence of rebel religiosity: every day at Frongoch internment camp ended 'with prayer. Our last act at night was to go down on our knees and repeat the Rosary and Litany of the Blessed Virgin. The Rosary was said every night in every hut in the Frongoch camp, not at the command of the camp leader, but out of the impulse to prayer which was in the heart of each of us. Nearly everyone had one or other of the holy images hanging over his bed. A kind friend had sent me a calendar on which there was a sweet picture of the Immaculate Conception. Every night and morning I knelt before it, and when I was released I brought it home with me – that dear companion of my exile. It hangs beside my bed to this day.' (pp. 90-91).
61   Robert Brennan, *Allegiance*, Dublin 1950, pp. 73, 93.
62   Mackenzie, op cit, pp. 93-94, 105-106.
63   Liz Curtis, *The Cause of Ireland*, Belfast 1994, p. 281.
64   W.P. Ryan, *The Irish Labour Movement*, Dublin 1919, p. 237.
65   Thomas Johnston, *Memories*, London 1952, pp. 238-239.
66   *The Woman's Dreadnought* 6 May 1916. On 13 May the paper carried Patricia Lynch's first-hand account of conditions in Dublin, 'Scenes From the Irish Rebellion'. According to one recent account, *The Woman's Dreadnought* was 'the most influential antiwar newspaper in England', see Barbara Winslow, 'Sylvia Pankhurst and the Great War' in Ian Bullock and Richard Pankhurst, *Sylvia Pankhurst: From Artist to Anti-Fascist*, London 1992, p. 114.
67   VI. Lenin, *British Labour and British Imperialism*, London 1969, p. 166.
68   A. Neuberg, *Armed Insurrection*, London 1970, p. 43.
69   Marcel Liebman, *Leninism Under Lenin*, London 1975, p. 172.
70   Lenin, op cit, p. 166.

Chapter VIII
In Time of Revolution

The Easter Rising began the destruction of the Home Rule party and the rise of Sinn Féin, an uneasy political alliance that encompassed both constitutional nationalists and uncompromising republicans. The execution of Pearse, Clarke, Plunkett, Connolly and the other rebel leaders turned much of Irish public opinion in all social groups against the British and served to discredit the Home Rulers who had committed themselves to supporting the British war effort. The decisive event in completing this process was the Conscription crisis of 1918 that saw Catholic Ireland mobilised against the war. The subsequent general election produced an overwhelming victory for Sinn Féin throughout the South. British refusal to engage with Sinn Féin precipitated the War of Independence with a reorganised Irish Republican Army taking on the British in a protracted guerrilla war. What part did the Irish labour movement play in this conflict? To what extent was social revolution on the agenda in this turbulent period? How far was the legacy of Larkin and Connolly squandered?

One point worth making here is that the explosion of working-class militancy that began in Ireland in 1917, the so-called 'second wave' of Irish syndicalism, was a national, not a Dublin affair. The focus of this chapter consequently shifts to a broader canvass.

Labour and the rise of Sinn Féin

When the Irish Trade Union Congress met at Sligo on 7 August 1916, only months after the Easter Rising, its chairman, Thomas Johnson made clear to delegates that now was not the time to discuss 'the right or wrong, the wisdom or the folly, of the revolt'. He did nevertheless propose a minute's remembrance for Connolly and the other trade unionists who had died fighting against the British but also for those Irishmen who had died fighting for the British in France and the Middle East. He made absolutely clear his own support for the Allied war effort. In this way, Congress with the acquiescence of the strong ITGWU delegation, quite deliberately refused to endorse the Easter Rising and similarly refused to oppose the War. Greaves, the ITGWU's historian, cannot help but express his surprise at the failure of 'this crucial test': 'no voice was raised to avow Connolly's programme of revolutionary opposition to the war, not even that of William O'Brien'.[1] This was partly to avoid precipitating a split with Protestant delegates from the North, partly to save the movement in the South from further British repression, but it also reflected the cautious moderation of the labour movement's leaders now that Larkin was in America and Connolly was dead. As one historian has aptly observed, Johnson was much more the Fabian than he was the Fenian.[2]

The labour movement's leadership, dominated at this time by Johnson, William O'Brien and others, regarded the national struggle as something altogether separate from their principal task of building strong trade unions and establishing a credible Labour Party. Rather than the labour movement providing the leadership in the national struggle or even entering into an alliance with middle-class republicanism, they saw its role as ancillary, as one of providing limited support for those actually engaged in the struggle to achieve independence. Labour's struggles were separate and apart from the republican cause though on occasions the strength of the working class would be mobilised in its support. Arguably, this handed political leadership in Ireland over to the Sinn Féin alliance, a surrender from which the Irish labour movement has never really recovered. As one contemporary critic put it: 'the Labour Movement entered into the compact as a vassal rather than a co-partner'.[3] While subordination to Sinn Féin was to be the political stance taken up by the labour movement in this period, as far as the trade unions were concerned, the years after Easter Week were to be a period of massive expansion, a period during which a second wave of syndicalist agitation engulfed both rural and urban Ireland. This explosion of militancy took place in the context of the Bolshevik Revolution in Russia and the spread of revolutionary ferment throughout much of Europe. On 4 February 1918 some 10,000 people assembled at the Dublin Mansion House to celebrate the Bolshevik victory and soon after the Socialist Party of Ireland had proclaimed that 'Ireland rejoices with you in your success, Ireland welcomes your Revolution, Ireland proclaims you Saviour of the working class'.[4] Both Johnson and O'Brien were in the leadership of the Socialist Party, an organisation founded by Connolly, but while they might welcome proletarian revolution in Russia, they had no intention of attempting such an enterprise in Ireland. Their support for Bolshevism was to remain rhetorical. In retrospect, the failure of the Johnson-O'Brien leadership of the Irish labour movement to use the increasing strength and militancy of the trade unions to, at the very least, place themselves in the forefront of the national struggle is one of the great missed opportunities in European labour history. It is, of course, certain that if either Larkin or Connolly had been leading the movement then events would have taken a very different turn, however, uncertain the outcome.

The increasing strength of the labour movement was most clearly demonstrated with regard to the opposition to British plans to introduce conscription into Ireland. The worsening situation on the Western Front forced the British to prepare for this regardless of the consequences. The result was to unite Catholic Ireland against them, completing the job begun by the Easter Week executions. The British effectively handed the political initiative to Sinn Féin and completed the discrediting of the Home Rulers. While Sinn Féin took the lead in opposing conscription (with the blessing of the Catholic Church) and the volunteers prepared for armed resistance, it was the labour movement that made the most effective demonstration of opposition. On 20 April 1918, the ITUC held a conference, attended by some 1500 delegates, to discuss the threat of conscription. The conference called a 24 hour general strike for 23 April. Despite the short notice the stoppage was a complete success everywhere except Belfast and the Protestant North. One leading republican acknowledged that

> the strike was a hundred per cent successful. Anyone who lived through the period will remember the sound of footsteps. No other sound was heard in the streets. All traffic was at a standstill. All factories and shops were silent. No newspapers appeared and in the hotels the guests had to wait on themselves. Labour had demonstrated its power ....[5]

It was an unprecedented display of the strength of the Irish labour movement, by now more than fully recovered from the effects of the Dublin Lockout. The importance of the general strike should not be underestimated: it was the first general strike against the War. As Arthur Mitchell points out, the anti-conscription campaign served as 'a demonstration of the power labour could wield when it took the lead in furthering national causes', while according to Emmet O'Connor, it 'shifted the entire nationalist community to the left'.[6] For many labour activists this shift involved, as we have seen, at least a rhetorical embrace of the Bolshevik Revolution in Russia with talk of socialism and of the Workers' Republic becoming increasingly widespread and red flags becoming obligatory on demonstrations. Plans and preparations were made for further industrial action when the British actually tried to implement conscription. A railway strike and local general strikes, including a protracted general strike in Dublin were mooted.[7] If it had come to a confrontation then there is every likelihood that British repression would have escalated the conflict, provoking increasing radicalisation. The War of Independence would have begun with mass working-class struggle. The consequences of this for the nature of the struggle would have been profound and at the very least would have established the labour movement as a major force in an independent Ireland, would have prevented the conservative outcome of the Free State. This was not to be. The

War ended with German military collapse and revolution in Berlin and Vienna instead.[8] Nevertheless, the labour movement had played a vital role in the crisis with its representatives taking part in the Mansion House conference called by the Lord Mayor of Dublin and with William O'Brien appointed one of the three members of its standing committee along with Eamon de Valera and the Home Rule leader, John Dillon. The strong position that the labour movement achieved in the course of the anti-conscription campaign was soon to be thrown away.

The Irish Labour Party approached the general election of December 1918 with its most radical manifesto, a manifesto that was in many ways an Irish echo of the Bolshevik Revolution. It proclaimed the party's objective as being: 'To win for the workers of Ireland, collectively, the ownership and control of the whole produce of their labour. To secure the democratic management and control of all industries and services by the whole body of workers, manual and mental, engaged therein'.[9] In the event, at a special conference held on 1 November the delegates accepted an executive proposal not to stand candidates by an overwhelming 96 votes to 23. This fateful decision was bitterly opposed by a militant minority led by Thomas Farren and Cathal O'Shannon, but to no avail. The party had surrendered to Sinn Féin pressure. The consequence of this momentous decision was that there was no labour representation in the revolutionary Dáil, that labour had no effective voice in the revolutionary movement that was to challenge British rule. The national cause had been voluntarily surrendered to Sinn Féin, to a party that was dominated by men who had little sympathy for the working class or for the trade unions and none for socialism.

A number of reasons have been put forward to account for the decision to withdraw: fear of alienating the Protestant working class (in fact, of course, Protestant Labour candidates actually did stand in Belfast, securing an average 22 per cent of the poll), a self-sacrificing willingness to give way so the general election could become a referendum on the question of the Republic, and fear that the party would actually go down to a crushing defeat at the hands of Sinn Féin. More important, however, was the unwillingness of the leadership to wholeheartedly commit the movement to a revolutionary challenge to British rule. Such a commitment would have involved considerable risks: Labour, for example, would almost certainly have been banned along with Sinn Féin. The truth was that Johnson, O'Brien and company were not revolutionaries and in the end they bowed to Sinn Féin pressure as a way of getting themselves off the hook on which Connolly's actions in 1916 had impaled them. Their cautious moderation was reinforced by the vociferous demands of Sinn Féin supporters within the labour movement that Sinn Féin should be left a free run against the Home Rulers. This need not have been the case. There can be little doubt that Labour could have used the threat to stand candidates across the country to secure a clear run for itself in Dublin. A Labour Party wholeheartedly committed to the republican cause might well have lost some support but would have won over others and, moreover, would have been considerably better placed in a future independent Ireland. While Brian Farrell goes too far when he regrets the Labour leadership's failure to recognise that they could have 'captured' Sinn Féin and turned it into 'a socialist sword', he is surely closer to the mark when he laments their failure to play an independent part in the revolutionary struggle.[10] Certainly neither Larkin more Connolly would have countenanced such political cowardice.

When the revolutionary Dáil finally met towards the end of January 1919, it proceeded to make a nominal gesture towards Labour. Johnson was asked to draft the new Republic's social statement, the Democratic Programme. In his draft he initially looked to Pearse for inspiration rather than to Connolly, repeating his Jacobin declaration in *The Sovereign People* that 'the nation's sovereignty extends not only to the men and women of the nation but to all the material possessions of the nation .... In other words no private right to property is good against the public right of the nation'. He claimed, moreover, 'the right of the nation's citizens to an adequate share of the produce of the nation's labour'. This general statement of the rights and obligations of the risen nation was accompanied further on by more specific, more controversial, more Connollyite commitments:

> It shall be the purpose of the Government to encourage the organisation of people into trade unions and cooperative societies with a view to the control and administration of the industries by the workers engaged in the industries. Finally, the Republic will aim at the elimination of the class society which lives upon the wealth produced by the workers of the nation but gives no useful service in return, and in the process of accomplishment will bring freedom to all who have hitherto been caught in the toils of economic servitude.[11]

In effect, Johnson was proposing to commit the new state to building up the strength of the labour movement and to recognition of itself as a transitional stage on the road to the emancipation of the working class and the Workers' Republic. As the historian Joseph Lee somewhat pompously observes, this 'was an attempt to foist on the Dáil a programme that had never been presented to the electorate', although in all honesty the Labour leadership regarded it as no more than recognition of the labour movement's contribution to the national cause, as payment for their decision not to stand in the general election.[12] What is particularly interesting, however, is the apparent belief that such a transformation in Irish society could be achieved without working-class struggle, indeed without the active involvement of the working class at all.

In the event, Johnson's draft was far too leftwing for Sinn Féin. It was to be a very different document, drawn up by Sean T. O'Kelly, a future President of

Ireland, that was adopted by the Dáil on 21 January. The Democratic Programme, as adopted, remained a Jacobin statement, but gone were the support for trade unionism and cooperation and for the ending of 'economic servitude'. Instead there was a commitment 'to promote the development of the Nation's resources ... and to adopt all measures for the recreation and invigoration of our industries'. The new Republic was to seek international agreement on measures to improve the lot of the working class, that is to say if the rest of the world's ruling classes agreed to improve the position of their working classes, the Irish government would do likewise.[13] Even this version was to remain empty rhetoric, designed to enlist working-class support in the coming struggle, rather than committing the government to any improvement in the working-class position in Irish society.

The Second Wave

The historiography of the Irish labour movement has traditionally focused on Connolly, Larkin and the ITGWU up until 1916. Only recently, however, has attention begun to shift to the post-1917 period, to what can usefully be characterised as the second wave of Irish syndicalism. The period from 1917 to 1923 saw an explosion of militancy and trade union organisation that exceeded in geographic spread and was more protracted than that of the earlier period. It has nevertheless been generally ignore. Both F.S.L. Lyons and John Murphy's early surveys of modern Irish history are altogether innocent of the phenomenon and the same is true of more recent surveys such as those by Ronan Fanning, Joseph Lee and Dermot Keogh. The eventual defeat of the second wave seems to have been so complete as to have excised it from national history.[14] Even E. Rumpf and A.C. Hepburn's otherwise groundbreaking *Nationalism and Socialism in Twentieth Century Ireland* missed the second wave of working-class insurgency.[15] The publication of Emmet O'Connor's pathbreaking *Syndicalism in Ireland 1917-1923* and Conor Kostik's *Revolution in Ireland: Popular Militancy 1917-1923* have hopefully made such neglect no longer possible.[16]

Trade union membership affiliated to the ITUC increased from under 100,000 in 1916 to 225,000 in 1920. The number of trades councils grew from fifteen in 1918 to forty-six in 1921. Leading the way was the ITGWU that increased its membership from 14,000 in 1917 to over 120,000 in 1920. In O'Connor's words:

Trade unionism exploded in all directions ... it assimilated the aggressive class consciousness fermenting since 1914, and the unprecedented frequency of strikes during these years consolidated an exceptionally assertive spirit at the base of the movement'. The workers 'spontaneously revived and developed pre-war Larkinite tactics' and looked forward to the Workers' Republic. It was a 'syndicalist moment'.[17]

One of the remarkable features of this upsurge was the spread of trade union organisation to groups of workers hitherto too weak or too difficult to organise. The key group here were the agricultural workforce who rallied to the ITGWU in their thousands. A census of ITGWU members in June 1918 revealed that of the 43,788 total, 9,634 were agricultural workers.[18] This breakthrough was sustained until 1923. Efforts were made to organise domestic workers.[19] And there were even trade union stirrings among the police.[20] In times of general working-class advance weak sections are able to win victories that would have been impossible in different circumstances. In March 1918, for example, Dublin barmen won union recognition and a pay rise after defeating a lockout. Another feature of the period was the local general strike. These demonstrations of solidarity took place in fourteen different towns, although in some of them more than once: Charleville, for example, had five general strikes. Moreover this industrial conflict had an important political dimension.

For Greaves, the architects of the movement were William O'Brien, Cathal O'Shannon and Thomas Johnson. He endorses their political stand as part of the left of the Socialist International as opposed to that taken by Jim Larkin, who was a founder member of the Communist Labor Party in the United States. This is perhaps somewhat surprising from a lifelong Communist, but Greaves emphasises the Bolshevik rhetoric that these men were capable of using when they felt it necessary. O'Shannon could quite bluntly declare that 'the Soviet idea was the only one that would confer freedom on Ireland'. Their actions, however, never lived up to their rhetoric.[21] Indeed, rather than O'Brien and O'Shannon leading the movement, a good case can be made that they rode it. The second wave was the product of a working-class revolt and the ITGWU leadership adopted an often revolutionary rhetoric in order to retain control over it. Their object was to build up a strong trade union movement within the capitalist system rather than to overthrow it. They were always social democrats, never communists.[22]

While there was a high level of militancy, accompanied by often revolutionary rhetoric and the parading of red flags, to what extent did this amount to a real socialist challenge? Was the movement really only about securing wage improvements or did it have the potential to change Irish society?[23] Oliver Coogan, in his study of County Meath, has commented on how 'from 1919 onwards one is struck by the way in which the wages movement and other union activities often were embellished with the paraphernalia and rhetoric of socialist revolution'. He goes on: 'Even in Meath the demand for a higher wage occasionally seemed to assume the form of a crusade for communism'. But was it really just a wages movement without any serious revolutionary implications. He describes an ITGWU boycott of a number of pubs in Dunboyne in April 1920 in protest against the price of porter and concludes that this 'was a far cry from the formenting of Trotsky's permanent communist revolution'.[24] To pose the alternatives this way shows a misunderstanding of the relationship between labour revolt and the struggle for socialism. It seeks to freeze opinion in order to assess its degree of radicalism at any one moment, rather than recognising that the key to understanding such periods is a recognition of their dynamism, of the dynamic interaction between political and economic demands and of how this carries the movement forward. The best account of this process is provided by Rosa Luxemburg in her *The Mass Strike*.[25] Moreover, one should certainly not dismiss a successful attempt to lower the price of a pint. What is clear with regard to the situation is Ireland is that at every point where the movement could have been carried forward, the leadership did their best to contain it. This was the crucial difference between the situation in Russia and Ireland. In Russia, the Bolshevik Party in 1917 was trying to push the struggle forward, to generalise it, whereas in Ireland in 1917-1921 the leaders of the labour movement, despite their often revolutionary rhetoric, were concerned to curb the struggle, to keep it localised, and subordinate to the republican government. They were not out to establish a workers' republic but to establish strong trade unions on the context of an independent bourgeois Ireland.

The Limerick General Strike of April 1919 provides a useful instance of their determination to restrain militancy. The strike began on 14 April in protest against the implementation of British Defence of the Realm Act regulations. As Liam Cahill has shown working-class consciousness in the city can be characterised as radical rather than socialist, as evidenced by the contents of the *Bottom Dog* newspaper. Nevertheless, militant action was taken, confronting the British authorities, and with the town passing into the hands of a strike committee which was known locally as 'the soviet'. There was clearly the potential for the struggle to develop in a socialist direction. It is worth remembering in this respect that in February 1917 when the first soviets were established in Petrograd, their consciousness too can be described as radical rather than socialist, but months of struggle was to change that. What happened in Limerick was that the strike committee's call for solidarity, for a national general strike in their support, was ignored by the ITUC, which instead recommended the evacuation of the city as a protest. Rather than extend the struggle, the ITUC acted to keep it localised, and having kept it localised, presided over its defeat in detail. Indeed, defeat was preferable to spreading and intensifying the struggle.[26]

One other point worth noting about the situation in Limerick is that it once again provides evidence of the Catholicism of the Irish working class. Ruth Russell wrote of how when she 'broke through the military cordon about the proclaimed city of Limerick' she found a 'Soviet supported by the Catholic Church'. When she asked Bishop Fogarty if this indicated that the people were 'priest-ridden', he replied that it was perhaps 'the other way about'. She describes, with obvious surprise, how the workers' guards got to their feet when 'St. Munchin's chapel bell struck for the Angelus' and blessed themselves.[27] There was not another European country where this would have been possible. Aodh de Blacam acknowledged as much when he wrote that

Catholic communities are generally hostile to socialism and so the socialistic enthusiasm which ran over Ireland during 1919 surprised and puzzled many. But there the fact was. Never was Ireland more devoutly Catholic than today after the great spiritual stirrings caused by the words and deeds of Pearse, the crisis of Conscription, the imprisonments and exiles – and yet nowhere was the Bolshevik revolution more sympathetically saluted. Books, pamphlets and letters and essays in the press debated socialism ….[28]

But while de Blacam could argue with considerable justice that 'nowhere was the Bolshevik revolution more sympathetically saluted' than in Ireland, the fact was also that nowhere in Europe was communism in its organised form, a Communist Party, weaker. When the Socialist Party of Ireland became the Communist Party of Ireland on 28 October 1921 it had only twenty active members. The new party proceeded, in the words of its historian, to ignore 'virtually every industrial struggle while it attempted to turn the Republicans leftwards'. At a time when Constance Markiewicz, by now the Minister of Labour in the revolutionary government, was warning her colleagues of the 'imminence of social revolution', the Communist Party was completely without influence and, even with only a handful of members, was nevertheless riven with factionalism.[29] The best militants were either committed to the syndicalism of the ITGWU, to the military activity of the IRA or to both. It seems clear that an opportunity to establish a strong revolutionary socialist presence in Ireland was let slip. W.B. Yeats, for example, complained that 'the execution of Connolly has given him many readers. I have already noticed Karl Marx's *Kapital* in the same window with Mitchel's *Jail Journal* and with *Speeches From The Dock*'.[30] What was missing was a Larkin or a Connolly, revolutionaries of sufficient stature and experience, to give a lead.

One factor that is often seen as militating against socialist prospects in Ireland is that unlike Tsarist Russia in 1917, the land question had already been solved. This is a gross oversimplification.[31] On the land there were two constituencies that could be won to the socialist cause: the agricultural workers and the small farmers. The ITGWU was to be triumphantly successful in organising the agricultural workers, but the ITUC never succeeded or even tried to organise the small farmers. And yet agrarian radicalism was developing in may parts of the country, an agrarian radicalism that caused Sinn Féin considerable problems. As Darrell Figgis, a determined republican opponent of social radicalism recalled, the revived land agitation presented a problem that the Republican Government 'could not neglect … Cattle-driving and death-notices accumulated, and led finally to violence of a nature that could not be neglected'. He wrote of how, in Co. Roscommon, a landowner was driven naked through a fair and in Co. Galway a landowner was shot. The Republican Government, he concluded, 'had to keep the national demand for freedom clear from class issues or be caught in the snare of a class war'.[32]

While it is clear that the Sinn Féin leadership was resolutely opposed to the republican struggle developing a socialist character, nevertheless the labour movement played an important role in the conflict. First of all, many union men and women were actively involved in the War of Independence as republicans, whether it be as Sinn Féin members or as IRA volunteers. Peadar O'Donnell is perhaps the best known of these, working as an ITGWU organiser before joining the IRA.[33] There were many others. Of the six men hanged for the 'Bloody Sunday' shootings, four were active trade unionists, one of them, Patrick Moran, a leading member of the Grocer's Assistants' Trade Union.[34] While Terence Mac-Swiney's death on hunger strike in Brixton Prison on 25 October 1920 is one of the key episodes in the War of Independence, two other men also died on hunger strike in Cork Goal only days before. One of them, Mick Fitzgerald, an IRA officer held for fatally shooting a British soldier, was secretary of the ITGWU branch at Clondulane mill, described by one historian as 'an IRA stronghold'.[35] He died on 17 October after sixty-three days on hunger strike. And, of course, the British themselves were in no doubt concerning working-class participation in the struggle. A British assessment of the situation in Dublin in 1920-1921 argued that 'Shop assistants and factory workers formed the backbone of the IRA'.[36] On a number of occasions, however, the trade union movement intervened directly in the national struggle.

The Limerick General Strike, a direct challenge to the DORA regulations, has already been mentioned. More important was the action taken by dockers and railwaymen. On 20 May 1920 dockers in Dublin refused to unload two ships carrying military equipment and material and were promptly locked out. The action spread to the railways where railworkers refused to carry troops or munitions. In many parts of the country rail transport came to a halt. The men involved were members of the National Union of Railwaymen (NUR) which refused to support the action even after the Trades Union Congress passed a resolution demanding British withdrawal from Ireland. Only after a protracted dispute did the ITUC call off the boycott in December 1920, effectively surrendering and leaving some 1,500 of the most militant railworkers victimised. According to Charles Townshend, the boycott had 'created severe difficulties, which could have become acute'. Indeed, he goes so far as to suggest that 'if the embargo had been made total in scope and indefinite in duration, it is hard to see how a functional military presence in the hinterland could have been maintained'.[37] More recently, Francis Costello has argued that the railway embargo 'was a major part in the breakdown of British governance in Ireland'.[38] Once again an opportunity was missed. On another occasion, in February 1921, following the arrest and summary execution of three railwaymen by the police at Mallow, County Cork, the men's British trade union, the Associated Society of Locomotive Engineers and Firemen (ASLEF), threatened a national strike, embracing both Ireland and Britain. The union demanded an inquiry into the shootings and a guarantee of the safety of its Irish members. The government made it clear that it would under no circumstances make any concessions on the issue and the union humiliatingly backed down.[39]

Most important as an indication of what might have been was the indefinite general strike called by the ITUC for 13 April 1920 in support of hunger strikers, who included a number of trade union prisoners, in Mountjoy Prison. With support growing and self-proclaimed soviets being established in many towns, the authorities backed down after two days and released the prisoners. Emmet O'Connor quotes the *Manchester Guardian*: 'it is no exaggeration to trace a flavour of proletarian dictatorship about some aspects of the strike'. While he goes on to warn against any equation of 'Irish red flaggery and Russian Bolshevism', he nevertheless concedes 'the extraordinary class triumphalism that had gripped the people'. What had emerged at this time was 'a consciousness that was not revolutionary of itself, but which signified the emergence of a political culture based on the wages movement and outside the formal consensus of the day. The counter-politics stood for the rejection of capitalism, and the celebration of solidarity, spontaneity, and direction'.[40] Now he is certainly correct that this level of working-class activity and consciousness cannot be equated with October 1917, but what took place in Russia was part of a revolutionary process that had been developing since February. What happened in Ireland in April 1920 can be usefully seen as part of a revolutionary process comparable with but not the same as early stages in the development of the Russian Revolution. In Ireland, however, the movement never developed into a socialist challenge for power. There are, of course, a number of reasons for this, but one of them is certainly the way in which the ITUC leadership was able to contain the movement.

Conor Kostick, in his account of the April 1920 general strike, states quite bluntly that it 'revealed that Irish workers had the power to defeat British rule'. This goes too far. While it is clear that the struggle in Ireland could have been given a mass character that would have been very difficult for the British to suppress, nevertheless victory was not ensured. Russia had its 1905 as well as its 1917. The general strike showed, however, that the struggle could have developed in a way that would have put Kostick's assertion to the test. The British release of the hunger strikers certainly indicated that the prospect of the working class as a class becoming actively involved in the struggle was not something they would welcome. Paradoxically, it was just as unwelcome to the leaders of Sinn Féin and of the ITUC.[41] The War of Independence remained a guerrilla war conducted by a relatively small number of IRA volunteers with the mass of the Irish people confined to the role of sympathetic onlookers. While there can be no doubting the extent of popular support for the republican cause, the strategy adopted by Michael Collins and his comrades, a strategy gratefully acquiesced in by the trade union leaders, was one that excluded mass struggle as far as possible.

There can be little doubt that this strategy was informed, at least in part, by fear of the radicalisation that popular involvement would have inevitably brought. The republican leadership were, by and large, conservative as far as the social order was concerned and certainly had no wish to precipitate a socialist challenge to British rule. The trade union leaders similarly had no intention of becoming involved in any socialist challenge and indeed were prepared to act as intermediaries for Sinn Féin with the British. In early April 1921, Foran, Johnson and O'Brien met with the Chief Secretary for Ireland, Edward Shortt, and indicated to him that Sinn Féin wanted 'an excuse to get out of the Republic pledge'. With Sinn Féin's private agreement they were prepared to issue a manifesto calling for a settlement on the terms of 'fiscal autonomy' in order to kick off the necessary diplomatic preliminaries for the opening of negotiations. Not even the Republic, let alone the Workers' Republic. This was not the role envisaged by Larkin and Connolly one need hardly say.[42]

The labour movement was by no means exempt from British repression. On 17 November 1920 Thomas Foran could report to the ITGWU executive that eight branch offices had been destroyed by British troops and three branch secretaries had been shot. Another thirty-two branch secretaries were at that moment in prison. In Bunclody, the British had broken a strike by arresting all the strikers, stripping them naked, soaking them in the freezing cold and violently scrubbing them with cane brushes. The branch secretary, Ignatius Redmond, was chased naked at bayonet point around the barrack square and threatened with summary execution if the strike was not called off. On 24 November 1920, following the Bloody Sunday shootings, troops wrecked Liberty Hall, causing £5,000 worth of damage, arrested many of the staff, and forced the union to move its offices to Parnell Square.[43]

Despite this the labour movement emerged from the War of Independence immeasurably strengthened. To a considerable extent its strength derived from the disturbed conditions that had existed in the country, but now it faced a new challenge. Employers were determined to push back the advance of trade unionism and were fully supported in this resolve by the rulers of the new state. In the conditions of economic depression that developed in the course of 1921 a major offensive against the Irish trade union movement and working-class living standards was almost inevitable. Two factors combined to prevent the employers from prosecuting their attack at this time. First, the country became embroiled in the Civil War so that the Free State army and police were too heavily committed fighting the IRA to be able to play an effective strikebreaking role. And secondly, the trade union rank and file offered a degree of resistance that was determined and militant enough to hold what they had. Disputes in the countryside were increasingly accompanied by violence and sabotage, while in the towns workers resorted to occupation as a tactic. During the course of 1922 there were to be some eighty soviets proclaimed, all disowned by the official movement, although local union organisers often played a leading role. Large numbers of workers were involved in seizing control of their workplaces and in many instances keeping production going. The high point of the occupation movement was in May when the Cleeve company locked out its workforce, who proceeded to take control of the creameries, mills and other plants. These occupations only ended in August with the arrival of Free State troops in the Suir valley.[44]

The Employer's Offensive

Once the Free State had effectively defeated its republican opponents, it quickly proceeded to the restoration of property rights and employers' prerogatives, deploying troops and police to break strikes and impose wage cuts. Indeed, the government itself quite deliberately led the way by imposing wage cuts on postal workers with the intention of provoking a strike. Even before the dispute began, the Postmaster-General James J. Walsh, had approached the British Postmaster General to ask for assistance in recruiting strike-breakers from among the Irish workers in the British Post Office. Walsh was himself a former postman and militant trade unionist before his rise to prominence first in Sinn Féin and now in Cumann na nGaedheal. He set about breaking the strike with a vengeance. The postal workers struck on 10 September, in defiance of a declaration that their action was illegal. Troops and police attacked pickets, beating men and women, and strenuous efforts were made to recruit strike-breakers. With the government determined to break the strike and without any solidarity action from other groups of workers, the unions admitted defeat on 29 September. They had assurances from President Cosgrave that there would be no victimisation, but Walsh refused to be bound by these. Not only were union members victimised, but Walsh also treated the strike as a break in service with serious consequences for pension rights and incremental rates. As the unions bitterly complained, not even the British had done this when they had supported the April 1920 general strike. Moreover, Walsh was quite clear about the implications of the dispute, remarking that 'at this critical juncture to smash such a well organised strike was a salutary lesson to the general indiscipline which has just seemed to run riot through the land'.[45] Private employers hastened to follow his lead.

The trade union movement suffered crushing defeats in the course of 1923. The decisive battles were the six month Waterford farm workers' strike that began on 17 May and was only called off on 8 December, and the Dublin dock workers strike that began on 16 July and was called off in October. The Waterford strikers held out in the face of severe repression carried out by troops, police and armed vigilantes, but in the end they went down to total defeat. The ITGWU in County Waterford ceased to exist and agrarian trade unionism throughout Ireland went into catastrophic decline. In Dublin, the dockers returned to work after accepting a wage cut.[46] The battering the movement received was made all the worse by the bitter divisions within the ITGWU, divisions that were exac-

erbated when Jim Larkin finally returned from the United States at the end of
April 1923. He mounted a strong militant challenge to William O'Brien's leadership of the union. How far was this a matter of personalities? How far was it
a question of politics? In his history of the ITGWU, Greaves is contemptuously
dismissive of Larkin: he was a fantasist, completely out of touch, his behaviour
'cannot be excused on any grounds' and, most incredibly, his 'egoism' had created the situation 'in which the employers could launch their general offensive
with the certainty of success'.[47] This stance is endorsed by Larkin's most recent
biographer, Emmet O'Connor.[48] While personalities undoubtedly came into the
conflict between the two men and their supporters, far more important were
questions of strategy: how to respond to the employers' offensive? O'Brien favoured retreat and attempts to reach an accommodation, while Larkin favoured
militant resistance.

Larkin in America

At this point, it is worth briefly considering Jim Larkin's activities in the United
States. On his arrival in early 1914 he threw himself into the anti-war and labour
movements. He worked as an organiser for the Western Federation of Miners,
spoke at socialist and anti-war meetings throughout the country, and in November 1915 was one of the speakers at the Wobbly Joe Hill's funeral. For a while, he
had close contact with German agents, but while he was prepared to cooperate
with them to keep America out of the war, he was not prepared to countenance
an alliance.[49] There is evidence that he knew of Connolly's involvement with the
IRB and of preparations for a rising. He actually sent Connolly instructions by
various means to the effect that he should 'pull out of it'. Later, he told Frank
Robbins that he had ordered Connolly 'to call it off' and that as far as he was
concerned Connolly 'had no right to be connected with the Insurrection; it
should have been left to Pearse, MacDonagh and the other poets'. Robbins, a
participant in the Rising, strongly disagreed.[50]

Larkin was subsequently extremely critical of the way the labour movement
subordinated itself to Sinn Féin. He complained in a letter to Thomas Foran in
Dublin, 'Are they all turned Sinn Féin?' In another letter to Foran he complained
that the Sinn Féin movement in America was 'anti-labour' and that it portrayed
the socialists as 'anti-Christs'. Republican speakers, including those from Ireland such as Hanna Sheehy Skeffington and James Connolly's daughter, Nora,
were making out that Arthur Griffith was 'a God-given saint' and that 'nobody
in Ireland had done anything but Sinn Féin'. The version of events being put
over was that 'Connolly and the other boys all recanted Socialism and Labour
and were good Sinn Féiners. My God it is sickening'.[51] Nora Connolly, he maintained, in remembering that her father was an Irishman, had forgotten that he
was also a socialist.[52] This certainly leaves little doubt as to Larkin's position, a
position which remained substantially unchanged since the time of the Lockout.
He was a champion of independent working-class politics and organisation,

subordinate to no one, and with the labour movement taking the lead in the national struggle. This stance was to be dramatically vindicated as far as Larkin was concerned by the lessons of the October Revolution in Russia and its international ramifications.

Larkin was won over to recognition of the importance of developments in Russia by John Reed, just returned from Petrograd, in April 1918.[53] He was to become a leading member of the left within the Socialist Party, arguing for an American embrace of Bolshevism, and at the end of August 1919 was one of the founders of the Communist Labour Party. It is very difficult to believe that, had he lived, Connolly's response to the Russian Revolution would have been any different. As for Larkin, he was to be swept up in the ferocious repression that was unleashed on the American left in the aftermath of the World War. He was arrested, along with hundreds of other, in the Palmer raids and eventually brought to trial for criminal anarchy in January 1920. He was sentenced to five to ten years in Sing Sing prison in New York State in May. Larkin remained in prison until he received a free pardon on 17 January 1923 and was eventually deported back to Ireland.[54] He arrived back at Westland Row Station in Dublin on 30 April a convinced Communist, and was met by a huge crowd of thousands of supporters who escorted him through the streets to Liberty Hall.

The Split

Back in Dublin, Larkin took on the role of a rank-and-file leader, leading both the resistance to the employers and an insurgency against O'Brien's leadership within the ITGWU. His stance had the support of the overwhelming majority of the Dublin membership. Elsewhere in the country, rank-and-file traditions were not so strong and O'Brien was able to retain control through the agency of the union's paid organisers. Larkin had no intention of starting a breakaway union. That decision was taken prematurely by his brother Peter, a man much closer to the IWW tradition than Larkin himself, while he was in Moscow.[55] Regardless of Peter Larkin's action in establishing the Workers Union of Ireland, it is certain that O'Brien would have made good his expulsion of Larkin and his supporters so that the outcome was really only a matter of timing. Moreover, a good case can be made that, regardless of either Larkin brother, some sort of breakaway from O'Brien's bureaucratic rule was on the cards. Such was to be the experience in London and Glasgow where dockers had to deal with Ernest Bevin's Transport and General Workers' Union. The Workers' Union was established on 15 June 1924, taking with it two thirds of the ITGWU's Dublin membership, but only twenty-three of the 300 provincial branches. O'Brien proceeded to ally with the employers against the new union.[56] Larkin was unable to turn the tide of defeat.

The catastrophic decline of the Irish trade union movement was certainly not due to Larkin or the establishment of the Workers' Union. In 1926, the ITGWU still claimed to have 40,000 members, but by 1929 this had collapsed

to only 15,000. The decline of the ITUC was equally dramatic, with membership falling to 92,000 in 1929. While this was undoubtedly due to the economic
circumstances, an important part was also played by the unremitting hostility
of the Cosgrave government. As for Larkin, there was now no labour revolt of
which he could become the voice. He was reduced to the leadership of a small
embattled union that was successfully contained by the employers together with
his enemies in the trade union movement led by William O'Brien. Larkin's figure still looms large, however, and this has led to him being blamed for, among
other things, the failure of Irish communism. According to Emmet O'Connor,
Larkin deliberately set out to prevent the development of an Irish Communist
Party and he puts this down, at least in part, to his supposed acute personality
problems.[57] This is not convincing. First of all, Larkin had been a founder of
the Communist Labor Party in the United States so that, whatever his political
weaknesses, he was clearly prepared to be part of a collective leadership where
it appeared that the movement could actually be built. Given this, it is much
more likely that he recognised that a Communist Party could not be built, at this
time, in Ireland. His Dublin-based Irish Workers' League was not an obstacle
to building a Communist Party, but all that could be built in the situation in
which he found himself, a situation where, unlike America, he was very much
a one-man band, whether he liked it or not. What is remarkable is how much
Larkin was actually able to hold together, at great personal cost, rather than what
he failed to achieve. On Lenin's death in January 1924 Larkin led over 6,000
mourners through the streets of Dublin, a remarkable achievement in Catholic
Ireland. In September 1927, his personal following was still strong enough to
secure his election as a Communist to the Dáil. He was denied his seat as an
undischarged bankrupt. But the movement had gone and not even his energy,
determination, courage and spirit could tell against that. His revolutionary spirit
was finally broken in the 1930s when he became reconciled to being the leader
of a small trade union and embraced Labour Party reformism. Jim Larkin finally
died on 30 January 1947, still incorruptible and with a large personal following
in Dublin.

Notes

1   C. Desmond Greaves, *The Irish Transport and General Workers Union: The Forma-
     tive Years*, Dublin 1974, pp. 75-76.
2   W.K. Anderson, *James Connolly and the Irish Left*, Blackrock 1994, p. 104. For John-
     son see J. Anthony Gaughan, *Thomas Johnson*, Mount Merrion 1980.
3   Michael Hopkinson, *Green Against Green: The Irish Civil War*, Dublin 1989, pp.
     45-46.
4   Tom Crean, 'From Petrograd to Bruree', in David Fitzpatrick, ed. *Revolution? Ire-
     land 1917-1923*, Dublin 1990, p. 146.
5   Robert Brennan, *Ireland Standing Firm and Eamon de Valera*, Dublin 2002, p. 114.

6   Arthur Mitchell, *Labour in Irish Politics 1890-1930*, Dublin 1974, p. 89; Emmet
     O'Connor, *A Labour History of Waterford*, Waterford 1989, p. 124.

7   David Fitzpatrick, *The Two Irelands 1912-1939*, Oxford 1998, pp. 73-74. See also
     Thomas Johnson's 'Memorandum to Local Defence Committees' in Gaughan, op
     cit, pp. 431-435.

8   For the extent of unrest in Britain in 1918 and after see in particular Brock Mill-
     man, *Managing Domestic Dissent in first World War Britain*, London 2000, pp. 252-
     296.

9   Michael Laffan, 'Labour Must Wait: Ireland's Conservative Revolution' in Patrick
     J. Corish, *Radicals, Rebels and Establishments*, Belfast 1985, p. 206.

10   Brian Farrell, *The founding of Dáil Eireann*, Dublin 1971, p. 44. For a different
     discussion of the longer term significance of the 1918 decision see Kieran Allen,
     Fianna Fáil and Irish Labour, London 1997, pp. 6-7.

11   Ibid, pp. 88-89.

12   Joe Lee, *Ireland 1912-1985*, Cambridge , p. 41.

13   Farrell, op cit, pp. 87-88.

14   F.S.L. Lyons, *Ireland Since The Famine*, London 1971; John Murphy, *Ireland in the
     Twentieth Century*, Dublin 1975; Ronan fanning, *Independent Ireland*, Dublin 1983;
     Lee, op cit; Dermot Keogh, *Twentieth Century Ireland*, Dublin 1994.

15   E. Rumpf and A.C. Hepburn, *Nationalism and Socialism in Twentieth Century
     Ireland*, Liverpool 1977. They write that 'If 1913 marked the beginning, then 1916
     marked the end of the social revolution in Dublin' (p. 20).

16   Emmet O'Connor, *Syndicalism in Ireland 1917-1923*, Cork 1988 and Conor Kostik,
     Revolution in Ireland: Popular Militancy, London 1996. The recent collection edited
     by Joost Augusteign, *The Irish Revolution 1913-1923*, Basingstoke 2002, suggests
     that this hope was in vain.

17   Emmet O'Connor, *A Labour History of Ireland 1824-1960*, Dublin 1992, p. 94.

18   There is a growing body of research chronicling the struggles of the rural work-
     ing class: see in particular, Dan Bradley, *Farm Labourers: Irish Struggle 1900-1976*,
     Belfast 1988; John Cunningham, *Labour in the West of Ireland: Working Life and
     Struggle*, Belfast 1995; Ross Connolly, 'A Rightful Place in the Sun – the Struggle of
     the Farm and Rural Labourers of County Wicklow' in Kenny Hannigan and Wil-
     liam Nolan, eds, *Wicklow: History and Society*, Dublin 1994; and O'Connor, *Labour
     History of Waterford*, op cit.

19   John Lynch, *A Tale of Three Cities: Comparative Studies in Working Class Life*, Bas-
     ingstoke 1998, p. 30.

20   David Neligan, *The Spy in the Castle*, London 1968, pp. 54-55.

21   Greaves, op cit, p. 235.

22   Adrian Pimley, 'The Working Class Movement and the Irish Revolution 1896-
     1923' in D.G Boyce, ed. *The Revolution in Ireland 1879-1923*, London 1980, p. 210.

23   See Laffan, op cit, pp. 209-210.

24   Oliver Coogan, *Politics and War in Meath 1913-1923*, Maynooth 1983, pp. 250-
     253.

25   Rosa Luxemberg, *The Mass Strike*, London 1986.

26   Liam Cahill, *Forgotten Revolution: The Limerick Soviet 1919*, Dublin 1990.

27   Ruth Russell, *What's The Matter With Ireland*, New York 1920, pp. 127, 136, 138.

28   Aodh de Blacam, *What Sinn Féin Stands For*, Dublin 1921, p. 105.

29   Mike Milotte, *Communism in Modern Ireland*, Dublin 1984, pp. 49-50, 62.

30   Elizabeth Cullingford, *Yeats, Ireland and Fascism*, London 1981, p. 116.

31   See in particular Paul Bew, 'Sinn Féin, Agrarian Radicalism and the War of Independence 1919-1921' in Boyce, op cit, and Tony Varley, Agrarian Crime and Social Control: Sinn Féin and the Land Question in the West of Ireland in 1920' in Mike Tomlinson, Tony Varley and Ciaran McCullagh, eds, *Whose Law and Order?*, Belfast 1988.

32   Darrell Figgis, *Recollections of the Irish War*, London 1927, pp. 292-293.

33   See Anton McCabe, 'The Stormy Petrel of the Transport Workers: Peadar O'Donnell, Trade Unionist 1917-1920', *Saothar* 19, 1994; Peter Hegarty, *Peadar O'Donnell*, Cork 199; and Donal O Drisceoil, *Peadar O'Donnell*, Cork 2001.

34   Kostik, op cit, p. 137.

35   Peter Hart, *The IRA and its Enemies*, Oxford 1998, p. 249.

36   Peter Hart, ed, *British Intelligence in Ireland 1920-21: The Final Reports*, Cork 2002, p. 32.

37   Charles Townshend, 'The Irish railway strike of 1920: industrial action and civil resistance in the struggle for independence', *Irish Historical Studies* XXI 83, 1979, p. 281.

38   Francis Costello, *The Irish Revolution and its Aftermath*, Dublin 2003, p. 176.

39   D.G. Boyce, *Englishmen and Irish Troubles*, London 1972, pp. 68-69.

40   O'Connor, *Syndicalism*, op cit, p. 45. for an interesting account of developments in one particular county see D.R. O'Connor Lysaght, 'County Tipperary: class struggle and national struggle 1916-1924' in William Nolan and Thomas McGrath, eds, *Tipperary: History and Society*, Dublin 1985.

41   Kostik, op cit, pp. 127-128.

42   Thomas Jones, *Whitehall Diary 3: Ireland 1918-1925*, London 1971, pp. 58-59.

43   Greaves, op cit, pp. 290-291.

44   See Crean, op. cit.

45   See Alexis Guilbride, 'A Scrapping of Every Principle of Individual Liberty: the Postal Strike of 1922', *History Ireland*, 200, and Kostik, op cit, p. 185.

46   See O'Connor, *Labour History of Waterford*, op cit, p. 183-208 and O'Connor, *Labour History of Ireland*, op cit, pp. 115-116.

47   Greaves, op cit, p. 319.

48   O'Connor argues that Larkin provoked the crisis in the ITGWU 'simply to gratify his vanity. Incredible as it may seem, the schism was entirely of Larkin's making …. This was not rational behaviour. It flowed from the needs of an unbalanced personality, in which arguably, egotism had given way to egomania', Emmet O'Connor, *James Larkin*, Cork 2002, pp. 70-71.

49   For Larkin's own account of his relations with Germany see Donal Nevin, ed, *James Larkin: Lion of the Fold*, Dublin 1998, pp. 298-312.

50   Frank Robbins, *Under the Starry Plough*, Dublin 1977, p. 164.

51   Emmet Larkin, *James Larkin*, London 1965, pp. 190-191, 199-200.

52   David M. Emmons, *The Butte Irish: Class and Ethnicity in an American Mining Town 1875-1925*, Urbana 1989, p. 357.

53   For John Reed see John Newsinger, ed, *Shaking the World: John Reed's Revolution-*

ary Journalism, London 1998 and Eric Homberger, *John Reed*, Manchester 1990.

54   For Larkin in America see Manus O'Riordan, 'Larkin in America: The Road to Sing Sing; in Donal Nevis, ed. *Jim Larkin, Lion of the Fold*, Dublin 1998; Claire Cullerton, 'James Larkin and J. Edgar Hoover: Irish Politics and American Conspiracy', *Eire-Ireland* XXXV 2000-2001; and also Emmet O'Connor, *Larkin*, op cit, pp. 54-69.

55   While Jim Larkin was in the United States, his brother, Peter, was in Australia, a member of the IWW, opposing the war. He fell victim to the suppression of the IWW and was one of the 'Sydney Twelve', sentenced to ten years imprisonment for treason in December 1916. He was eventually released in August 1920 and returned to Ireland. See Frank Cain, 'The Industrial Workers of the World: Aspects of its Suppression in Australia 1916-1919', *Labour History* 42, 1982 and Ian Taylor, *Sydney's Burning*, Melbourne 1967.

56   For a recent account of the split see Mark Farmer, 'James Larkin and the Workers' Union of Ireland', *Etudes Irlandaises* 2001.

57   O'Connor, *Larkin*, op cit, pp. 80-93.

58   For Larkin's embrace of reformism the best and most recent account is Ibid, pp. 94-112.

Conclusion

The defeat of both the first and second waves of Irish syndicalism saw the Irish labour movement successfully marginalised in the Free State with consequences that are still with us today. While these defeats were obviously not responsible for everything that followed, if defeat had been avoided then the subsequent history would have been very different. At the very least, the Irish labour movement would have played a much more central role in developments in the late 1920s, the 1930s and beyond. Ireland would in this way have had more in common with the experience of the rest of Europe.

Nevertheless, what lessons can be drawn from this period of unprecedented struggle? First, there was the remarkable success that Larkin and his comrades had in organising and mobilising a Dublin working class that seemed condemned by the harshness of circumstances to passivity and despair. The tactics that the ITGWU developed (solidarity, blacking and the sympathy strike – all predictably illegal in New Labour's Britain PLC) enabled the union to take on the Dublin employers and bring them to terms. Only the intervention of Ireland's most powerful capitalist, William Martin Murphy, a man with the clout necessary to unite employers, Church and state against the union, was able to put a stop to its apparently irresistible advance. The intervention of the Catholic clergy against the Larkinites was absolutely predictable, but what is significant is the refusal of a Catholic working class to be intimidated by this intervention.

The union's success did not, of course, rest on tactics. The determination with which the Dublin working class stood by the ITGWU derived from the way that the union came to embody a distinctive social vision, the vision of an Ireland where labour had come into its own. The ITGWU was committed to both a socialist reordering of society and to the establishment of an Irish Republic. Indeed, in the years immediately before the outbreak of the First World War the ITGWU was the largest and most important republican organisation in Ireland.

The union and the working-class revolt that it gave form and voice to can be legitimately described as Larkinite. The locked out workers who marched through the streets of Dublin singing 'I am One of the Horrible Larkinites', would have had no argument with that. Larkinism remains a working-class movement of great historical significance.

The Dublin Lockout that defeated the first wave of Irish syndicalism was not, it has to be insisted, just an episode in Irish history. It was also a crucial moment in the history of the British working class. Syndicalist and socialist militants, activists and sympathisers throughout Britain rallied behind the Dublin workers in a tremendous display of solidarity. An important section of the women's movement took up the cause. While huge sums of money were contributed to help sustain the ITGWU in its war of attrition with the Dublin employers, in the end victory would have required solidarity action, the blacking of Dublin traffic. The British trade union leaders set their faces determinedly against this. All attempts to launch unofficial solidarity action in the docks and on the railways were successfully put down, with the railwaymen's leader, J.H. Thomas, a future Labour minister and defector to the National Government, playing a crucial role. The failure of the left to overcome official opposition to solidarity action defines the limits of the syndicalist movement in Britain, marks the extent of its influence. And this was at a time when unofficial action, when revolt against union officialdom, was very much a feature of working-class advance.

Even though Larkin and the ITGWU were defeated there is clear evidence that the union still had the support of a very substantial section of the Dublin working class. It was intimidation, pure and simple, victimisation and the blacklist, that forced men and women to give up their union membership. There was no significant split in the Larkinite ranks despite the enthusiastic efforts of clergy, employers and Hibernians to manufacture one. Larkin's bitterest enemies acknowledged that even in defeat he remained the leader of the Dublin working class. Without any doubt, the Lockout and its aftermath constitute one of the great heroic struggles of the international working class and still provides inspiration and example, a lesson in class warfare.

The ITGWU retreated to its core membership on the docks in the face of defeat, but still saw itself as having an important political role. The union campaigned against partition and opposed the outbreak of war in 1914. Indeed, 1914 saw the union attempt to capture the leadership of the national movement, pushing aside Redmond and the Home Rule party. Larkin and Connelly urged that the war provided an opportunity to force concessions from the British – dominion status, along the lines of 1782. Redmond's hold was too strong and support for the British war effort too widespread. The failure of this attempt to mount mass opposition to the war and win independence saw Larkin depart for the United States, handing the leadership of the union over to Jim Connolly. It was Connolly who was to enter into a secret alliance with the republican underground, an alliance that culminated in the Easter Rising of 1916.

The politics of Easter Week are still the subject of considerable controversy. Was the Rising a serious calculated attempt to defeat the British or a deliberate blood sacrifice? Did Connolly see it as a blow struck in the socialist cause or as a desperate attempt to save 'the soul of Ireland' from national apostasy? Should Connolly have waited? The overthrow of Tsarism was less than a year away. What was the attitude of Socialists outside Ireland to the Rising? Was it a Catholic affair? These questions are likely to continue to exercise historians, socialists, republicans, and indeed everyone interested in the Irish fight for national freedom and in the struggle for socialism. While this volume puts forward answers and deploys argument and evidence, this is necessarily as a contribution to a continuing debate.

What of the aftermath of Easter Week? Here the focus shifts from Dublin to a broader landscape. The second wave of Irish syndicalism, inevitably coloured by the Russian Revolution, was much more of a national phenomenon. In a historic display of militancy and struggle the Irish working class at least temporarily shifted the balance of class forces in Ireland and played an important role in the War of Independence. This militancy, however, was accompanied by a subordination to the republican movement that it is hard to imagine either Larkin or Connolly countenancing. The result, in the short term, was the defeat of the second wave by the Free State government and the rolling back of working-class advance, most decisively in the countryside. In the longer term it began the marginalisation of the labour movement with politics dominated by the parties that emerged from the Civil War. This remains the case even in the very changed circumstances of contemporary Ireland. However, the ghost of the Larkinite insurgency and its ramifications has still not been laid to rest and continues to haunt the victors. It could have been, and still can be, different.

Index